A MARXIST LOOKS AT JESUS

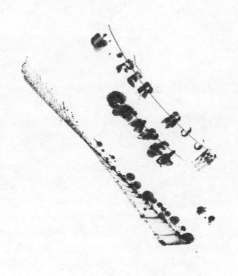

A MARXIST LOOKS AT JESUS

MILAN MACHOVEČ

with an introduction by
PETER HEBBLETHWAITE

DARTON, LONGMAN & TODD
LONDON

DARTON, LONGMAN & TODD LTD
89 Lillie Road, London SW6 1UD

ISBN 0 232 51260 4

A Translation of
JESUS FÜR ATHEISTEN
published and © by Kreuz Verlag Stuttgart 1972

This translation
© Darton, Longman & Todd Ltd 1976
First published 1976

Printed in Great Britain by offset lithography by
Billing & Sons Ltd, Guildford, London and Worcester

Reprinted 1977

PUBLISHER'S NOTE

The English translation was made from the German edition, at the author's express wish, rather than from the original Czechoslovak manuscript of chapters II–VI. Chapter I was originally written by the author in German.

The R.S.V. text is used for biblical quotations. In some cases in the original Czech version the author had made his own translation of biblical passages; but there seemed no point in retranslating these personal versions, so the passages concerned are merely listed here for the record: Deuteronomy 18:20; Psalms 2; 22; Isaiah 2:4; Daniel 7:13–14; Matthew 5:1–7, 29; 13:33–46; 16:17–23; 25:31–40; Mark 8:27–29; 14:21–25; 15:16–36; Luke 1:46–55; 2:10–19; 7:36–50; 10:29–37; 17:20–24; 24:13–35; John 1:10–14; 17:1–21.

CONTENTS

Introduction by Peter Hebblethwaite   8
I.   Jesus for Atheists?   18
II.   The Sources and their Significance   39
III.   Jewish Religion before Jesus   51
IV.   The Message of Jesus   74
V.   The Christ   119
VI.   The Significance of Jesus   192
     Appendix: The Life and Thought of Jesus as an
     Object of Research   205
     Index of Subjects   221
     Index of Biblical References   228

INTRODUCTION

Dr Milan Machoveč was Professor of Philosophy at the Charles University in Prague from 1953 to 1970. He remains a loyal Marxist, but has nevertheless written a book on Jesus which is far removed from the crudities and evident hostility of previous Marxist works on the subject. One might say, before reading Machoveč, that to have a Marxist writing respectfully and intelligently about Jesus is in itself a remarkable fact. And so it is. But Machoveč is much more important than that: even if one does not agree with all he says, he makes a contribution to our knowledge of Jesus by looking at the evidence about him through a Marxist lens. Theology, one could say, is too important an activity to be left to believing theologians. It is important to know how it strikes unbelieving contemporaries.

The fact that Machoveč began teaching in Prague in 1953 is of some significance. He became professor in the worst days of Stalinism – and Novotny in Czechoslovakia was a very thorough and faithful Stalinist. The horrors of that period are discreetly evoked in this book when he speaks of 'painful human tragedies' and 'judicial errors' which millions of men had to undergo (p. 26), and of the sufferings of those who were 'victims of the abuse of centralised power in the show trials' (p. 27). Machoveč does not attempt to deny the fact of profound injustice, and indeed provides a Marxist interpretation of 'carrying one's cross daily': there will be times, he notes, when a Marxist will have to choose 'to suffer injustice rather than contribute to it' (p. 34). Marxism in its communist form – others are possible – had become a state religion, pronouncing its bans and excommunications, and backing them up with force.

By the early 1960s there was a perceptible change of atmosphere. Stalin had been denounced. Pope John in the encyclical *Pacem in Terris,* which was almost his last will and testament, had recognised that communists could have worthy aims, despite their ideology. The ice-blocks of the cold war began to melt. In Prague, always a cross-roads of ideas, Professor Machoveč organised a seminar on Christianity and Marxism. Soon he was able to invite foreign theologians and Marxists to take part. Most of those mentioned on p. 19 passed through Prague and joined in the seminar. If Machoveč had an influence on his guests – and theologians like Moltmann and Metz have revealed a sophisticated awareness of Marxism – they also influenced him, as this book bears witness. Prague had invented something wholly new in Christian-Marxist relations: dialogue. It startled hard-liners on both sides. They reached for their pens and wrote with high indignation about naiveté and fellow-travelling.

Could Christians seriously say that they had something to learn from atheistic communists who had persecuted and were still persecuting them? And could Marxists likewise admit that they had something to learn from people they held to be deluded survivors from an earlier historical period, sunk deep in alienation and fantasy? The surprising answer to both questions was 'yes', but a necessary condition was that both sides should show a minimum of good will. In making comparisons it had been traditional on both sides to contrast one's own best performance with the worst the other side had to offer; lofty idealism about oneself combined with unflinching realism in dealing with the other. It was not difficult to win arguments set up in those terms; the cards were marked. So much propaganda, pro and contra, was for home consumption, designed to reassure and bolster up prejudice which is an attitude characterised by rigidity, obstinacy and ignorance. Once dialogue starts and one is dealing not with straw men or caricatures but with men of flesh and blood, then it becomes possible to compare one's own 'best' with the 'best' of the other. There must, of course, be equality, and it is only in fiction that the commissar holds dialogue with his prisoner.

In Machoveč's seminar, prejudices began to be dissipated. But that was only a necessary preliminary. The next stage was that Christians should read Marx, and Marxists the New Testament, with an attempt to understand. The sources, the title deeds, the classical texts, would not be read to build up an arsenal of arguments and counter-arguments, but rather for the light they

threw on present-day situations. Thus the Christian might begin
to appreciate how Marx's views on the development of ideology
as the way a group legitimates its interests and responds to
threats, were reflected in the way dogma had evolved in the
Christian Church; and the Marxist might recognise in the
description and denunciation of 'Pharisaism' a type of mind with
which he was only too familiar as the revolution settled down
into a period of comfortable assurance. Or both might find surprising convergences in, for example, the way mere theorising is
not regarded as enough. There is an obvious parallel between
Marx's eleventh thesis on Feuerbach – 'The philosophers have
only interpreted the world; the point, however, is to change it' –
and the scriptural insistence that what counts is not 'word and
speech' but 'deed and truth' (cf. 1 John 4:16). It is not really surprising that there should be these parallels and cross-references,
since Marxism and Christianity have common roots in the Jewish
prophetic tradition.

To have and utter such thoughts in the Prague of the early
1960s was to gamble on hope. In view of the actual political
situation in Czechoslovakia, they could appear as no more than
wishful thinking. But ideas have a life of their own, they have a
way of burrowing underground and suddenly emerging and
proving useful at the right moment. That explains why, happily,
thought-crime can never be totally eradicated. The ideas that had
been discussed quietly in the Machoveč seminar were the subject
of the first ever full-scale meeting of Marxists and Christians held
on communist soil. It took place at Marianské Lazné, better
known in the West as Marienbad, in the spring of 1967, and was
organised by the West German *Paulusgesellschaft*. The date is important. The brief Dubcek period still lay in the future. At the
time it was alleged that that arcane body, the Central Committee
of the Czech Communist Party, had approved the holding of the
Marienbad meeting only by the narrowest of majorities and that
it was infiltrated by government spies. There were undoubtedly
some suspicious-looking individuals present, but there was no
means of checking either story.

What became perfectly clear, however, was that Machoveč
and his colleagues represented a Marxism that was somehow
'different'. Here one had to proceed cautiously. To call them
'revisionist' harmed them in the eyes of the party bosses, and

Machovec's discreet reflections on the relations between the intellectual and the *apparat* are a reminder of the danger. To call them 'liberal' did them equal harm. 'Modern' was perhaps the least injurious epithet, and it is interesting that Machovec here adopts it and spends much of his first chapter discussing what it might mean. But whatever name one gives them, what Machovec calls the 'Prague School' certainly existed. It was a loose grouping of non-dogmatic Marxists who were ready, and felt the need, to learn from other philosophical views. At Marienbad, they were out in force. At the opening meeting, Dr Josef Macek, an historian who has written on Jan Hus, spoke of the tolerance which had been written into the constitution of the Kingdom of Bohemia in the fifteenth century, and then let slip some remarks, jejune enough in themselves, which were astonishing to those who remembered Stalinism. He declared that science (*Wissenschaft*) was international, and that just as science refuses today to be the handmaid of theology, so also it refuses to be the handmaid of ideology. Dr Macek said that the members of the conference were there to 'test their systems against reality'. These simple observations left gaping holes in volumes of Marxist theorising.

More wreckage followed. Milan Pruha, then a thirty-one year old professor of philosophy, pleaded for a certain 'pluralism' in Marxist philosophical work. He believed that Marxists ought to study and learn from Wittgenstein, Husserl, Heidegger, Merleau-Ponty and Teilhard de Chardin as a matter of intellectual honesty. Pruha had studied in Moscow and Paris, and his reading list alone was enough to alarm any intellectual spies present.

Behind these exchanges lay the echo of the great Marxist debate of the 1960s. It started in Poland with philosophers like Adam Schaff and Leszek Kolakowski. The discussion was ostensibly about Marxism and humanism, but the real problem was whether Stalinism, by now officially denounced and discredited, had been the aberration of a demented individual or was a danger inherent in the system, and in either case, how it could be checked. When Machovec writes with considerable understatement about 'the problem of power' (p. 33), he is alluding to this debate. For the Stalinists there had been no problem. As Brecht, the great East German poet had sung: 'The Party has a thousand eyes, the individual has only two' (in *Die Massnahme*). But many began to feel that this approach gave the Party *carte blanche* for arbitrariness and abuses of all kinds, and that morality could not simply be defined according to the sliding scale of alleged working-class interests. Kolakowski objected strongly: 'When a man is dying of hunger and you can give him something to eat, there is no combination of circumstances in which it would be right to say: "It would be tactically better to let him die" ' (*Die Mensch ohne Alternative*, Munich, 1964, p. 248). These and other assertions of Marxist humanism led many to the view that there had to be some built-in restraints, some degree of public discussion of issues, in order to prevent the resurgence of Stalinism. In this way the theoretical ground was broken for what was later known in Czechoslovakia as 'socialism with a human face'. Without this intellectual preparation, the 'Prague Spring' of 1968 would not have happened or would have had a different character.

At Marienbad in 1967, one year earlier, Machovec̆ prepared a paper called 'Christians and Marxists in a common quest for the meaning of human life'. His main point was that, although Marxists rejected religion as a mystification, the problem of the meaning of life nevertheless remained. It could not be spirited away in any exercise of the dialectic, since it was rooted in human existence:

> When we find that there is no one 'out there', then we are left with our knowledge and our culture which become an end in themselves, and are therefore meaningless, since meaning can exist only in relation to something or someone else. When this Titan has succeeded in overthrowing the gods, he has no meaningful task left and so he must despair.

Moreover, added Machovec̆, the post-religious situation made people particularly susceptible to pseudo-gods and surrogate transcendence: it is difficult to live with the void, substitutes come rushing in to take the place of the abandoned absolute, and men begin to worship the state or the party or the march of history or the future. Here one could comment that one of the heuristic reasons for faith in God is that it enables one to be very properly sceptical about much else, that it locates faith in a worthy object. But naturally this was not the point Machovec̆ was making. He insisted, however, that genuine Marxist atheism was not a counter-dogma, was not simply theism turned upside down, but was a matter of *critical method*. Dialogue, he concluded, was neither tactical nor political, it was not a Trojan horse; it was rather an existential need, without which the Marxist – and the Christian – would remain morally backward.

An important question, then as now, was how far Machovec̆ was representative of the Communist Party. If he were simply some Marxist lone ranger, a maverick Machovec̆, he would be of less interest. But he was not alone. From 1966 to 1967, Vitézslav Gardavsky, Professor of Philosophy at the Military Academy of Brno, was publishing articles in a Prague literary magazine, *Literárm noviny*, in which he tried to justify his atheism and at the same time to come to terms with the Christian intellectual inheritance. These articles were belatedly published in English under the title *God is not yet Dead* (Pelican, 1973).

However, there is an interesting difference in method between Gardavsky and Machovec̆. Gardavsky is radically reductionist, that is, he believes that the assertions of Christian theologians are thoroughly mistaken, but that they may retain some interest because and in so far as they express deep human problems. The Christian 'hidden agenda' may have a certain value, but its formal statements have first to be rescued from their mythological or obscurantist language. This approach involves a sort of psychoanalytic 'listening' technique, in which what a man says is of less importance than his 'unconscious meaning'. The method can be traced back to Marx himself, who believed that he had demonstrated that Hegel's metaphysics was 'really' mystified economics. Feuerbach in his *Essence of Christianity* had subjected Christ and Christianity to this treatment. Gardavsky is faithful both to Marx and Feuerbach when he says that he is not interested in the historical existence of Jesus as such, since 'Jesus exists for us in a much more positive form: as an embodiment of a symbol, a symbol for a specifically Jewish way of looking at the world and mankind', which is characterised by love understood as 'a passionate desire for life on a more elevated level' (p. 49) and involving a decision which 'breaks open the womb of the future' (p. 51). It is possible that this type of reductionism is more dismissive than straightforward rejection, since it both explains and explains away. However it was courageous and original of Gardavsky to be interested in Christianity at all. The originality of Machoveč goes further: he does not lump all mythologies together, and he makes a serious study of Jesus. In his completeness and thoroughness, he has no rivals among his fellow Marxists. He is a pioneer. Even Kautsky's 1906 book to which he refers (p. 23; p. 216) is not strictly in competition, since Kautsky's aim was to undermine and reject, while Machoveč is trying to understand.

The result is a picture of Jesus from which Christians, though they may demur, have much to learn. Machoveč is critical of Bultmann, but at the same time dependent on him, and his Jesus is haunted by the eschatological vision of the future and his own role in the impending events. This is a useful corrective to the picture of a majestic Jesus, unruffled and unmoved, who goes through life *une rose à la main*, knowing exactly what is going to happen in the future (and therefore missing an essential aspect of what it means to be human), who has so often been presented in Christian preaching and devotional works. Technically known as 'docetism' and involving the suggestion that Jesus was not 'really' man but only appeared to be, this heresy gets rough treatment from Machoveč. Machoveč goes to the other extreme, which is hardly surprising. But though he 'reads into' Jesus his Marxist preoccupations – and who can blame him for that, since we all have to appropriate what we can of the richness that is Jesus, 'from whose fulness', he writes, quoting the Gospel of John, 'we have all received' (p. 193) – Machoveč does not deliberately distort Jesus in order to exploit him. Thus, for example, he does not accept the now widespread contention of the 'Catholic Marxists' that Jesus was a political revolutionary, points out that he did not become a Zealot, and acknowledges that the revolution in the name of the future for which Jesus called goes much deeper and is concerned with more fundamental needs than are touched in revolution understood as a political event.

The crucial point at which most orthodox Christians would have to part company with Machoveč is in the radical, unbridgeable distinction which he makes between the Jesus of history and the Christ who is preached, between what he calls the 'dogmatised image of Jesus Christ' and 'the image of the man Jesus of Nazareth' (p. 203). This is, of course, another familiar

Bultmann theme, but here it is pressed with all possible rigour, and the more human, accessible and intelligible he makes Jesus, then the more he has reasons for maintaining that faith in Christ came later and was an invention – largely, he suggests, of Peter. Given Machovec's presuppositions, and the methodological exclusion of God and transcendence from the scheme of things, no other course was open to him. In a wholly immanent world-view, Jesus can be no more than a man. In the end, then, Machovec too is thoroughly reductionist; but he spends more time getting there.

En route he has much to say that is stimulating and of value. On this point it is interesting to note that in the 1960s Marxists and Christians employed a comparable intellectual strategy in dealing with each other. When two absolutist systems meet, neither will be content until and unless it has encompassed, explained, coped with, and consequently disarmed and to some extent 'recovered' the other. Thus Karl Rahner's theory of the 'anonymous Christian' was admirably designed to lay bare traces of latent Christian virtues in the manifest non-believer. It was irrelevant that the un-believer might deny with some vehemence that he was 'anonymously' anything of the kind: in his goodness and moral striving he was borne along by grace, and all grace is grace of Christ. Without knowing it, he was mysteriously related to Christ. In this way, at least theoretically, Marxism could be fitted into the Christian scheme, and the merits of Marxists could be ac-counted for. But this delicate process was in a sense merely the reverse of the Marxist reductionist method in which Jesus is valued for what he contributes to human self-understanding. There is another aspect to this mutual intellectual om-nivorousness. If the Marxists could succeed in spelling out con-vincingly the *human content* of Christian assertions – 'the secular meaning of the Gospel', then Christians would gain from this ex-ercise a greater degree of relevance; and conversely if Christians could persuade Marxists to look once more at their theory and at-tend to its as yet unrealised potentialities, then they too would gain. Thus a novel form of the *tu quoque* argument began to be developed.

The *tu quoque* had been standard practice in the days of cold war polemics. Predictably, tediously, it was always the other side that was to blame. If someone spoke of the excesses of Stalin, then the Holy Inquisition was dragged in. If political prisoners languished in communist jails, then they were said to be just as badly off in Spanish ('Fascist') jails. Nothing could be heard above the din of rapid verbal gunfire. But the new form of the *tu quoque* argument invited the partners in dialogue to rise to the level of their highest ideals. So here Machovec̆ is found reproaching Christians not with living according to the Gospel but rather with not living according to the Gospel (p. 194). Conversely, at the 1966 dialogue with Marxists at Herrenchiemsee in Bavaria, Giulio Girardi reproached Marxists not for being Marxist but for being insufficiently Marxist (the text of his speech later appeared in his book, *Marxism and Christianity*, Gill & Son, Dublin, 1968, pp. 173–204). In both cases the shoddiness of the present and the dead weight of the institution are judged in the light of critera derived from the authentic sources.

It gradually became apparent that in the Christian-Marxist dialogue one grew not only in knowledge of the 'other side' but also in the critical understanding of one's own tradition. There was a need to be 'radical' in the sense of getting down to roots. Much ballast and bric-à-brac would have to be discarded. One of the most intriguing accounts of the Marienbad meeting was written by Dr Erika Kadlecova, a sociologist, who became minister responsible for Church affairs in the Dubc̆ek government, a post she relinquished, under compulsion, in September 1968. She stressed the point I have just made: 'Fidelity to basic values and to original aims not only does not exclude critical judgment, constant verification, separation of myth and representation, but it entails them' ('Die Gespräche in Marienbad', in *Dialog*, 1, pp. 101–9). For a time there was a glimpse of a world in which it would be possible to combine convictions with openness, firmness with tolerance, orthodoxy with self-criticism. The vision quickly faded. The dialogue failed, at least in the sense that, after the Marienbad meeting of 1967, there were no more in Europe of comparable scale and importance. The future lay in Latin America rather than Europe, where the invasion of Czechoslovakia in August 1968 discouraged any further immediate attempts. The Christian-Marxist dialogue in Europe now seemed to have been taking place in the stratosphere. The high hopes it had aroused could be dismissed as so much moonshine. The cynics said: 'We told you so'. But that did not mean that the dialogue had been a waste of time. Erika Kadlecova had answered this objection in advance. She wrote:

There were many complaints at Marienbad about the powerlessness of intellectuals who can make fine speeches but have no power to put them into effect. That is both true and false. Of course they do not have armies and prisons, they can neither make promises nor pronounce bans. But they can create a spiritual atmosphere in which change is possible. (ibid. p. 108)

Those who have armies and prisons and power have taken over again in Prague. Machoveč is working privately. But his book will help powerfully 'to create a spiritual atmosphere in which change is possible'. The time will come when his thought is needed, when an institutionalised Marxism loses its systematic hostility towards the immediate past and feels the need for dialogue or even simply for more broadly based support. The situation will not remain static, since you can do anything with bayonets except sit on them. At the end of Chapter I Machoveč expresses his conviction that 'the Marxism of the twentieth century can be truly faithful to itself only when it has the courage to open itself whole-heartedly to this fruitful dialogue with the central problems of 3000 years of Western tradition' (p. 38), and that the dialogue between Christians and Marxists which began so tentatively and yet promisingly in Czechoslovakia in the 1960s was not just a transitory episode over which we can now draw a veil but was the beginning of something radically new and of decisive importance for the future of the world.

A Marxist looks at Jesus, then, has immense symbolic importance: it can stimulate and challenge Christians, and open the eyes of Marxists; it is a minor but indispensable Marxist classic which will replace Kautsky as a study of Jesus; it is a memorial and a tribute to the debates of the 1960s, but also a pledge of hope for the future.

Oxford, 1 March 1976   Peter Hebblethwaite

CHAPTER I

Jesus for Atheists?

The attentive reader of this book will realise – perhaps to his surprise – that I am a self-confessed Marxist and yet that I write about Jesus with enthusiasm and passion. That may make him wonder whether I am 'really' a Marxist, how far my writings are truly representative of contemporary or future Marxism, or whether I am not simply ploughing an eccentric and lonely furrow.

A still more careful reader will notice that my statements about Jesus of Nazareth are by no means simply a repetition of the familiar and widespread Marxist clichés, but rather that, like a historian, I not infrequently concern myself with quite specialised problems and 'subsidiary' questions, with apparently insignificant biblical texts, with the complicated controversies of early Christianity which had hitherto remained the exclusive preserve of the exegetes. This approach may arouse a certain interest and make the question raised in the preceding paragraph even more urgent and insistent: what has all this got to do with Marxism as we know it? What has it to do with the Marxist rulers in Moscow or Peking, or with the socialism of the students in Western universities?

It is not the first time that such questions have been asked. During the sixties well-known leading Christian theologians spoke appreciatively about Karl Marx, and indeed about Lenin and his heritage. But the converse was also true. Well-known and leading Marxists from East and West found themselves agreeing about Jesus and the Christian tradition and even – and for Marxists this was extremely difficult – about the role of Christianity in contemporary society. Was this welcoming attitude on the part of Christians simply the result of 'humility' which involved them in 'dialogue' as an artificial and conventional exercise lacking any meaningful content? And was the attitude of the Marxists anything other than a subtle tactic in a complicated power-game? There is perhaps some truth in both these suggestions. But the friendly and fruitful collaboration over so many years of people like Hromádka, Gollwitzer, Rahner, Casalis, Moltmann, Girardi, Metz on the Christian side, with Bloch, Fromm, Garaudy, Luporini, Lombardo-Radice, Farner, Gardavsky on the other, makes it ridiculous to speak of convention or routine or tactics or intellectual over-excitement. There has been a real transformation in the relations between Christianity and Marxism.

It is true that the causes of this embryonic, changed relationship are many and may vary from person to person. But in the last analysis, at least as far as the most important causes are concerned, they have a rationale and are therefore intelligible. Some causes are common to both sides, such as the increasing dangers to which the world is exposed, especially in the form of possible nuclear suicide, or the reduction of progress to what is in the interests of the super-powers. Other causes are comparable on both sides. There are similar disappointments among thinking people, who are sometimes regarded on both sides as impatient fools, with the mediocrity, the deadness or the compromises of their own institutions. Finally there are specific causes on each side. They correspond to the earlier traditions and the particular strengths or weaknesses of each side. Both movements can find in their sources principles which lead naturally to 'dialogue' and 'openness', and at the same time obstacles, inhibitions, prejudices, tendencies to fanaticism and to the universal and exclusive claim to possess the key to salvation.

Before we discuss in more detail the causes of the recent metamorphosis in the attitudes of Marxists to Christ and comment in more detail on Christ himself, we must consider at least briefly the 'obstacles' which come from an older tradition. In this way we shall be able to distinguish the rational from the emotional or the accidental, and the insuperable oppositions from the differences that can be overcome. This is the only way to plan the near and distant future responsibly.

One thing is clear from the start: it would be naive to underestimate the burden of prejudice that Marxists bring to the question of Jesus. The prejudices are deep-rooted and so firmly held by hundreds of thousands of communists that they seem unassailable and not open to argument of any kind. For such people

there is indeed no occasion even to think about such questions, or
to consider the arguments for and against. Instead there is an *a
priori* attitude which is regarded as self-evident and obvious and
which derives from an age-old emotional hostility and a rigid
and petrified 'thesis' – what we might call in theological terms a
'dogma'. True, it has never been solemnly proclaimed by any
pope or college of cardinals, and yet this attitude has been confirmed by similar hierarchical structures and through the almost
total dependence of hundreds of thousands of men on its acceptance. In such a situation many Marxists, especially those who
wield most power, are not really 'free' to abandon the old theses,
for this would threaten them in their position of power, and
nothing is more important to them than to maintain it. What or
whether one thinks about Jesus is therefore a question of secondary importance. Those who do turn their minds to it generally
assume that the radical rejection of Christianity is part of the
'sacred heritage'. They found this judgment on more or less
clear memories of the reactionary and anti-social role of the
Church in the nineteenth century which, unfortunately, is not
just a matter of past history. The idea that the Church purveys
'opium for the people' cannot be corrected by any available new
experience, since it represents the fossilisation and institutionalisation of one stage of Marxist thinking and therefore *must* be true.

The attitude of such Marxists to Christianity remains hostile
'on principle', even when they come across Christians like Pope
John XXIII (though not all Christians resemble John XXIII!),
since their position is not something which is open to question-
ing, but is rather a self-evident truth upheld by the ideologically
closed institution. On the other hand, have the attitudes of non-
Marxist and even Christian politicians in the present century to
Marxism – or indeed to Christianity itself – been any different?
In a highly centralised and monolithic institution these attitudes
naturally find a harsher and more striking expression. But should
not the committed Christian use this evidence from the non-
Christian world in order better to understand the process of
'dogmatisation' which took place in his own Christian history?
Was it always and only reasons of faith which led the early
Christian aspirations to become embodied in hardened 'dogmas'?
Or did the growing institutionalisation and the developing
hierarchical structure play an important part in this process?

There is something else which is part of the Marxist tradition about Christianity: the Marxist method by which so many thinkers and scientists — mainly intellectuals, therefore — have been influenced. In our present context the dialectic itself is not so important as its methodological basis in so-called historical materialism, and especially the tendency to explain all 'historical ideas' by socio-economic interests and developments, in other words to explain the 'ideology' by its 'economic basis'. This is more important than the materialistic world-view in itself.

We may begin with what is less important, the so-called materialistic world-view. Christians often allege that this is the biggest obstacle to our coming together, but there is a mis-understanding here. For the 'materialism' of Karl Marx and most of his disciples is by no means a 'cult of matter' or 'physicalism' — for this Marx had not the slightest inclination. The materialism of Marx means unambiguously the supremacy of man and of the human principle in the cosmos. It is not that Marx and his followers turn lifeless matter into a 'counter-ideal' to God, but rather that *man* with all his intellectual and spiritual gifts and values fulfils this role. As for atheism, if we leave aside the in-fluence of the institutionalisation already mentioned, in other words from the point of view of pure theory, its real content is not something affirmative but something *critical*. Atheism has meaning only as a critique, limited in place and in time, of cer-tain dominant models used in contemporary religious faith. Marx developed his 'atheism' as a critique of the conventional nineteenth-century representations of God, and should these change, then the genuine Marxist would have to revise his criti-que. Twentieth-century theologians have worked out new and more dynamic models for thinking about God, so that often we Marxists no longer know whether we are still atheists or not in their regard. One thinks of Rahner speaking of God as 'the ab-solute Future', of Braun who understands God as the question about the ultimate 'Whence' and 'Whither' of my existence, of Hromádka who sees God as the reason why man can refuse to give in to power, of Buber with his I–Thou relationship. It is difficult to know why we Marxists should feel obliged to reject all these notions. Of course Marx criticised dogmas, including the dogma of the existence of God, but this was to free his followers for their task of radical criticism, not to create a new 'dogma of the non-existence of God' for all eternity. Politically, then, and on the philosophical level, there are dozens of more urgent and pressing questions for Christians and Marxists to discuss, questions which also have the advantage of being rather more soluble than 'what happened in the beginning' (and, in any case, no one seems able to give a reasonable account of this 'beginning'). For thinking Marxists such purely theoretical questions do not constitute a vast obstacle.

In the heritage of classical Marxism, and also in modern Marxism when it has not betrayed its heritage, the historical-materialist methodology is of much greater importance. One of its most elementary principles is the teaching that developments and transformations in the realm of the human 'spirit' or 'mind' – which give rise to political, moral and religious ideas and other ideas with a historical origin – are ultimately explicable by the developments, contradictions, interests and changes that take place in the socio-economic infra-structure. It is true that only relatively few Marxists have applied this doctrine systematically and with 'desperate earnestness' (although some did attempt to explain the fundamental differences between Aristotle and Plato purely in terms of socio-economic considerations), yet it is nevertheless deeply anchored in the consciousness of all Marxists as a method which is according to reason and fruitful for the understanding of history.

Now what does all this mean in practice in relation to the principal positions of Christianity? How does it affect Jesus' uniqueness and central messianic role for all humanity? Marx could admire Jesus' love of children, Kautsky the revolutionary and utopian-communistic tendencies in early Christianity, modern Marxists can be inspired by particular biblical episodes, but every Marxist, even the most 'modern' (and in the eyes of the party bosses often the most 'revisionist') has taken over this method from Marx as a 'classical inheritance'. It has often, and understandably, been transformed from 'a capacity to explain ideas by their socio-economic conditioning' into 'an incapacity to explain even the most sublime human ideals by anything other than the socio-political conditioning'. There is a vast distinction here. I can use a 'capacity' whenever I like – this is for example how the artist works; but I cannot rid myself of an 'incapacity' any more than a scientist can rid himself of his knowledge and methods.

In relation to Jesus and early Christianity this means that no Marxist, even one who is most open to dialogue with Christians, can avoid the urgent and insistent question: what socio-economic conditions were there in the period from Gaius Gracchus and Marius up to Nero and Trajan, between the first and the second conquest of Jerusalem, which necessarily produced the ideals of 'salvation' and 'redemption' and therefore a of a 'saviour' and a 'redeemer' and enabled the preachers who proclaimed such ideas to play such a transforming and decisive part in world history? This is how in the end all Marxists think, and they cannot think otherwise. It is another matter whether they apply this method with stupidity or intelligence. The first and in a sense classic result of this method was Karl Kautsky's book *Foundations of Christianity* (1908). Thousands of later propaganda pamphlets fell far below the level of Kautsky, because they nearly all lacked the most important factor: knowledge of the subject they were discussing.

Even if we leave aside these feeble efforts as the waste-paper of world history, from Kautsky onwards and in other relatively competent Marxist writers such as Archibald Robertson, the following positions have been clear and constant: (1) It was the socio-economic situation of the Roman Empire – from the fate of the peasants to the revolt of the slaves – which gave rise to the primary and original form of the 'quest for salvation', while the early Christian and other 'ideologies' were secondary and necessarily *had to* come into existence after the failure of reforms and the collapse of the slave revolt. (2) These 'ideas', even the most splendid of them, were thus produced and borne along primarily by socio-economic interests, and only secondarily by the person of the founder and his apostles and disciples. (3) The actual historical figures with their ideals and illusions are at best interesting and determining only as a second instance, for it is in the end a matter of indifference how many apostles there were and whether Peter really spoke with a certain Jesus in Caesarea Philippi. Likewise irrelevant, therefore, are all miracle stories, along with pseudo-rationalist attempts to explain them away whether by chance, fraud, error or self-deception, by cunning or stupidity. For ultimately historical determinism and the 'iron logic' of the socio-economic processes are so powerful that it is not a 'miracle' that Christianity came into being; the 'miracle' would have been if it had *not* come into being. In clumsy hands the application of this method can be naive and almost comic, as when for example certain hard-line atheists claim to 'know' that Jesus never existed. They have so simplified and distorted the method that he does not 'need' to have existed. But every movement has its feeble-minded supporters and one should not underestimate the greatness and the historical importance of the movement because of their stupidity. It is a plain fact in the mind of every Marxist that the historical-materialist method determined the development of Christianity and that other factors such as emotion were subordinate to it. That is why he finds it impossible to 'believe' in a 'saviour', since he is compelled by his methodology to ask how the idea of a 'saviour' should enter history and catch on.

This method is always in the foreground of every Marxist's consciousness, and it little matters whether the individual Marxist has a feel for 'purely religious' questions or not. Most Marxists are not interested anyway. And so they often tend to overestimate other factors, and especially the socio-economic influences; this happens in Kautsky's book on Jesus and in almost every instance where there has been some form of political co-operation between Christians and socialists. But even Marxists who have a certain feel for religious questions are still impelled to ask questions about the socio-economic roots, and this affects the way they respond. It is true also of the modern Marxist, even though other experiences may have led him to fill out and partially modify the method.

We must now raise an important question: What is meant by 'modern Marxism'? Or to put the question less ambitiously: what does the author understand by 'modern Marxism'? How does this Marxism differ from the classical Marxism of the nineteenth century? And what chance does it have of success?

Modern Marxism cannot be a 'revision' of classical Marxism in the sense of a betrayal or softening of the goal of an international classless society. It is in no way 'revisionist'. Modern Marxism is nothing other than classical Marxism, providing that the latter is allowed to survive intact into the twentieth century, in other words providing that it has lost none of those essential characteristics which enabled it to bring such a fruitful and dynamic element into the nineteenth century. But if someone now, one hundred years after Marx, simply repeated or re-emphasised what he once said, then this 'fidelity' to the conceptual system would be an abandonment of the original real and alert sense for what is new in history. There can be no doubt that Marx wanted to *organise* all reformist, progressive people through a strict and sober *scientific* analysis of the fundamental problems of *his* historical period so that a basis could be created for a *more human society* in which *human individuality* could develop more fully and freely. Should any one of these elements be missing, a caricature would result that would frighten the reformists away. *Corruptio optimi pessima.* The corruption of the best is the worst. If, for example, one loses the ability to analyse new social tendencies and new instances of alienation, the resulting 'Marxism' is quite contrary to Marx's own intentions, even if one conjures up his shade a hundred times a day. One would have to be a liar or a cynic to deny that the twentieth century has most certainly seen new tendencies and factors of which Marx had not and could not have had the slightest inkling. Marxism can therefore be modern only if it assimilates the most important new phenomena of the twentieth century and has entered along paths which are accordingly new in relation to its classical goals, or at least made the attempt. The following factors should be noted:

(1) The methods and discoveries of the second technological revolution in which science already imitates the processes of the human brain and through its nuclear techniques and cybernetics inaugurates a period of complete rational planning and the conquest of the cosmos;

(2) The dynamic and by now irreversible awakening of the peoples of the Far East, of countries having intellectual traditions totally different from that of Europe which up till now have been almost totally undervalued and misunderstood;

(3) New facts in the classical countries, whether capitalist or now socialist: capitalism has reached a stage of relatively lasting and efficient prosperity, while in the states which arose after a Marxist revolution and where Marxism is the politically dominant power, there are new forms of the struggle between good and evil.

It is the third of these factors which is of the greatest importance in discussing the relation of modern Marxism to the world of the Bible and of Jesus, since it has given hundreds of thousands of Marxists new moral and 'existential' experiences which previous generations could not have had. The second factor has a certain importance, since entirely new insights can be gained both for Christianity and for Marxism by studying what happens to Marxism when it is implanted in non-Christian soil. The first factor we can in practice leave aside. This is because, although nuclear dangers can increase fear and therefore encourage a greater readiness for encounter and dialogue, they do not add to our understanding of the Bible.

Let us therefore concentrate on the third factor, and see how it brings Marxists closer to Jesus of Nazareth. Wholly new experiences were inevitable after more than fifty years' existence of Marxist states, especially since Marxist states have come into being in countries with very diverse intellectual and political traditions. On the one hand, Marxism had 'something to show' as it transformed a once backward agricultural country into a world power, and thus demonstrated that it was not simply 'utopian'. But there was another side to the question. Millions of men in these countries underwent painful human tragedies, ranging from judicial errors to the simplest sufferings caused by illness or human shipwreck because of unrequited love, failure, misunderstanding by one's comrades etc., and in view of this one can and must correct certain 'paradisiac' ideas which had been typical of the founding fathers and of the majority of pre-revolutionary socialists. Early socialism had the concept of a totally different, incomparably 'other' future. It was thus 'radically eschatological' and much closer in mentality to some of the prophetic figures of the biblical tradition than anyone in the nineteenth century, Marxist or Christian, was prepared to admit. This was mainly because almost anything 'old', whether 'bourgeois morality' or 'Christian myth', was scarcely worth speaking about: after the dispossession of the capitalists and the ending of the principle of exploitation, the early socialists expected life to be so different and human beings so much nobler in every respect, that to be concerned about the past seemed a mere waste of time ... Repeatedly in history we come across the same harsh and 'unjust' judgement: 'Leave the dead to bury their own dead: but as for you, go and proclaim the kingdom of God' (Luke 9:60) and 'Do not look back or stop anywhere in the valley' (Genesis 19:17).

But it is very difficult to go on 'waiting' with such intense concentration and in so 'eschatological' a way fifty years *after* a Marxist revolution; and it is difficult to believe that the expropriation of private property, given the correction of a number of faults that happen to have been made *en route,* will eventually have such wonderful consequences as to bring about an 'absolutely different' form of life and soon put within everyone's grasp all possible beauty and pleasure. Early Marxists were often enchanted by the prospect of 'a leap into the realm of freedom', and indeed bewitched by it; and this is a partial explanation for the tremendous dynamism and power of Marxism, as also for the possibility of its abuse. But it took twentieth-century Marxists a long time and involved much pain to learn how difficult it is in fact to make any real progress without secretly reviving the demons of the 'past' in some new guise. The 'leap' is no longer made – and this makes a critical view of other systems of thought much easier. In much the same way Christians of the early period, as they ceased to look forward to the imminent second coming of the Son of Man in all his glory, began gradually to develop a more critical and accurate view of the thought-systems of the ancient world. Dialogue began . . .

Thus the deepest reasons for these changes are to be found not, as one might superficially suppose, in failures or broken promises, in the betrayals or the abuses of Marxism. These factors played a part, as they always do in history. One cannot forget, for example, the sufferings of those who were the victims of the abuse of centralised power in the show trials; it naturally hurts more or less all socialists, even those who did not suffer directly. The deepest causes of the changes, in general and in relation to Christianity, should be sought rather in certain successes of classical Marxism. The simple fact of the rapid and enormous diffusion of Marxism – the first result of the dynamic enthusiasm that Karl Marx had been able to arouse in his first supporters – must have had some effect, as did the later successes under Lenin's banner. In the communist-ruled states, Marxism has won the sympathy of hundreds of thousands of intellectuals, teachers, philosophers, artists, scientists of varied tendencies. Thus Marxism has become the business of people who are professionally concerned with thought and with the inner reasons for possible human salvation or failure. These are mostly people who even in communist states are admittedly in some way (certainly financial-

ly) dependent on the ruling institution, but who nevertheless for
the most part refuse to become simply cogs in highly disciplined
organisations – and not because they are exposed to influences
other than those deriving from the tight economic structure and
the administrative-political institutions. The paradoxes inherent
in the fate of an ex-revolutionary in a by now hierarchised institution do not affect them so much: pain is more easily
recognisable, a possible revolt against the happiness of 'organisation man' finds readier ammunition. Of course there are also individuals in these situations who would prefer to pursue anti-
socialist or egoistic goals, but most genuine Marxist intellectuals
will sooner or later – although they might not be understood or
commended for it by their Marxist political leaders – tread the
paths of modern Marxism we mentioned above. The reason for
this is that there is at work today a certain historical determinism,
an 'iron logic' of the twentieth century, which demands that all
the above-mentioned problems must sooner or later be solved.

Naturally it will not be easy: there will certainly be setbacks,
disappointments, dead-ends, sacrifices. But precisely in what are
still such chaotic and hard-to-analyse battles, the moral factor
will play an increasingly greater role as the years go by. Once
again this is something which brings the Marxists closer to the
problems of early Christianity. Thousands today claim to be
Marxists not only because they are convinced of the truth of
Marxism and its humane mission, but also because it happens to
be the dominant power. So they are Marxists for the same reason
for which weak-spirited men have always kowtowed to the
powers that be: simply because they are the powers that be, and
because yes-men always profit outwardly. There is nothing new
about that, and it exists in every relatively powerful group or
movement. But in the modern highly centralised and complex
systems – and this does not apply only to the socialist system – it
takes on menacing and more deplorable forms.

For it is precisely the man who believes in 'nothing', that is
who does not take any human ideal seriously, who is by nature
capable of becoming a thorough-going conformist, whether out
of naiveté, opportunism or Machiavellian calculation. Thus internal conflicts developed among socialists and Marxists of which
Karl Marx and the eschatologically-minded earlier Marxist
generations had no inkling. Marx had supposed, and he was

right, that he was starting a vast and epoch-making movement which would win millions of supporters. But how double-edged and full of contradictions are these concepts of 'winning' and 'supporters'. Marx did not devote much thought to these questions. Yet one can 'win' the hearts of men in so many ways. An ambitious and unscrupulously clever demagogue can toy with a somewhat limited but still sincere Marxist, or a cynical careerist and conformist can arraign and destroy as a traitor a colleague whose only crime is not being a yes-man: but there is nothing new in this, even if it comes in Marxist dress. However — and here the Christian suspects that we are reaching the heart of the matter — if thousands and hundreds of thousands of sincere socialists and Marxist intellectuals and even 'apparatchiks' should have so frequently and painfully lived through such experiences, then it is obvious that such men will no longer believe eschatologically that a 'wholly different' life is just round the next corner. Their experience will make them appreciate certain situations which are described in the Bible and which centre on the figure of Jesus. The European Marxist of the twentieth century can find no models or clear indications in earlier Marxism either for spiritual aspirations in a sated consumer society or for the trampling on human dignity in the world of industry or for the painful moral conflicts already mentioned or for the better understanding of other intellectual traditions and their way to humanity and fulfilment. The situation impels the Marxist to take a fresh look at other positions. Although this does not mean that he is on the point of becoming a Christian, it would be difficult for him to ignore the fact that the Judaeo-Christian tradition has been concerned with these problems and contributed certain models towards their solution. Even the atheist can find that the Psalms, for example, are thoroughly 'up-to-date' and provide a dramatic description of what he is living through in the twentieth century.

Let us illustrate this often paradoxical change by one classical example. Marx and his early followers criticised mercilessly and justifiably that system of society which among other things was guilty of leaving the alleviation of human suffering to private initiative (basically on the principle of so-called 'charity'), in other words, to chance. Three or four socialist generations knew perfectly well what G. B. Shaw described in his plays: that Good

Samaritans do not alter the basis of exploitation in capitalist society, and that instead they encourage the illusions of the pious, strengthen the Pharisaism of the rich and powerful, and contribute to the self-deception and ease of conscience of both. Charity was therefore a fraud to be swept away! It all ought to be organised from scratch on scientific principles and not simply left to the hazards of private enterprise. So very usefully and logically the socialist states made themselves responsible for social security, the care of the sick, industrial injuries, the handicapped and so on. There are few people in Europe today who would question the reasonableness of this principle – though America is different. But how could the nobleminded socialists of the nineteenth century know that in the twentieth century thousands of men could come to believe that *only* 'official' institutions should be responsible for help and care and ministering to human needs? Or that the state and its institutions would take over the 'totality' of social life and attempt to take the place of the compassionate and generous heart? Or that in the end a man does not have to feel any distress, indeed should not feel any distress, when someone in his neighbourhood suffers, whether 'deservedly' or not? So there is no compassion, no responsibility for one's brother, when he is a casualty of 'historical forces' . . . That is not what the early socialists dreamed of and fought for. Age-old human egoism, cowardice and Pharisaism reappear in new disguises.

In short, if the Marxist of 150 years ago opened the Bible at all, after a few pages he would be saying to himself: 'Heaven, animals, paradise, sin, Eve with nothing on – this is all tedious mythology, a fairy story, an old wives' tale.' But today, after his experiences in established socialist society, the Marxist can read the same pages of the Bible and, without finding reasons why he ought immediately to become a Christian, approve of the question 'Where is your brother Abel?' and find it highly relevant and interesting. He sees more in the Bible, is more understanding and less critical, less put off by the 'mythological' element.

Christians should know this basic fact: if many modern Marxists now have a different relationship to the world of the Bible and to the person of Jesus Christ, it is not chiefly because they have been exposed to more effective influence from Christians, and not because they are in fact able to understand Christianity better and more deeply, but above all because they want to work out from their own Marxism a deeper, more rigorous and more modern view of life. Philosophers, artists and others who are professionally concerned with 'existential' questions, will come more easily to these tasks than scientists, economists, technicians or mere 'officials' of whatever organisation (though there are always exceptions), but ultimately these questions concern, or will concern, everyone, since the very roots of human existence are at stake.

The situation, therefore, is not always as Christians imagine it to be. One cannot say that the less someone is a Marxist, the more he will be inclined towards Christianity. The contrary is true. The more deeply and rigorously a Marxist understands himself and the vastness of the tasks which lie ahead and therefore the more he is a Marxist, the more will he be able to learn from the Judaeo-Christian tradition and to welcome Christians as potential allies and brothers. It is not, then, traitors and renegades who are able to perform for Christians the service of opening up new and liberating vistas, but only men who have remained faithful to the good of the working class and the living future of Marxism and who are ready to suffer for their views.

The same principle works on the other side. Hundreds of thousands of Sunday or conventional or fellow-travelling Christians or so-called Christian politicians could do nothing: only Christians like Pope John XXIII or the Czech Protestant theologian Hromádka could create a situation in which Marxists had to start thinking about religion in a more subtle way; for only such deeply Christian spirits could not be denounced, even by the strictest 'guardians of Marxist orthodoxy', as mere pawns of capitalism or as dispensers of opium to the people. They almost compelled Marxist thinkers to re-examine certain traditional Christian positions, and they achieved this not through harshness but through openness and love. This process is by no means at an end, but the movement has begun.

It was inevitable that the changes we have discussed would have an effect directly or indirectly on the central figure of Christianity. Nearly all the older Marxists thought that Jesus in his human destiny was a noble and attractive person and with the rallying cry that 'Christianity began with a dreamer and has end- ed with a well-fed clergy' have tried to usurp all the pleasant-sounding moralisms of the New Testament to serve their own cause. There was almost no genuine interest in Jesus and his teaching. Certain quotations from the Gospels were known, but they were for the most part interpreted as exhortations to passivity, as something which hindered the class war, as something typically 'religious' in the worst sense of the word, as 'opium for the people'. Spiritual consolation and the promise of eternal life were regarded as tranquillising pills, which might make people for a time and in some sense happy but which diverted them from the real struggle in the real world. Although this criticism was almost always over-simplified, one can regret that Christians began to take it seriously only very late in the day. How many religious socialists of the stamp of Kutter or Ragaz were alive in the time of Marx or Lenin?

The modern Marxist can be critical too, and he knows how to mock certain miracle stories in the Gospels with an irony worthy of Voltaire. But it is striking how rarely Marxists actually do that today, and, when they do, it is with considerable hesitation and only after being provoked by unyielding Christians. As time goes by they are ever more capable, for the reasons that we have already given, of stressing other elements in the Jesus tradition and of interpreting the traditional themes differently.

The conflict of Jesus with so-called 'Pharisaism', which runs through the whole of the Gospels, seemed at one time to be a historical curiosity, an obsolete controversy; at best one could find a use for it by applying certain modern-sounding phrases to one's political opponents, denouncing for example the 'Pharisaism' of bourgeois-humanist literates. But after a certain experience of how easy it is in any ideological or social position to adopt similar Pharisaic tendencies – when, for example, the cult of dead heroes is used as a cover for the contemptuous treatment of the living – thousands of people begin to see the Gospel passages in a new light and to value them. Even if they do not appeal to 'God', there are men who are proud and self-satisfied and delighted that they are 'not like other men' (Luke 18:11). And even though it is no longer a matter of the chair of Moses, modern men often have the feeling that scribes and Pharisees have sat down there (Matthew 23:2); whether justifiably or not is not particularly relevant here.

For the modern Marxist, the central problem in the Jesus question is almost always the different interpretations given to reconciliation and especially pacifism, as they are described in the Sermon on the Mount (Matthew 5–7). It is here that the contradiction between the teaching of Jesus and that of Marxism seems insuperable. Marx undoubtedly laid especial emphasis on the place of force in history and the socialist revolution. How could one dispossess the owners of the means of production without force? Yet many things are beginning to shift even in this controversial area. It is true that Marxists continue to reject pacifism in so far as it is merely another word for *petit bourgeois* narrowness, the self-satisfaction of the rich and the defenders of the *status quo*. But there are other problems. One needs to be more critical than ever of tendencies which do not distinguish clearly, unambiguously and indisputably between Marxist force and criminal force. Marx wanted to transform the social situation, property relationships and the administrative system by means of a radical – 'violent' – break with the past, but his concept of violence had nothing in common with the heedless shedding of blood, the arbitrary use of force (frequent with the powerful) or the principle of 'temporarily' suspending human rights, as it has not seldom been interpreted since Marx's time.

Precisely because power was used so thoughtlessly in the Marxist movement, and indeed abused, so that thousands of honest men have suffered, many Marxists began to wonder whether there was not a deeper and more legitimate interpretation of force and its limits than had hitherto been in use. When in the final analysis it is lasting progress and systematic activity which are at stake, force ought to be only a momentary, a fringe form, not the principal form, of this activity, and it must later be replaced by other motivations which are compatible with humanism. Thus Marxists too begin to wonder whether the pacifism characteristic not only of the Sermon on the Mount but of Jesus' entire ministry could not be joined perfectly harmoniously to the most rigorous forms of Marxist commitment to progress. Most leading Christians begin to understand that American bombers over Vietnam, for example, did not exactly help Marxists to understand how this could be done. It is not only on the Marxist side that there are obstacles and barriers.

In this connection, many twentieth-century Marxists have had daily experience of new and deeply painful problems, so that when a Marxist who cares about honesty and truth wishes to serve his movement, he finds that he 'must take up his cross'; and this gives him a new insight into the texts mentioned above which seemed simply to be recommending passivity. His own experience of life now teaches him that there are many situations in which he must suffer injustice rather than contribute to it. In this way he stands on a threshold where the deepest mystery of the New Testament appears no longer as mythology but as a profound and highly relevant truth. An atheist who takes his life and his work for his beloved movement really, 'deadly', seriously cannot be undermined by any cynicism or by opportunist considerations and can recognise that Jesus' victory was one of the greatest moments in the history of mankind and humanity, as Peter discovered – even though there was no apocalyptic miracle on Calvary, no *deus ex machina,* only a tormented dying on the cross – and that Jesus is still the victor. I do not say that the majority of Marxists have put this experience so clearly into words. I can only bear witness that hundreds of thousands of them are on the threshold of this knowledge. It depends partly on Christians whether they go any further.

When the modern Marxist atheist has experienced comparable situations a number of times in his life, he begins to think everything through again from scratch, including his historical-materialist method. None of its basic principles is changed, of course, because the Marxist is still unable to repress the question of how this or that moral or philosophical idea of the Bible, especially the basic concept of 'salvation' itself, derives from this or that socio-economic situation. But having witnessed in such painful forms the depravity and formalisation of moral and ideal values in the twentieth century and often, perhaps, experienced them himself – in the consumer habits of bourgeois affluent society, but also in his own systems and institutions – even the Marxist begins to wonder whether the most important and urgent task of the Marxist philosopher is merely to interpret moral and other values and their devaluation. That can often mean, and in the eyes of a wider public it is often true, that one 'explains away' moral and other ideals and dismisses them, because as pure reflexes, as mere camouflage for socio-economic interests, they do not really exist! This is the greatest distinction between the older Marxists (up to Lukacs) and the so-called 'modern' Marxists. The latter are already only too aware of the danger of explaining spiritual values away into the indifferent realm of the unreal and are beginning to combat it in an attempt to salve and revive Marx's original humanistic legacy.

Modern Marxism, then, understands the historico-materialist method as follows: even though it is fully justifiable, indeed necessary, to look to the socio-economic roots of ideas, that does not exhaust the matter. It is only after the 'roots' have been clearly recognised that the really important task begins. One has to ask: which of these ideas offers positive and true knowledge about man's being and existence as well as inspiring ideals, models and norms of value without which even the best-organised, affluent and technically perfect society would remain impoverished and indeed barbarous. And one has consciously to encourage, develop and diffuse these norms of value precisely as a materialist who expects no help from on high! For example, even though one may already know the historical and social reasons why people should tell the truth in one situation and lie in another, that does not mean that the principle of 'love of truth' and the principle of 'lies and tactical deception' are to be placed on the same level. Only truthfulness can provide a lasting principle for a humane society. And that also means that Marxists can never realise their aim of a classless humane society without promoting an unshakable love of truth.

Here is another example. Although Christianity has certain mythological features which cannot be incorporated into a scientific view of the world or be 'believed' without adjustments, this does not mean that one mythology is as good as another. The early Marxists often did not distinguish Christianity from myths about Osiris, Heracles, Adonis or Perseus. What matters is not the mythological form, but asking which genuine and effective ethical ideals, values and models may be contained in this or that mythologically coloured structure; whether we can live in a way that is worthy of human beings without them; whether we can simply set them aside and 'dialectically negate' them. Even when one does not believe in a divine revelation, one can still concede that Christianity has articulated certain important ideas about the human situation, as Feuerbach already knew and Marx never doubted – it was only later, because of Engels and Kautsky, that 'explaining away' by economic forces came to be regarded as

'Marxist orthodoxy'. Once the twentieth-century Marxist has understood this point, his old conflict with 'idealists' and also with theologians begins to take on new forms: from now on he begins to 'compete' with Christian theologians in an effort to grasp the biblical ideals more deeply, to adapt them to our own age, to bring them to life and to extend them further. In the sixties the 'Prague School' of Marxists achieved something along these lines.

At the purely philosophical level the message of Jesus – especially its kernel, the teaching on the coming 'Kingdom' and the need for metanoia, that is for the immediate conversion of every individual in view of the Kingdom – can help the modern Marxist atheist (even though he remains an atheist) not to betray his own classical inheritance – the quasi-eschatological orientation towards the future – even in the post-revolutionary period when the tendency to pragmatism is strong, not to consign it with a sad smile to the museum of memories, but to renew, purify, adapt and develop it.

Thus in the twentieth century, Marxists have painfully discovered how easily a onesided stress on the paradise to come, which alone would be a genuinely human society, can lead to a fanaticism which abuses and ill-treats the present-day members of society. Christians have often had similar experiences in the history of their own movement. But what is also dangerous and for true Marxists just as painful, even though it does not bring such evident tragedies, is the onesided 'de-eschatologicisation' which can jeopardise everything: the only victor would be a consumer pragmatism with its mediocrity, lack of ideals, frantic search for pleasure (all of which earlier Marxists called *petit bourgeois*). This creeping and ever-spreading indifference has just as catastrophic results for Marxism and perhaps for humanity generally as fanaticism. The Marxist movement, which did not allow itself to be destroyed either by the Scylla of Stalin's cult of the future with all that went with it or by the Charybdis of Krushchev's pragmatic realism, has been fighting since the sixties for a sublimer form, one more adapted to the age. It is now involved in a laborious struggle, not always with full awareness, and so there are new and painful crises ahead; for what is at stake is ultimately the proper post-revolutionary form of the authentic and original Marxist vision of the future! The movement will reach this goal, for it must be reached.

The dialectical unity between future and present belongs to the nature of man. Only in this way can modern man, including the atheist, carry in his heart the highest human ideals and goals – as the early Christians carried the Kingdom of God in their hearts, and at the same time keep alive a humble and compassionate feeling for the 'greyness' of the everyday, for the 'petty suffering' of abandoned, injured, weak and therefore 'unhistorical' man. A genuine 'kingdom' (*basileia*) demands an immediate 'conversion' (metanoia).

The author, having, like hundreds of thousands of others in the twentieth century both in East and West even though in their different ways, experienced all these conflicts, anxieties, threats and hopes, and not from reading about them but through more than twenty years of active participation in the life of a socialist country, that is, of a country striving for socialism in a post-revolutionary situation, has year by year come to understand all these problems more clearly. However, because at the same time he is among those who have some small understanding of the world of the Bible, Judaism and Christianity, and because he has noticed ever more striking analogies, he has had no option but to turn once again to a study of the sources of information about the master of Nazareth in an attempt to discover in the tangled synoptic tradition an answer to the question of 'how it all came about'. That is the origin of this book, which I admit is only a beginning in the positive encounter of the modern atheist with Jesus.

The author has recently stressed several times that although he has a good deal of sympathy with Jesus and his conceptual world, he does not therefore consider himself to be a Christian, that on the contrary he has reasons for remaining a Marxist or 'disciple of Marx': the principal reason is that, although he has opted positively for the 'Christian cause', there remains at the heart of his way of thinking a radical critical approach which leads him to subject everything to scientific criticism, as Karl Marx taught his disciples. However, he regards criticism not as something purely destructive but rather as a radical reconstruction of an authentic image of man and of its realisation in the society of the future. This can never happen without a strictly scientific critical approach, but equally it can never be created by scientific methods alone; for although modern science provides man with knowledge, it does not provide him with conscience. No science of itself gives direct reasons why a man should behave more morally, truthfully or virtuously or make personal sacrifices. Personal sacrifice is never in the name of science alone. No branch of science is able to provide, absolutely and inalienably, the basis of man's self-discovery and growth as a person. This can be realised only in a profound dialogue with the sources of our Western history, from Abraham's restless wandering, the Exodus of Moses and the Psalms of David to the Sermon on the Mount and Augustinian and Faustian unrest. The author is convinced that the Marxism of the twentieth century can be truly faithful to itself only when it has the courage to open itself wholeheartedly to this fruitful dialogue with the central problems of 3000 years of Western tradition.

The way to truth takes the form of dialogue, as all genuine thinkers since Leibniz, Lessing, Kant and Hegel have known; but perhaps we can go further and say that truth itself consists in dialogue. It may be that the metaphysics of human existence can be realistically grasped only when it is expressed in terms of dialogue. The authentic West has been shaped equally by the austerely scientific approach of an Aristotle and the prophetic images of an Isaiah. If this fact was later obscured — in both Christianity and science — should we not today be trying to sharpen the two foci of the ellipse again and bring them into a fruitful and dynamic tension based on dialogue? Then the dialogue between Christians and Marxists which took place in the 1960s would remain not just an episode in history or the business of a handful of naive or idealist outsiders, but would appear rather as the modest beginnings of a radically dialogical future — and most genuinely new phenomena in history have quite modest and unspectacular beginnings. In this way new vistas would be opened up through the inspiring tension between these two elements, so that one could work with patience for the highest goals and at the same time with enthusiasm for the humblest: 'As you did it to one of the least of these my brethren, you did it to me' (Matthew 25:40).

CHAPTER II

The Sources and their Significance

Long ago in the region of the Lake of Galilee ... The rocks crumble in the heat and seem to cry out for rain. The River Jordan wends its way through gentle hills towards the earth's deepest hollow, away to the South, the region of death, the Dead Sea. Here in Galilee, in the North of the country, there appeared a man called Jesus (*Jeshua, Jehoshua*). That was a common enough name. As soon as people began to take an interest in him, he was called Jesus of Nazareth, after the small town in which he grew up, to distinguish him from others with the same name. And as news about him and then he himself travelled beyond the boundaries of Galilee, especially towards the South, towards Judaea, the real centre of the country, he became known as Jesus of Galilee. He had pupils, disciples. He travelled about the land, preaching, teaching, doing good. But he was taken prisoner and executed after only a very short period of active life – perhaps three years, perhaps less, certainly not much more.

The outward course of his life and his public activity were in no way unusual for his time. That explains why he received so little attention outside the limits of his own disciples and supporters. Preachers and religious reformers, self-appointed teachers, all manner of Zealots and rabble-rousers abounded, as happens in times of crisis. Among them were men of zeal and uprightness, but there were too, as also tends to happen in history, impostors and charlatans, 'false prophets' (Matthew 7:15). Some of them, carried away by the hope and interest they aroused, were hunted down and condemned for their rebellion against the Roman occupation; others protested passionately against the tepidity, the corruption and religious indifference of the Jewish people and especially of its spiritual and political leaders. The first group were persecuted and executed according to Roman political law; while the religious protesters often met a similar fate, perhaps because the authorities were too casual to bother to distinguish them, and so they became the victims of the Roman indulgence towards home rule and local leaders especially in religious matters. Death on the cross, which could be inflicted on Romans only if they were slaves, was used in the colonies against any sort of protester. There was nothing unusual about it. Every year hundreds died in this way – dreamers, rebels, non-conformists.

In the course of history there have been many outstanding figures who had an effect on millions of people: Confucius, Buddha, Socrates . . . After centuries, sometimes after thousands of years, their memory is not dimmed. But what happened when this man no longer walked through Galilee and Judaea, what began to happen 'in his name' (Acts 3:16) has, in its range and intensity, no parallel in history. And the names that were given to him have no parallels. He was and is honoured by millions as 'Saviour of the world', as 'Son of God', indeed as a person 'of one substance with the Father', which means that he is equal to God and in some sense divine. His ideals and teachings have been handed down along the generations and have inspired remarkable individuals and whole nations, historical eras and movements. Martyrs have died with his name on their lips – while others have killed in his name. Evil men as well as good men have confessed his name. Profound thinkers have spent the whole of their lives meditating upon him and his message, to discover what he is and what not, and what he really taught. The dramatic character of the bimillenary history of the continent which so far has been the most enterprising and influential depends on the appeal to his name, on his 'message', the Gospel ('Godspel' being the Old English translation of the Greek/Latin *evangelion/evangelium* meaning Good News). But there have also been the bitterest conflicts on the interpretation of his message, and the most diverse interpretations.

Was it all a mistake? Was this 2000-year-old history simply the result of a chapter of accidents, was it based by deluded Westerners on one man who really was not very different from dozens of others? Even someone who reaches this or a similar conclusion has not put an end to the questionings, because one of the most important and interesting questions of human history still remains: what is the meaning and influence on human thought of the traditional picture of Jesus? It involves distinguishing between truth and falsehood in this tradition, between human illusions and the depths of progressive self-knowledge, which have often been confused, and finding an explanation of what it is that has led minds repeatedly for thousands of years to intense speculation and bitter conflict. Is it all just a collection of mistakes and stupidities? Ultimately even stupidities can reveal something of great importance for human beings, so much so that to ignore them can lead to catastrophe. Even if at the beginning it was a matter simply of one mistake, after 2000 years it has become implicated with something of the utmost importance. Those who try to make a radical break with this tradition ought in their own interests to realise that it is not at all easy to dispense with a tradition for and from which our civilisation has lived for 2000 years. From the point of view of human history as a whole, the Jesus of tradition, the 'kerygmatic' Jesus (*kerygma* = preaching) is incomparably greater in importance and effectiveness in human minds than the so-called 'historical Jesus', that is, the earthly life of Jesus of Nazareth. But usually such traditions do not emerge from nothing, without some stimulus from a real person. Thus it is perfectly legitimate to ask to what extent the kerygmatic Jesus, the Jesus who is preached, corresponds to the real, historical Jesus of Nazareth.

However, this task of trying to reconstruct the life and thought of the real Jesus of Nazareth, using the most advanced methods of historical and philological criticism, which are indispensable today, has turned out to be unbelievably difficult, and in certain respects totally impossible. It is only at first glance that the sources on which we have to depend seem rich and full. They consist in the first place of the four Gospels – in order of composition Mark, Matthew, Luke, John; then the rest of the New Testament; and then the non-canonical writings, especially certain apocryphal gospels, Thomas for example. It is true that these sources contain much rich and varied information and in places are certainly unique, but at the very best they are documents from twenty to thirty years after the earthly ministry of Jesus (the letters of Paul); while the Gospels, which at first glance seem to be so much fuller and more detailed, date from a period which was forty to sixty years after his death. They are beyond any doubt of outstanding importance as religious documents and witnesses to the thought and experience of the men of the period in which they were written, but are they so valuable as information on the life of Jesus? And yet it is on the basis of documents written decades after the events that the scholar, the would-be biographer of Jesus, has to build his guesswork reconstruction. The time-lag alone should give us pause for thought and act as a warning.

There are still further difficulties. For example the Gospels contain striking contradictions in their narratives. Thus in John's Gospel Jesus speaks almost exclusively about himself, while in the first three Gospels he hardly speaks about himself at all. Modern scholarship has shown that there are so many and serious difficulties, so many contradictions and uncertainties, that in the end only two facts emerge as certainly proven: that Jesus first appeared in Galilee and that his earthly pilgrimage soon came to an end on a cross in Jerusalem. All the rest is problematical, and has been defended or challenged with good and bad arguments.

The third difficulty arose towards the end of the nineteenth century when the scholars finally recognised and admitted that, throughout the whole of the New Testament, Jesus is seen from the point of view of the early Christians, that in other words he is seen through a theological prism, through the eyes of faith which understand and shape absolutely everything in the light of the 'Easter experience'. The early Christians were not interested in the past or in history but were entirely directed towards the future. Is it, then, at all possible to separate historically reliable tradition from the theological and religious attitudes of the writers of the Gospels? It is true that they used existing material and especially oral tradition in their work, but they had no critical approach to their sources. Further, we have practically no documents for comparison from non-theological sources, since first-century non-Christian documents which mention Christianity (for example Tacitus and Josephus) are not only very disputed but also so unimportant that they can practically be ignored. For practical purposes the value of other sources such as the Talmud is equally questionable and adds nothing of importance. Finally one must add that the Gospels have come down to us in Greek, a language which is very different in its basic structure from the Aramaic spoken by Jesus and his companions and very different from Hebrew, in which the Jewish Old Testament tradition is enshrined.

Are there, then, any traces at all of the historical Jesus of Nazareth in the image of Jesus Christ as it was developed towards the end of the first century? The question has to be faced, especially in view of the countless 'biographies' of Jesus written in the nineteenth century and on into this century. Karl Kautsky rightly compared the efforts of the New Testament critics with the work of an art restorer who tries to discover the original picture beneath the many layers of paint. The results of the heroic efforts of many generations of critical theologians and New Testament scholars are certainly impressive if one considers the intellectual power they have displayed, the wide range of cultural and historical material used, the sources of comparative religion drawn on etc., as well as the immense number of subtle and ingenious hypotheses put forward, and yet despite it all there remains only uncertainty, the uncertainty of all previous hypotheses and solutions. This fact will never basically change, even if one found some new source which differed in time and in content from existing sources. The discovery of the Qumran manuscripts after the Second World War, however important the knowledge it made possible, led to no sensational or revolutionary results. Consequently every New Testament scholar (who has to reckon with a literature so extensive that it is often easier to propound a new theory than to find out whether someone else has already put it forward) knows perfectly well, if he is honest with himself, that the ground on which his researches take him is very shaky indeed.

The remarks which we have so rapidly set down here are depressing and thought-provoking for strict historical science. It is therefore no accident that as early as the end of the eighteenth century, radically sceptical and nihilist views began to be developed which culminated in the rather curious hypothesis that Jesus probably never existed at all and that everything in Christian tradition, including Jesus, was entirely the fruit of man's mythological invention. The author of the present book does not underestimate the human capacity for myth-making. Indeed he starts from the assumption that it plays an essentially greater part even today than most modern men imagine. Yet it would be unreasonable to reject the Christian tradition, to go against the evidence of expert analyses and refuse to see behind the early

Christian texts of the Gospels any great and moving religious figure whose teaching and ideals were soon adopted and broadcast by many disciples and followers. It is certain that in this process new elements were introduced which had nothing to do with the historical Jesus: the contradictions of the written Gospels are evidence enough of that. But when the contradictions of the Gospel are put forward as an argument for the alleged non-existence of Jesus, one must ask whether this theory would not be more convincing if there were *no* contradictions in the Jesus tradition. It would be better if a harmonious, perfectly consistent 'myth' without any contradictions had emerged from the first century. Most genuine myths are usually perfectly consistent.

One can advance further and, in our opinion irrefutable, arguments in favour of the existence of Jesus. For example, if according to the 'mythological school' Christianity arose exclusively from the myth-building capacities of the Hellenistic world, and so not in Israel proper, why should this 'myth' be historically rooted in Palestine? How could it have been invented by Jews, even diaspora Jews, whose myth-making propensities were still significantly weaker than those of other oriental peoples? And if Jews developed the myth in a Hellenistic milieu, why should they deliberately locate Jesus' home town in Galilee rather than in Judaea, since it was in Judaea that the birth of the Messiah was awaited? The Galilean aspect of Jesus, along with many other facts which no myth would be interested in setting down and which indeed might be embarrassing for the myth, forces us to ask whether the contradictions of the Gospels, no matter how late the Gospels were committed to writing, are not the best evidence for the historical existence of the person of Jesus; for these contradictions show how as early as the second half of the first century different traditions, some of which early Christianity could only reluctantly accept (for example the 'brothers and sisters' of Jesus in Mark 3:32,JB), already encountered theologico-orthodox tendencies. Such traditions were not the result of myth; on the contrary they hindered any tendency to mythologise.

Furthermore, we cannot call to mind any outstanding, original figure, political or religious, with a positive contribution to world history to his (or her) credit, whose psyche was not complex, whose views did not undergo a sometimes painful development, who had not an inquiring mind, who did not react

THE SOURCES AND THEIR SIGNIFICANCE

differently to different situations; who therefore never said anything that could contradict another statement uttered in another context, and who therefore does not have disciples and followers who interpret his utterances in very different ways. This is surely universal, but particularly likely to occur in times of crisis, conflict and new challenge. We know that the first century throughout the Roman Empire, but most particularly in Israel, was a period of extraordinarily violent conflict which eventually erupted in two great revolutions and led to the destruction of the Jewish state and the expulsion of most of the population from their homeland. When within a generation of Jesus' death the revolution proper broke out, the climax of a whole series of conflicts dating back to long before Jesus' time, can we imagine that in view of this general situation a figure could emerge and exercise a tremendous influence on succeeding generations whose life and teaching were *not* extremely elastic, capable of being viewed from many angles, laden with tension, and therefore patient of many interpretations and understandings? The contradictions in the written Gospels, the contradictions in Jesus' own utterances – for example, 'I have come on earth to bring not peace but a sword' (Matthew 10:34) and 'All who take the sword will perish by the sword' (Matthew 26:52) – the contradictions between Jesus and his fellow-countrymen, the contradictions between the historical traditions and those who helped to frame them – all these are not only arguments in favour of the historical existence of Jesus but also keys to an understanding of the original form of his teaching.

Even if it were possible to challenge some of these arguments for the historicity of Jesus, the irrefutable fact remains that the early Christian conception of the faith (second half of the first century) which already regarded Jesus as a divine being, the 'Son of God', finds minimal support in the Gospel tradition. It therefore arose as a secondary element. The dogmatic and theological development of the early Church did, of course, partly modify the ancient tradition concerning Jesus, but had it had to *invent* it, the result would have been quite different, much more theological. This fact, which practically speaking no reputable scholar today would question, clearly shows that the development took place exactly the opposite way round: from the historical Jesus to the theological Christ, not from the mythological Christ to the allegedly historical (or historicised) Jesus.

On the other hand it is equally obvious that one cannot offer a detailed and unassailable reconstruction of the original teaching of the historical Jesus; and unless one can, there can be no question of a 'biography'. The stories about Jesus were given literary form at a time when the oldest traditions about his teachings and fate were still strong enough to hold their own against theological tendencies, but no longer so strong that they could not be combined with new tendencies. Christians at the end of the first century did not distinguish their own situation from that of the time when Jesus appeared; consequently they did not always distinguish very carefully the message of Jesus from teaching about Jesus. This means that sayings could later be attributed to Jesus which were in fact the product of the community or, often, of the theological preoccupations of the Christian communities towards the end of the first century. And Jesus is often placed in situations which read as if they owed more to the ideas of his followers than to the accounts of ancient tradition. The figure of Jesus, as it appears at first sight, that is without a study of the synoptic tradition, is therefore a synthesis of all these traditions and tendencies. This makes it extremely hazardous to assert the certainty of any particular saying, event or parable. An admission of uncertainty must preface any discussion.

But that should not lead to complete scepticism. That Mark, Matthew and Luke were not 'writers' in the modern or the ancient sense of the word but rather 'editors' who tried to give an overall view of the traditions about Jesus, and that in their compositions there are at least three levels of the so-called synoptic tradition (Greek *synopsis* = general view) allows us to distinguish between what did or must have arisen between the years 60 and 90 A.D. as a result of the situation or theological effort of the Christian community and what could not have come from this period and must therefore be of earlier origin. It is then even more difficult to say precisely what 'earlier' would mean; one cannot here speak of what 'must have' or 'could not have' happened, at least as far as individual *logia* or thoughts are concerned. That means that even at this stage one cannot distinguish with certainty what Jesus himself 'really said' and what disciples trying to think in his spirit said long before Mark and Matthew set about their editorial work. Apart from two or three very general affirmations – such as that Jesus preached the coming of God's Kingdom (just as every prophetic figure had probably in some form or another), there is not only no certainty about the life of Jesus but also no certainty about his teaching. And someone whose interest in history and in the world generally is limited to that kind of certainty can happily ignore the entire centuries-long controversy about the exact content of Jesus' preaching. One might well ask, however, whether people looking for this type of certainty have themselves any certainty as to the content and meaning of their own lives.

When we come to establish the truth about many significant historical figures, particularly those who wrote nothing themselves (one thinks of Socrates and Confucius; but there are others like Napoleon or Goethe who have been presented by admirers in totally different ways), the question arises whether the demand for guarantees for particular statements attributed to them is not the height of folly. Even if we could never decide with total certainty which individual sayings were pronounced by Jesus himself and which should be attributed to a later period, to resign oneself consequently to the hypothetical reconstruction of the first two levels of Christian history would be unrealistic; yet a study of the two different levels of the synoptic tradition enables us to reconstruct the main lines of Jesus' thought with a high degree of probability. The simple fact of Jesus' impact on history leads one to conclude that his sayings could not have been totally chaotic, that they must have had a certain structure, must have hung together as an organic whole, must have been organised around certain basic, central, determinative ideas. For in the end the great figures of history usually have only a few ideas; it is people of average talent who have a lot of ideas running through their heads. Once we have ascertained these pillars of Jesus' thought, what Jesus 'really said' in every particular case will not seem important. We shall be much more interested in knowing not only whether his sayings as they have come down to us in their logical structure and internal coherence enable the men of our time to gain a rational understanding of the basic structure of his conceptual world, but also whether, rightly viewed, they enable us to understand our own lives more fully through the life of Jesus, the living springs of our being through the living springs of early Christianity, to discover a creative harmony of knowledge and action, feeling and willing, joy and pain. Modern man, a product of the fetishistic needs of an industrial civilisation which he no longer or not yet understands, scarcely knows how deeply he stands in need of 'redemption' and how he has to solve the problem of meaning in his own life, sufferings and loves through dedication to something which transcends the empirical order. It is true that he can read about Jesus, he might even understand something about him, but as long as he himself has not become alive in a human way, he will not see the living Jesus.

One final remark is needed here. Jesus is not just one historical figure among others, someone about whom monographs can be written as they are about Moses, Augustine and others. For millions Jesus is also the 'Son of God', the 'Redeemer of the world', in whose election and central role in history people believe in a religious sense. That is why for an immense number of people considerations about Jesus are far more than matters of mere 'historical research'; they coincide with a life style, with certain experiences, including 'Sunday' experiences, feelings of being raised above the everyday and its meaningless rhythm, with certain 'ultimate questions' too, experiences of being threatened, of the proximity of death, experiences of failure, weakness and guilt. They also encounter Jesus in the experiences of overcoming life's difficulties and the cruelty of chance and fate, as consolation in the disillusioned longing for freedom, in unrequited love. For other people, however, Jesus is the central concept of one of the greatest and most deplorable errors in human history: the Christian religion.

I do not personally think that the world has already been 'saved', but neither do I regard Jesus' ministry and the entire 2000-year 'salvation' history of the interpretation of his message as pure error or as a deplorable lapse in human history. The dramatic greatness of this history − a history characterised by 'blessings of heaven above, blessings of the deep that couches beneath' (Genesis 49:25) as Jacob said to Joseph, who was the first to try to bring the 'God of Abraham' and the 'God of Israel' to a non-Jewish people of the West − matches the greatness of the questions posed by Jesus' message, in whose name the 'long march' of Western thought through history really began. After the experiences of Auschwitz and Hiroshima, but also after the tremendous efforts of Albert Schweitzer, Rudolf Bultmann and other Protestants to 'demythologise' Christian tradition, and after the revolutionary first attempts to face 'the world', 'the present', evinced by the Christian Churches, including Catholics with the boldness and faith of John XXIII – after all this 'believers' too have a growing interest in 'what it has all come to'. For the question is inescapable: what is the meaning of the command to love one's neighbour (Mark 12:31) if today, despite the scientific study of the social and political situation both in East and West and all the factors to which Marx and the movement based on him have drawn attention, it is not yet established how in the near future a more human life can be effectively brought about.

But 'unbelievers' too, especially those for whom 'unbelief' is not just an empty negativism but an aspect of the positive effort to establish a new form of social life which would be more in accord with human dignity (and only this sort of atheism can have a positive meaning for the disciples of Marx and Lenin), will have to become aware, with greater urgency than ever before if all is not to collapse in ruins, of the magnitude of our epochal crisis, one which not merely is economic but also threatens to destroy our whole European civilisation with its millennial traditions. They will have to understand clearly that this crisis cannot be solved by economic and political means alone, but that we shall have to delve into the depths of our tradition so as to master the problems of today and not totally fail, humanly and morally, in the encounter with the expanding cultures of the Far East. The critical study of the three pillars of the European tradition – Greek culture, the Roman concept of the state, and Judaeo-Christian faith – is of fundamental importance even for the radically secularised atheist of the twentieth century, if he wishes to know his own hopes and the causes of his failure.

The indispensable conditions of this enterprise are an unshakable adhesion to the truth – an adhesion which transcends the prejudices of both unbelievers and believers – and the conviction that historical truth cannot be gained on the cheap. One must draw on all the critical possibilities of previous scientific research with cool understanding and exercise the greatest scepticism with regard to easy hypotheses, whether someone else's or – more particularly – one's own. That does not mean, however, that the

results of the work must be 'value-free', neutral between the op-
posing sides, between good and evil, distinguishing truth and
error only as mathematics distinguishes positive and negative
quantities. The interested researcher – writer or reader – should
not remain an indifferent spectator when confronted by a conflict
that raises moral and human problems or by a struggle between
good and evil or the attempt 'that the light should shine forth,
and the darkness should not master it'. To put this in more
modern terminology, he cannot be indifferent in the face of the
battle for a fuller and more responsible humanity, the sincere
striving for honesty, conscience and the meaning of human life.
Wherever – even after the full exercise of critical scepticism – we
encounter a deep and inner struggle for something which is important for mankind, even though the struggle is not yet at an
end or has not yet succeeded (and what human project ever really 'succeeds'?) or is on the fringe of what needs to be done, we
ourselves are involved in this struggle and transformed by it. The
result of our preoccupation with our present theme, now of so
many years' standing – and not just *our* theme, but in some sense
the theme of the dialogue between Marxists and Christians which
took place in Prague in the 1960s – is not something that can be
set down as though it were a thing of the past that no longer
affects us; we have rather to say with the first disciples of Jesus:
'Did not our hearts burn within us while he talked to us on the
road . . . ?' (Luke 24:32).

CHAPTER III

Jewish Religion before Jesus

I am the Lord your God, who brought you out of the land of
Egypt, out of the house of bondage.

You shall have no other gods before me.

You shall not make for yourself a graven image, or any
likeness of anything that is in heaven above, or that is on the
earth beneath, or that is in the water under the earth; you shall
not bow down to them or serve them; for I the Lord your God
am a jealous God, visiting the iniquity of the fathers upon the
children to the third and fourth generation of those who hate
me, but showing steadfast love to thousands of those who love
me and keep my commandments . . .

Hear, O Israel: The Lord our God is one Lord; and you shall
love the Lord your God with all your heart, and with all your
soul, and with all your might. (Deuteronomy 5:6–10; 6:4–5)

Two questions need to be clearly distinguished from each
other: the causes and directions of the rapid spread throughout
the Roman Empire in the first two centuries of faith in Jesus as
the 'Saviour of the world', and the development of the thought
of Jesus and his personality. The speedy diffusion throughout the
whole Roman Empire of the news about Jesus cannot be understood without a study of the whole socio-political situation,
which was one of extreme crisis. It was an age which looked for
'salvation', that is, which sought for a 'way out' and yet which at
the same time denied it to many millions of ordinary people. In
the end it stimulated an unappeasable longing for some illusory
principle of salvation and was therefore an ideal seed-bed for the
rise of a religion of salvation. In contrast to this, only the immediate circumstances of the political situation and the religious
development of his own homeland are relevant to the develop-

ment of the thought of Jesus and his first disciples. They lived in a country known successively – according to the ethnic groups who fought over it in history – as Canaan, Israel, Palestine. The movement which starts with Jesus derives partly from the influence of the concrete situation of the country in the first century (A.D., our reckoning), and yet it is also conditioned by the independent intellectual development of the Jewish people, who are indisputably one of the most remarkable peoples in human history. They have been the most persecuted, yet from among them has emerged a disproportionate number of outstanding personalities who have deeply affected the course of history, from Moses, Jesus and Paul to Marx, Freud and Einstein.

In order to understand the thought and personality of Jesus, the first task is to attempt to grasp the specific character of the thought of the pre-Christian period, especially the period immediately before his coming, and in particular its religious features. But this cannot be done without some reference to the historical development of the Jewish people as a whole. It will be important here to stress certain aspects and tendencies of Jewish thought at that time which differ essentially from the current attitudes of our own time and thought patterns, even if in certain only externally inconspicuous details. Since our purpose is to try to arrive at an at least relatively sound historical knowledge of Jesus, nothing could be worse than simply to open the Gospels and expect these texts to inform and inspire us without more ado. If he does no more than that, modern man almost inevitably projects his own in part quite different concepts and attitudes involuntarily into the text, so that he reads something other than what is written there, confuses the essential with the accidental, and often reaches the very opposite conclusion to that which the apostles and evangelists were trying to express.

A second and closely connected point must be made. Jewish religion of that period was stamped with the vivid feeling that man is a threatened being, that his existence is a struggle between life and death, that in fact everything is a struggle, both for the individual and for the people as a whole. Perhaps this was the reason why religion developed here more swiftly, more profoundly and more colourfully than elsewhere. Life was not only never easy, it was almost always entirely at risk, existence in the raw. This followed partly from the geographical situation.

The country had always been at the crossroads of varied and mutually hostile political interests: first of all between the Egyptian empire and the states of Assyria and Babylon on the Euphrates and the Tigris, later between the Persian Empire and Greek colonisation, shortly after that between the states which succeeded to the Empire of Alexander the Great: the Seleucids and the Ptolemies. Finally the country formed part of the disturbed and never thoroughly pacified frontier region of the Roman Empire. For the purpose of this book we can leave aside the fact that this exposed frontier situation continued into the Middle Ages and is particularly evident in our own time.

New peoples constantly invaded the land, while others were always being driven out of it. We have to remember that the Jewish people never had this land to itself, even in the rare moments of its relatively greatest expansion, for example under King David. The first Hebrews who were attracted into this land, long before they had consciously attained national or political unity, before they were really Israel in other words, found there an older Semitic but non-Jewish people, the Canaanites, which is why it was known as the land of Cenaan or Canaan. There followed bitter battles with the non-Semitic peoples of the South, the Philistines: very much later, the Romans called the country Palestine after the Philistines, as if they wished to root out the original name. From the North there came the Syrian-Aramaic peoples towards Galilee, the homeland of Jesus. They mingled increasingly with the Jewish people and their language displaced Hebrew for centuries even in the everyday language of the Jews. Yet the Jews remained Jews, with full consciousness of their distinctiveness. There can be no possible doubt that this sense of being different in religion, together with the racial unity to which it led, would prove to be of the utmost importance. It provided a permanent response to threat and danger.

From what is, seen from our standpoint, the dawn of history, at the time of the Jewish sojourn in Egypt about thirteen centuries before Christ, there developed from this in the course of history one of the most remarkable features of the Jewish religion, which is found in no other people (though there are traces of it among the ancient Romans): the fusion of religious feeling with the historical consciousness of the race. They interpenetrate each other to such an extent that on the one hand historical events acquire a sacral, consecrated, messianic quality, while on the other every problem of the 'divine' is drawn into the historical struggles of mankind. Some kind of mingling of history and the idea of the numinous is found among all peoples, especially at the beginning of their history. It can be seen in the myths and sagas relating to the origins of the race. Yet everywhere else the two elements are soon separated from each other: various stories about the gods are handed down, and alongside them stories about profane history, but they are not linked together, except perhaps when some 'miracle' has to be explained. The Jews, on the contrary, did not have two sorts of history, a sacred history and a profane history; from the beginning the divine voice is heard exclusively giving commands for precise historical actions. The very oldest stories of the race are told in this way, stories about the patriarchs, about Abraham, Jacob and Joseph of Egypt. There can be no doubt that they incorporate certain distant memories of the travels and struggles of some groups of the semi-nomadic tribes from whom in the first half of the second millennium before Christ Israel was gradually formed. Of course the definitive redaction and canonisation of the text belongs to a later period, possibly the time of David.

If in particular we compare Greek or Indian myths with the accounts of the period of the Jewish patriarchs, there appears a basic difference: in the Greek and Indian narratives the stories are about the fates of gods or demi-gods or heroes; in the Jewish stories the action concerns exclusively human beings, the tribe, its patriarch, and the voice of God is heard in and through this human action. From the point of view of the amalgamation of religion and history, it was above all the memory of the Exodus of Israel from Egypt which played a decisive role for the whole of the rest of Jewish history. They were led out under the leadership of Moses, who was, of course, in his turn led by the 'voice of the Lord'. We cannot here discuss to what extent this or that detail of the narrative was founded on historical fact. Something much more important is involved: the commemoration of something *historical,* of that 'great night' in which the lamb was sacrificed and the people freed from slavery, became the greatest religious feast of the Jews, on which for centuries tens of thousands of Jews poured into Jerusalem. This feast, the

Passover, later played an important part in Jesus' destiny.

It was not only faith in God himself but also this fusion of sacro-religious sentiment with meditation on the history of the race which led to another remarkable and extraordinary characteristic of this people, something that is not found to the same extent among any other people: the astonishing capacity to endure and resist, to bear generation after generation with the toughest conditions, exile, slavery, and yet to ward off outside pressures and to refuse the evident advantages of assimilation. Thus the people was not destroyed, even when David's kingdom was annihilated – it had reached its zenith about the year 1000 B.C.; and it still survived when first of all the North of the country, known at that time as Israel, was conquered in 721 by the Assyrians, and when later in 589 the Babylonians conquered the Southern part, Judah, and carried off into captivity a great part of the population, in particular, obviously, its élites:

> By the waters of Babylon, there we sat down and wept,
> When we remembered Zion.
> On the willows there, we hung up our lyres.
> For there our captors required of us songs,
> and our tormentors mirth, saying,
> 'Sing us one of the songs of Zion!'
> How shall we sing the Lord's song in a foreign land?
> If I forget you, O Jerusalem, let my right hand wither!
> Let my tongue cleave to the roof of my mouth,
> if I do not remember you,
> if I do not set Jerusalem above my highest joy!
> (Psalm 137:1–5)

All Christian peoples later accepted as their own similar experiences recorded in the Psalms and made them a permanent part of Christian worship. Yet when they really found themselves in comparable situations, 'on foreign soil' (we may recall the fate of tens of thousands of Czechs and Slovaks in America), it did not help them at all, for after two generations the language has usually disappeared, and after another two, the memory of it is gone, the assimilation is complete. Why did that not happen to the Jews? How did they manage to survive for centuries and greet each other so confidently with 'See you next year in Jerusalem'?

It cannot simply be explained by some theory of 'racial vitality'. It must be somehow linked with the circumstances out of which the Bible, Jewish religion and Jesus himself came. It must derive from what is most essential in the thought of the Jewish people, from their concept of God and, therefore, indirectly from their concept of man, of themselves (both as individuals and as a race), of the meaning of human existence and the human struggle. That their way of thinking was essentially different from that of the men of our industrial civilisation today is obviously to be explained by the different circumstances, especially through the predominantly agricultural way of life of ancient Israel and the less developed nature of the division of labour. The individual's self-awareness was not so strong as it was later to become (or as it already was among the Greeks with their technical and more advanced civilisation), and so there was for example not so much clinging to individual destiny, to survival after death, which was to become the basis of the search for happiness, and at the same time the cause of incalculable suffering, for the majority of men in modern European and in general Western civilisation. At that time in Judaism people felt more involved in events which concerned the race, the cyclic course of life, the fate of their country. In this respect we can today find parallels in Asiatic countries rather than in the countries of 'Christendom'. For similar reasons – agricultural work was still absolutely predominant and there were as yet no 'problems of work' – there could be no contrast at that time between the spiritual and the material principle. Yet in the end we are unable to derive the special character of Jewish history and the origin of the Bible from these circumstances; for hundreds of other tribes lived in a similar way without making their mark on human history. It is easier to describe how the concepts of God and man developed among the Jews than to explain why the development of a deeper form of religion happened so much more swiftly than among any other race or people in human history.

There is of course in Jewish religious traditions too something which resembles the mythico-religious representations of other ancient peoples. One example is the myth about the creation of the world which is found among other Semitic and Aryan peoples. Roman history begins with the story of Romulus and Remus, where likewise there is the murder of a brother as in the biblical story of Cain and Abel. Like Abraham, Oedipus and Aeneas wander about the world, engaged on a quest, led by destiny. Iphigenia must be offered in sacrifice by her father as Isaac is. The fairy-tale theme of the one chosen out from among his brothers is familiar to many who have never heard of Joseph of Egypt. Niobe was punished in the same way as Lot's wife. Examples could be multiplied. If one insists on seeking further parallels in this direction, one will find them, and yet they do not in the end explain the phenomenon of Moses, Isaiah, Jesus and Paul. They do not touch the essential.

Even monotheism, the exclusive cult of the one God, of Yahweh, although it was the basis of Jewish religion from the start, had elements, especially in its earliest stages, which recall other religions current at that time elsewhere. A hint of this is to be found in the fact that God was originally a tribal God, not the only one, but merely superior to the other gods, in the sense in which the tribe put its own interests before those of other tribes. In the oldest strata of the biblical tradition his appearance is sometimes linked with fire, and this suggests that the tribal god was honoured as a volcanic divinity (of fire), or perhaps as the God of atmospheric phenomena generally (rather in the way the Greek Zeus ruled over thunder). There are also features of a war-like divinity which are easy to explain by the constant warfare and strife in which the tribe found itself. Moreover one can follow for centuries certain hints that alongside the history of Jewish monotheism and even in some forms of its own culture, there survived vestiges of the more primitive cults of the Canaanites, especially in the North of the country, which was never completely won for orthodoxy.

Yet in the end these details are not very important. What really counts is that we have in the oldest levels of the biblical tradition a refined and coherent concept of monotheism that is found nowhere else. It is only among the Jews that the idea of the absolute uniqueness and the universal character of the godhead and the non-existence of other gods wins through explicitly and successfully. What is more important still is that this God should forbid representations and images of himself, that he should refuse to make things easy for those who wanted to believe in him, and that he should order them to act and think in ways which often ran counter to their immediate worldly experience.

In this fashion he demanded a greater surrender of the human intellect and will. There were of course other attempts to overcome primitive anthropomorphic ideas of the gods from the Egyptian Pharaoh Akhenaton to the Greek philosophers, but only the Jews managed to make it something for the whole people. Whether this was really the work primarily of Moses, as the oldest biblical traditions narrate, one can today neither affirm nor deny; yet there is on the whole no reason to disbelieve the tradition that he played the principal role in the development of monotheism. It is no accident that the Bible describes the prodigious difficulties and resistance which Moses had to overcome among his own people. That he succeeded in imposing monotheism irreversibly can perhaps be partly explained by the trials which the people had to undergo in the Exodus from Egypt and which helped to arouse their spiritual powers. It is true that hundreds of other tribes in the course of history found themselves in situations which seemed to be similarly menacing, and yet they did not develop any such ideas in response. One thing is certain: the further religious development, with regard both to the light thrown on the existential situation of the individual in Job and in the Psalms and to the vision of the future for mankind described by the prophets, would have been unthinkable without this first phase, without the movement towards a radical and strict monotheism, towards a God who refuses to be reduced to the mere instrument of human wishes and ideas.

This explains the deeper reason why in Jewish mythology Yahweh has a totally different role from that of Zeus in Greek or Shiva in Indian mythology: Yahweh speaks, forbids, gets angry, but he does not act, at least not in human form — *it is man who acts.* Only in this way can one understand the important idea of the covenant between Israel and God: Yahweh imposes on them a duty to act. He does not behave like a director of the cosmic play, nor is he someone who guarantees the meaning and corrigibility of human activity, nor is he simply someone who fills in the gaps in human knowledge or satisfies emotional needs. That all these conceptions should have played a greater or lesser part in Christian history must be traced back rather to Greek and Roman than to Jewish influence. If one reads the Old Testament and to some extent the New Testament without being aware of such concepts, one will read into the texts something which is alien to them.

Precisely because our ideas are shaped by 'culture' and civilisation (at least as far as knowledge is concerned, since from the
moral point of view modern man is still in a position to show
perfectly well how fragile civilisation is) and are therefore bound
to attitudes which have been established for centuries, it is
difficult to arrive at an even approximate idea of what the God of
Abraham really meant for the men of the time of Jacob, Moses,
and David, so long before the development of classical Greek
culture. Whether we are atheists or believers, centuries-old
traditions lead us almost inevitably to conceive of God as a 'Person', 'Lord of all', Creator of nature, Lord and Master of the
historical processes. It is this conception of God that has been
obstinately preserved, whether one believes in such a God or not,
and when modern man opens the Bible, he assumes that Moses
and David must obviously have had the same idea of God,
because others are ostensibly impossible. *Either* God is like Apollo
or Hermes – and in the Bible he plainly is not, *or* he is an abstract
philosophical principle, 'Spirit', the unitive principle running
through the whole of nature, the cause of movement, the
guarantee that the world has a meaning, the protector of
mankind from absurdity and from the sense of being lost in the
meaningless infinity of material processes. Modern man does not
understand that the second limb of this alternative is just as
'Greek' in its origins as are the concepts of Apollo and Hermes.
He can grasp only with difficulty that the world of the Old
Testament is completely different from the world of Plato. Moses
and David had no reason to look towards what we might call
the Platonic-Stoic conception of God. The ancient Jews did not
study either nature or causality: why then should they develop a
concept of God which later arose from such a study in Greece?
They abandoned primitive polytheism and anthropomorphism in
quite a different way from the Greeks in their passage from
Xenophon to Plotinus.

Yahweh is neither a God of nature nor a God of causality. The
Jews were not concerned with these questions. The fact that God
was not clearly delineated does not mean that he was some sort of
abstract principle in contrast to the visible statues of polytheism.
But what then is this Yahweh? What sphere of human life is his
own sphere? The most decisive thing of all is that Yahweh *speaks*.

Yahweh speaks to man, addresses him as 'thou', makes demands on him and on the whole people. As God of the covenant, he is a God who makes claims, gives commands, issues summonses. His sphere is not that of cosmic and natural events but rather that of human self-awareness, of need, guilt and the possible mission of the man who is thus addressed. 'But I will establish my covenant with you . . .' (Genesis 6:18): this is the theme, the strongest and most frequent thread in the Jewish sacred texts. This is why Yahweh – after the collapse of polytheism, nature worship and primitive adoration of the tribal divinity – becomes not anything vague like 'God in general', but the 'God of Abraham', the 'God of Isaac', the 'God of Jacob' (and not 'the God of Abraham, Isaac and Jacob').

What sort of relationship is this, which is not common even to a community as tight as that of 'grandfather, father and son'?

It is the most personal and inalienable sphere of every human 'I'; indeed, it is in some sense the human 'I' itself, in so far as the latter is the fully experienced and conscious I identical with its mission. It persuades us to leave behind the sense of being lost in daily reality – frequently such a miserable reality at that – and to acknowledge the supreme claims of life and exert ourselves to the maximum to answer them. This God is a long way from being the object of feelings of bigotry or nostalgia, but is a God with whom one struggles, a God one must be able to resist and oppose, even violently (Genesis 32:28). He is therefore an expression of the tension between the higher and lower components of human subjectivity. Human subjectivity here does not mean withdrawal into one's self, into the intimate realm of purely personal experiences, but subjectivity in the sense of consciousness, of conscious activity not only of the individual but of the whole tribe. It is the human 'self' acting consciously in the spirit of the covenant.

It is for this reason that the only possible 'name' of this God is the one with which he reveals himself to Moses, one of his greatest heralds: 'I am who I am' (Exodus 3:14). When one's thinking has been influenced by the Greeks, by the natural sciences and rationalism, it is difficult not to understand this phrase in an Aristotelian or medieval or supposedly modern sense in terms of an ontology of substances. But that is thoroughly misleading, even when, as many have been recently inclined to under the influence of the dynamism of the last generation, one translates it as 'I am the one who happens'.

For the Jews were neither Aristotelian-Scholastic philosophers nor the creators of some sort of dialectical ontology. This expression – if we neglect a certain Delphic obscurity which always characterises religious utterances – means rather something like 'I am the one that really is'. That is: I am the occasion of your and every possible human 'self', I am the 'I-principle' of humanity and the whole world. It is in other words saying the same thing as the non-generalisable expressions we have already noted – the 'God of Abraham', the 'God of Isaac', the 'God of Jacob'. He is a God who makes claims on *you* in the name of his covenant, with which he binds human beings to action.

This could be put philosophically in a different way: the downfall of polytheistic ideas and nature worship is understood in Mosaic monotheism as the defeat of the divinity of 'things', and therefore as the downfall of God as an 'object'. Hence his lack of clarity or definability. The divine is transferred exclusively to the realm of the subject and is brought into the relations between the higher and lower levels of the 'self' and into the 'I-thou' relationship.

But are we then dealing any longer with religion? The ancient Jews certainly had a definite cult and a form of sacrifice, they had a definite 'credo', a priesthood, and so on. In a sense, that is a more profound religion than any other. Later generations of Jews were unavoidably and constantly among pagans and idolaters and were to some extent influenced by them and tempted to honour the 'golden calf' (Exodus 32:4) in a form of cult which resembled that of neighbouring peoples. Especially when things were going well, many of them lost their taste for the true inheritance of Abraham, Jacob and Moses (Deuteronomy 32:15).

In this way Jewish history is certainly a history of unfaith as much as faith, the story of the overcoming of superstition and bigotry as of falling away from the covenant with Abraham and Moses into superstitions in which God is scaled down and reduced to being no more than the product of one's own desires and the projection of one's own yearnings into religious ideas.

But on the other hand, and precisely through this 'God of Abraham', the God who addresses every human 'I', the God who forbids all images of himself, the specifically religious sphere is in

some sense if not destroyed at least extended and therefore confused. That is why it is no accident that the biblical tradition gave
rise to the most varied tendencies which in some way transcended
the horizon of religion. In the twentieth century a host of
thinkers – the most important among them being Karl Barth,
Erich Fromm and Ernst Bloch – have tried with varying success
to interpret the biblical tradition as something which is basically
non-religious. Barth of course attacks religiosity and piety,
although he keeps the idea of 'the Word of God' and understands
the revelation of God to man as the contrary of religion, which
he sees as the attempt to develop a merely human doctrine of
God. The other two authors draw conclusions from the Bible
which are unreligious, humanistic and atheistic. This is possible
since the God of the covenant is a God who expressly forbids
what lies at the root of all religion, namely images,
anthropomorphism, the projection of human desires. Not only
does he make this development possible, he makes it strictly inevitable.

The essence of the Jewish ideological tradition, as it appears especially in the Bible but also in the Talmud and in post-biblical
Jewish literature, can thus be interpreted in two totally different
ways. Even its intellectual high points like the Psalms, the Book
of Job and Ecclesiastes, can on the one hand be understood as
religion at its deepest, most demanding and sincere; or they can
be read as an account of complicated and profound problems of
human existence, as an important contribution towards man's
self-discovery, and from this point of view they might be considered more important than the high points of other religions or
Greek and Roman antiquity. Certain basic situations of human
life are uniquely expressed, for example, in the Psalms: situations
of struggle and failure, of hopeless depression, and the overcoming of these by new hope; the injuries inflicted by the pains
of life and by betrayal by friends, and then a restored faith in
mankind; the nearness of death or danger, and the courage to
face them; the shame and misery of everyday life, and the lifting
up of one's eyes to 'the hills, whence comes our salvation' (Psalm
121:1). Taken over by Christianity and spread throughout the
world, the Psalms have for centuries furnished models of the experience and mastery of elementary human situations. It is not
easy to overcome these situations without the human 'self' being

finally overwhelmed, and these models provide no guarantee that one will succeed; yet when one lives intimately with the Psalms, one has something to rely on in order not to go under in the distressing situations of life, and one can gather enough moral and emotional strength to win through. In so far as modern man no longer has such models, in spite of all the veneer of civilisation and perhaps his superior knowledge in specialised fields he is morally and emotionally on a lower level than those who do have such models.

The ancient Greeks laid most of the foundations of modern science, technology, specialisation, of cultural and artistic forms, of individualism and rationalism. Thus they endowed humanity with books – hundreds of them, led mankind to prodigious successes and opened up to men the horizon of the real mastery of nature and the cosmos. But there also came into being – especially in the modern period when this 'Greek principle' became the basis for the life-style of millions – a type of man who has read hundreds of books but who experiences none of them deeply. What he has read goes in at one ear and out at the other, and perhaps leaves behind certain traces of knowledge; but it does not shape him intimately. The Jews gave mankind not books but *the book,* and that in a sense is more. The reason is that in this book there are models which are capable of influencing the conscience, the will and existential attitudes, and which give a feel for 'ultimate questions' – questions concerning the meaning of human life, effort, love, suffering and man's situation between life and death.

The Jewish people itself often ran the risk of losing its appreciation of the far-reaching content of the covenant. It was led to this by success and ease rather than by frightful catastrophes, which could revive moral strength. But even when, in the vertigo of success, the dazzlement of power and the magic of Epicurean delights, everything was lost and the heritage of Moses was reduced to the purely external formalistic fulfilment of the Law and ritual ceremonies, there came prophets who inveighed against all that and renewed the vitality of faith in Yahweh. They appear in almost every century between Moses and Jesus, from Elias to Daniel, the Second Isaiah and John the Baptist. They provide a first hint that man has always to be starting again, that his reform either is permanent or does not exist at all.

When, in desperate situations like the Babylonian captivity, and also in personal trials, the prophets gave hope and strength to the people of Israel, and when they described how everything could and should be better, they discovered for man something hitherto unknown and which was perhaps the greatest discovery of human history – provided that we do not look on it simply in an external way but regard it as the story of man's gradual self-discovery – the *dimension of the future,* a living future which draws us forward, which makes demands on man in his present, and in this way makes the 'present' for the first time something real, something deeply appropriated. Without some knowledge of the content and meaning of the prophetic movement, as the important link between Moses on the one hand and early Christianity on the other, one cannot hope to understand the thought-world of Jesus and his first disciples.

Of course there are prophets and seers in all religious systems. We have only to think of the Roman augurs and diviners. But whereas elsewhere they do not rise above the level of naive 'guesswork' about some coming events, among the Jews – and this is certainly linked with the deepened function of religion, analysed above, from the tone of Moses' monotheism and the Psalms of David – the prophets became an influential political and social force, which in protest and opposition often developed tendencies which were either directly revolutionary or at least paved the way for revolutionary radicalism. Indeed there gradually developed in the Jewish prophetic movement a whole system of so-called eschatological thinking (from Greek *eschatos* = last), that is to say, a way of thinking in which there was a radical critique of the present state of society combined with the expectation of a dramatic upheaval in the future either through God's direct activity or through a hero chosen by him.

In its description of this coming Kingdom of happiness, the prophetic movement quite naturally begins with mankind's age-old memory of some original society, of a 'golden age' or a 'paradise'. In this context 'repentance' is seen first of all as a return, an end to the falling away from the original faith in Yahweh; but it does not remain there. Something wholly new comes into existence because on the one hand this tradition is involved with the most radical social criticism in that it begins to express the social yearnings of the oppressed and to criticise

kings, tyrants, the rich, traitors; and on the other the transference
of its vision from an ideal state to the foreseeable future makes it
possible to regard it now as the concern of human striving, activity and moral duty. Israel will be saved in the future! Indeed,
the whole world will be radically different and will be liberated.
The ideal Kingdom will come in which oppression and bloodshed are no more, in which 'swords are beaten into ploughshares'
(cf. Isaiah 2:4), in which there is peace not only between man
and man but in the whole of nature. The harsher life is – the oppression of the innocent, alienated work, suffering – the more
eagerly do the prophets paint a picture of the coming Kingdom
and give men hope and the moral strength to resist and persevere.
They are themselves persecuted, exiled, stoned, of course, but
they do not give in.

The closer one comes to the generation of Jesus, the more
different aspects of the prophetic-eschatological message were
developed. There was for example the idea of a sudden chiliastic
(from Greek *chilioi* = a thousand) upheaval of history: that
precisely at the highest pitch of suffering the 1000-year Kingdom
of happiness and freedom would come. There arose colourful
apocalyptic images (Greek *apokalypsis* = unveiling, revelation) of
the climax of the catastrophe with all the horror of the 'last
battle', but also of the happy state which would follow. The
thought of thousands fastened on this future age; thousands of
pure hearts thought they were let into the secrets of life and
human existence more deeply and accurately in the revelation of
this apocalypse than in the greyness of everyday reality. So from
inconspicuous seeds began to mature something which later –
when the Christian and Marxist missions had carried it to other
peoples – was to display an extraordinary power to transform the
actual existence of millions with all their hopes and tragedies.
The future began to appear to mankind as the most important
thing possible.

As always and everywhere in history these desires for redemption were linked with the hope that some powerful figure would
come and inaugurate the new age of salvation or at least prepare
it. Memories of the great heroes of the past, of Moses who led the
people out of their Egyptian labour camp, and especially
memories of the most famous king of Israel, David, helped to
awaken the hope that a similar hero would appear who could

lead the people of Israel to new prosperity and fame. But just as the eschatologico-prophetic movement in Israel was not the concern of the majority but captured the imagination only of a section of the resistance movement and of the revolutionary fringe, so the concept of a future hero of Israel was neither clear nor widespread. The greatest hope of the widest public could, without any great intellectual effort, conjure up the pure Davidic idea, namely that there would come an extraordinary hero 'anointed' like a king (Hebrew *Maschiah,* from which we get Messiah; Greek *Christos* = anointed one, and then by extension 'Redeemer', 'liberator'). Finally the concept of the 'anointed one' was transferred to possible liberators even when they were not kings. Since the belief was widespread that a period of terrible suffering would precede the Kingdom of blessedness, indeed that the Kingdom of God would break into the world *as a result* of the very extremity of suffering, it is not surprising that already in some of the Psalms and in particular in Deutero-Isaiah hopeful looks should be directed towards the suffering figure who would be 'Servant of the Lord' (*ebed Yahweh*). He would take upon himself all suffering and in this way inaugurate the era of salvation. This tells us a good deal about the psychology of the Jewish revolutionaries in their wars with Rome. They persisted in the struggle even when all real prospects of victory were lost. They hoped that their last-ditch resistance and their endurance to the end would bring about the messianic transformation. This perhaps helps us to understand something of the human destiny of Jesus. It was still not clear whether the coming saviour would appear as a purely earthly rebel or king, or whether he would be a supernatural, apocalyptic hero rather as the prophet Daniel thought of him — the strange and mysterious 'Son of Man' who appears on heavenly clouds, the cause of eternal prosperity for all the nations (Daniel 7: 13–14). The two images, it is true, do not exclude each other, yet they did not necessarily have to be found together. Of course these ideas — like prophetical thinking in general — never became very widespread or generally accepted, and obviously they were stronger among those who tended to heretical views and deviated from strict orthodoxy. Similar contradictions were found in the Middle Ages and also in modern times.

Palestine had practically never been at peace since the time the

armies of Alexander the Great had traversed it. There were
already very good grounds for the critique of the prophets and
for the messianic aspirations of the people. In the three centuries
immediately before the coming of Jesus, there were conflicts of
all kinds, and ever more violent and despairing efforts to solve
them. The country had freed itself from the sphere of Persian influence and then from the domination of the Egyptian Ptolemies,
but it then became Hellenised under the Syrian Seleucids in the
third and second centuries. Thus for the first time it came into
contact with what was in many respects a more developed
culture, that of ancient Greece. This showed itself above all in the
thought and life-style of the upper classes, but also in the
strengthening of the old antagonism between the orthodox
South, Judaea, and the North of the country, Samaria and
Galilee, which were less able to resist Syrian and Hellenistic influences. It was at that time that the so-called Samaritan sect
seceded from the central Jewish cult, and from then on Jewish
mistrust of the Samaritans lasted right up to the time of Jesus.
Even though the Maccabean revolt against the Syrians was
successful in the second century, Jerusalem was conquered by
Pompey in the year 63 B.C. and the country became a colony,
part of the Roman Empire. For two centuries that was the fate of
Israel. It led after revolutionary struggles to the complete destruction of the country and the dispersal of the Jews to the four corners of the world, but paradoxically, it was also the basis for the
future fate of the Roman Empire. The movement which started
from Jesus grew out of social conditions similar to those which
led to the two great rebellions in the years 66–70 and 132–5
A.D.; and when shortly after this Rome became the centre of the
worship and glory of the Prophet from Galilee, it was one of
those fantastic reversals of history in which it is difficult to say
who is really the conqueror and who the conquered.

Finally, the last century before the coming of Jesus was also
characterised by great intellectual activity and clarification in
Judaea, even to the extent of controversies on the nature of
orthodoxy in the very centre of orthodoxy, in Jerusalem itself.
Under Herod the Great (37–4 B.C.), who achieved a certain
measure of independent sovereignty thanks to a cunning policy
of repressive terror against inconvenient people at home combined with servility towards the Romans (and it is worth noting

that the people were more ready to forgive Rome than to forgive Herod: hatred of him lived on long after his death in the legends about Jesus' birth and Herod's terrible death), the political parties and sects who were later to play a direct part in the story of Jesus were founded. Their squabbles over the meaning and nature of the Mosaic Law were not simply a matter for purely academic or theological discussion. They carried with them socio-political implications. And among the questions raised was doubtless that of how the country was to be saved from its present crisis.

The religious group best known to us, the Pharisees (Hebrew *Perushim* = Singled out, Called, Exclusive with regard to the interpretation of the Law), were inclined to all kinds of reforms, to which the contemporary influences deriving from Hellenism and Neo-platonism opened their eyes. They formed a kind of liberal wing of the Jerusalem middle classes which strove for a compromise between conservative traditionalism and popular radical tendencies. No doubt they attached importance to the conversion of each individual: but it is far from certain whether the tendencies rightly criticised in the New Testament were really so prevalent among them, and whether Jesus really saw them as his principal enemies in polemic, as appears from a first reading of the synoptic Gospels. In the end it seems that some of them became Jesus' disciples and were not so opposed to him as Jesus appears to have been to them in the synoptic tradition (cf. Luke 7:40ff; John 3:1ff; Acts 5:34–9). The synoptic tradition and perhaps Jesus himself criticise rather the 'Pharisaic principle' – hypocrisy, superficiality, self-satisfaction – which may have been verified only in some of them. One cannot go so far as to say that they played a part in the rise of Christianity, on the grounds that they were the first to emphasise the idea of resurrection. It is more significant that it was from their circle, from among those who stressed not so much the Law as inner religion, that Paul emerged, who was later to free early Christianity definitively from the bonds of the Law (Acts 23:6).

In contrast to the more liberal Pharisees, the Sadducees (Hebrew *saddik* = pious, just) represented a sort of priestly patriarchy (the 'scribes' of the New Testament), the conservative wing of Jerusalem's highest class. They stressed the absolute unalterability of the Jewish Law and the need for a strict formalistic adherence to it. They rejected all demands for reform, whether from Hellenistic or popular sectarian-prophetic movements, they opposed all forces of renewal and became the mainstay of the collaboration with the Roman occupying forces on the basis of a strict separation of political and religious authority. According to every tradition of the New Testament, the principal responsibility for the condemnation of Jesus belongs to them. There can be no doubt that, unlike the Pharisees, they were utterly opposed to any movement of renewal.

While the two movements we have mentioned were found above all in Jerusalem, all more radical movements and groups developed rather outside in the country areas and were focussed on the peripheries of the country: Galilee, along the Jordan and round the Dead Sea. As regards their constitution and aims, there were two main types of popular opposition movement, as always happens in times of similar crisis. On the one hand there were groups and also individuals who pressed for armed revolutionary struggle, rebellion, the driving out of the Romans and the vigorous punishment of collaborators, and who adopted whatever aggressive action opportunity or their strength allowed them. On the other hand there were other individuals and groups who were no less radical in their rejection of the present state of society but whose rejection took the form common to hermits, monks and sectarians: in other words flight from the evil world, anywhere at a distance from it, and the attempt to achieve moral renewal, especially in themselves. This they regarded as the basis for a better society for the future. No doubt these were not two completely self-contained and mutually exclusive tendencies. Between them there was a certain amount of give and take, and those who were either not completely satisfied with one approach or utterly disillusioned by the other, switched sides – and often changed back again later. What, according to Marx, both these tendencies have in common, despite all differences of religion and revolution, namely the rejection of the world as it is, has as its effect that in all ages and centuries secret bridges exist between monks and revolutionaries, bridges that have not gone unused.

Was one of the reasons for the success of Jesus' movement the fact that he offered a third and different way? That in spite of its undisputed and well-proved contacts with both tendencies, early Christianity chose neither the path of armed conflict nor the path

of sectarian pacifism? It is a fact not only that many of Jesus'
followers came from the movement of John the Baptist who was
a typical representative of the monastic denial of the world, but
also that there were Zealots in his wider circle of friends as well
as among his closer disciples (Greek *zelos* = passion, enthusiasm),
as the nicknames of many disciples (Luke 6:15; Mark 3:17),
together with many other events and stories, show. It was a
movement whose adherents were then fighting a partisan war
against the Roman power in the Galilean hills and who were
later the most radical fighters in the two revolutionary wars. It
was their intransigence which later led to the complete destruction of Jerusalem, at least according to the Jewish historian
Flavius Josephus, who belonged to the priestly hierarchy. If Peter
himself came from among the ranks of these men who so detested
Rome, as Carmichael has suggested, then the fact that he could
become the basis of Rome's new claim to fame and glory would
be another of those remarkable paradoxes of history which it is
easier to read about than to create.

Especially from the works of the historian Flavius Josephus and
the philosopher Philo of Alexandria, it has long been known that
among the radical sects was one called the Essenes (perhaps from
the Aramaic *chassajjá* = pure, pious) who are said to have existed
throughout the whole country. There was therefore considerable
astonishment, when the taste for historical research began to
develop in the modern period, that the Essenes are never mentioned in the synoptic tradition and indeed in the entire New
Testament, even though their teachings bear certain obvious
similarities (as well as containing notable differences). Theories
were proposed as early as the end of the eighteenth century,
notably by Venturini and Bahrdt, which suggested that Jesus had
been a member of an Essene group and that his death and apparent resurrection had been engineered by the Essenes; the
silence of the biblical texts could therefore to be explained only
by deception. Firstly, this theory is altogether too fanciful; and
secondly, it is scarcely likely that such conspiratorial secrets
would have been respected by the highly diverse group of people
who became responsible for the handing on of the Christian
tradition of the first century. Yet astonishment grew still more
after the Second World War when certain important new
manuscripts were discovered, particularly during the excavations

at a settlement resembling an extensive monastery on the West bank of the Dead Sea at a place called Qumran. Texts of the Old Testament were discovered, among them the oldest we know, dating from the second century B.C. to the first Roman War (i.e. 70 B.C.). But extensive and hitherto unknown original writings were also discovered which seemed to be very close to what was known of the thought-patterns of the so-called Essenes and which therefore showed that, towards the beginning of Christianity and not very far from Jerusalem, there existed a by no means insignificant group of an Essene character, perhaps a part or even the headquarters of the Essene movement itself!

The Qumran discoveries have not so far been fully published or evaluated; but they have significantly increased our knowledge of the ideas and way of life of this Jewish monastic sect at the time when Christianity originated, and have disclosed certain other significant analogies with the thought of early Christianity (as well as differences) and made the complete silence of the New Testament texts on this movement an even more puzzling question. Among the parallels are important facts such as that the Qumran dwellers knew of a 'Teacher of Justice', who was abandoned by a part of his followers and persecuted, but who nevertheless in the Essene faith — and this is the crucial point — would return at some future date. There are analogies with the thinking of John (the struggle between the sons of light and the sons of darkness) and also with the Epistle to the Hebrews (the idea of the Messiah as High Priest); riches are criticised in a comparable way, and there are rites reminiscent of baptism and the eucharist; naturally they also stress the imminence of the eschatological catastrophe which was expected to come after the highest pitch of suffering. This was evidently a common feature of all popular prophetic movements.

There are, however, no less important differences. The most important is beyond doubt the sectarian-monastic, consecrated and élite character of the Qumran movement, and linked with it the strict and complicated rituals of the chosen 'pure ones'; all this contrasts with the completely unsectarian nature of early Christianity which was open to the world. The fact that Jesus' beginnings are set in Galilee, which is inexplicable if taken to be pure legend, means that he cannot be identified with the Qumran 'Teacher of Justice' or indeed have any close links with the

Qumran community. How could legends about the principal figure of an élitist sect take on the characteristics of Jesus, who had friendly contacts with the Romans, with their collaborators the tax-gatherers, with prostitutes? That is against all logic and experience: mythologising, legend-making tendencies do things the other way round. Although this explains the non-identity of the two groups, it still does not explain the silence of the early Christian texts on the Qumran and Essene communities. The New Testament does not usually avoid polemics. Many theories have been devised to answer this question. It has been suggested for example that perhaps the Qumran community appears in the synoptic tradition in the person of John the Baptist and his disciples. On that hypothesis, the New Testament polemics against ritualism, the blind sanctification of the Sabbath, the ostracism and hatred of enemies, would be echoes of the real polemic which Jesus' movement had with the Qumran-Essene movement; while at the same time Jesus' personal relations with John the Baptist, attested in tradition, would explain a certain reticence and indirectness in these controversies.

Without denying a certain justification for this theory, we should like by way of conclusion to discuss the opinion according to which the silence of the New Testament on the Qumran-Essene sect, despite all unanimity on some important ideas, has ultimately the same causes as the almost complete silence of Jewish and Roman texts of the first century on early Christianity: in the confusion and turmoil of that century, each movement must have looked on other from the standpoint of its own particular 'world', so that for it the 'others' – the Christians for the Roman historians and politicians and Jewish men of learning, the Essene-Qumran hermits for the first enthusiastic apostles of Christianity – were simply 'not there'. They were at the very edge of their field of vision, if not actually outside it. One must try to imagine what it was like for the first apostles of Christianity: they were only a handful of men, they aroused only mockery or pity in their immediate acquaintances, and they had no importance whatsoever for serious historians and politicians. Yet they set off on immense journeys throughout the countries of the Mediterranean so as to 'go into all the world and preach the gospel to the whole creation' (Mark 16:15), and 'make disciples of all nations' (Matthew 28:19). What could have been the im-

portance for them, for their world-view, of a few introverted
hermits who for the last five or six generations had atrophied in
their clausura, nourished by pride in their status as the Elect?
Provided that we are not taken in excessively – 'postitivistically'
– by the external similarity of the teachings, the Qumran-Essene
movement was probably only one of the symptoms of the age in
which Jesus' movement emerged, only an off-shoot of the same
trunk from which Jesus, Peter and Paul grew, but for that very
reason had disappeared from history by the end of the first century. We do not know whether one can apply to this dis-
appearance the words reported by all the evangelists: 'I am not
worthy to stoop down and untie the thong of his sandals' (Mark
1:7 & par.). This leads us directly to that historic moment in
which so many people – political rebels and religious dreamers –
in their longing for salvation were impatiently awaiting him in
whom they could at last believe that 'the time was fulfilled . . .'
(Mark 1:15).

CHAPTER IV

The Message of Jesus

The time is fulfilled, and the kingdom of God is at hand; repent, and believe in the gospel. (Mark 1:15)

The man who will later have an extraordinary fascination for the thinking and feeling of thousands almost always appears unobtrusively on the scene. His childhood remains a mystery. Certainly no one is brought up with the aim of effecting an upheaval in history. Suddenly the man is 'there', he appears, he comes out of the unknown. Something which is truly 'new' and which ushers in a new period in the development of natural or human history regularly emerges – as Teilhard de Chardin remarked – in the shadow of the only apparently new. The apparently new attracts all the attention of the old world, its hate, its resistance, actions designed to sustain its power.

From the point of view of the powerful and educated – those who wielded the sword and the pen – the apparently new element in the first century of our era in the Eastern part of the Mediterranean was certainly not Jesus and his first disciples. In the eyes of the Roman administration, the most urgent threat came from the groups of radical freedom fighters, the Zealots, who were fighting a guerrilla war and preparing a general revolt; these groups were gradually growing in strength, were united in their detestation of Rome, and no doubt did genuinely represent the greatest threat to the civil power. From the point of view of the clerical and theological circles of Jewry, the most important problem was that posed by the radical sectarian groups of the Qumran-Essene type: these men protested, complained, hated. They could not be reconciled to official policies, they were a cause of the greatest concern to the Jewish and the Roman authorities. When Jesus was later put to death, clearly on the condemnation of both authorities acting in concert, it was more than important for his followers, but for the authorities themselves it must have seemed a tiny incident, a routine episode. Their attitude towards Jesus' movement was for a long time one of bored uninterest. This is the only way one can explain how it was that even a long time after the first Roman-Jewish War of 66–70 which had drawn everyone's eyes to Palestine, neither the Jewish nor the Roman sources bothered with Christianity, apart from a few trivial and unreliable mentions; and yet this was already a generation after the Pauline Epistles. In this way it was possible for what was of the greatest importance for society to pass unnoticed, unobserved, lost in the shadow of other events.

That is why it is the Gospel of Mark which beyond any doubt describes with relatively the greatest historical accuracy the beginnings of the public activity of Jesus, since in Mark Jesus suddenly appears alongside John the Baptist and nothing is said about his childhood and youth. Plainly that did not interest Mark, any more than it concerned Paul at an earlier date. This lack of interest was doubtless characteristic of the admirers and followers of Jesus during his life and in the first generation after his death. And he himself, like all those who are gripped by a revolutionary vision, must have had a similar attitude towards his mother and his relatives as the one expressed in the following episode:

And his mother and his brothers came; and standing outside they sent to him and called him. And a crowd was sitting about him; and they said to him, 'Your mother and your brothers are outside, asking for you'. And he replied, 'Who are my mother and my brothers?' And looking round on those who sat about him he said, 'Here are my mother and my brothers! Whoever does the will of God is my brother, and sister, and mother.' (Mark 3:31–5)

That is not an isolated incident. There are several similar motifs in the synoptic tradition.

Paul and Mark know nothing about the influences which Jesus underwent in his youth or of his contacts with his family, which anyway had probably ceased by the time of his public life. One can take as certain only that he grew up in the North of the country, in Galilee, in the town of Nazareth, and that his mother

was called Mary (Miriam). He probably left the house of his
parents early on, so filled was he with the vision of his future
mission. And then he gave no more thought to his family. It was
only later when, in the memory of thousands, Jesus was already
the dearest and best-beloved person, when he no longer worked
through the immediate power of his personality, his vision and
his stories – 'The eyes of all in the synagogue were fixed on him'
(Luke 4:20 & par.) – that it seemed obvious to his followers that
such a man must also have been loved in childhood. Since all
mothers love their children – or if not alas all, at least all those
whose children enter life with trust in love and with generous
hearts and are not undermined by bitterness, cynicism or
pessimism – his followers of the second and third generation
were unanimous that his mother must have loved him. There
must once have been a young woman who, like most mothers,
dreamed of a wonderful future for her child; at the first stirrings
of her child in the womb she must have had exalted feelings as
she imagined his future, and perhaps they took this form:

My soul magnifies the Lord,
and my spirit rejoices in God my Saviour,
for he has regarded the low estate of his handmaiden.
For behold, henceforth all generations will call me blessed.
(Luke 1:46–8)

And when, as the child grew, his unsophisticated mother
perhaps no longer understood him – 'And they did not understand the saying which he spoke to them' (Luke 2:50), that moment of exaltation, of longing presentiment, of desire that her
child would grow up to bring mankind something great counted
more than the harshness of everyday reality, more than misunderstanding, disappointment, despair. True, none of this has
anything to do with historical science, which relies on verifiable
and recorded facts. But can man be reduced to documented
dates? Do mothers put down their feelings on paper as they rock
the cradle? Do they tell investigators just how they felt after the
execution of their child? What the majority of mothers feel, the
mother of Jesus must have felt: the followers of Jesus were convinced of that. And how strong her feelings must have been after
giving such a son to the world!

Such thoughts did not occur to the first disciples and admirers of Jesus. They were overwhelmed by his preaching and the strength of his immediate effect. The only thing they knew about his youth was that he came from Galilee, as was evident from his accent (Matthew 26:73 & par.); yet in their hearts they harboured quite other desires. People who await some extraordinary and transforming event have not the interest of biographers. Only two items from the early days of Jesus have come down to us, and we can regard them both as highly probable: the first being the report that the beginning of his public life was somehow linked with the ministry and the movement of John the Baptist, though they soon were separated; the second that he spent some time in the wilderness, in solitude. These two facts we can take as practically speaking certain, not only because later tradition would have had no interest in inventing them, but especially because similar things happen in some form or another in the lives of every exceptional man. By means of a close relationship to a mentor (which can often, by normal standards, seem exaggerated), the exceptional figure of the future first develops his personality in a difficult process of self-enlightenment (only average men find everything perfectly clear from the start) and gradually learns to distinguish the essential from the accidental in his own thinking. Through the period of solitude which then follows, whether it takes the form of the periodic wandering existence of the Persian, Indian or Chinese heroes or the withdrawal into oneself as in the countries of Western traditions, the maturing exceptional individual on the one hand frees himself from the persisting, disturbing influences of his youth and on the other resists being too strongly overshadowed by his mentor's personality, and thus becomes not merely a continuator or imitator but 'himself'. Both the period in which Jesus was with John the Baptist (and perhaps also in contact with the Qumran-Essene movement), and the time of solitude probably lasted many years: only in this way could he begin his mission at the height of his powers. Tradition casts this into dramatic form – as it always does in similar environments and similar situations – in two brief episodes. But the synoptic tradition taken as a whole makes it clear that they were not just episodes.

One cannot say with certainty whether tradition has minimised, exaggerated or recorded without substantial alterations the

differences between John the Baptist and the mature Jesus. It is
the concern of tradition to present Jesus as something absolutely
extraordinary and superhuman, and therefore to stress the
differences and contrasts that marked Jesus out from others. Yet
since John the Baptist soon came to be regarded as the
'forerunner', tradition was not fully effective in this particular
case. There need be no doubt that the central idea of John, just as
much as of Jesus, was the 'coming of the kingdom of God' (cf.
Matthew 3:2 & par.), for that as we have already mentioned in
connection with the Qumran-Essene sects was probably a universal phenomenon of all popular-prophetic opposition movements
and groups within Judaism at that time. Nor is there any reason
to doubt the tradition according to which John the Baptist was a
typical hermit, an ascetic, a figure as if stemming from the roots
of the Old Testament prophetic resistance: 'Now John was cloth-
ed with camel's hair, and had a leather girdle round his waist,
and ate locusts and wild honey' (Mark 1:6). He was different
from Jesus in his life-style: the eccentricity of his outward
appearance, the severity of his diet, the harshness of his criticism,
his intransigence towards sinners, and his radical attitude to the
powerful. And there are features that one does not find at all in
Jesus: his emphasis on self-humiliation, puritan moralism linked
to certain ritual acts and especially baptism (Jesus himself did not
baptise, though his disciples were later to do so). When the synoptic tradition reports that Jesus, unlike John, had certain absolutely 'worldly' characteristics, there can be scarcely any
doubt: such reports cannot have been legendary inventions.

We may presume that his long stay with John the Baptist's
group (which had close connexions with the Qumran-Essene
movement) helped Jesus gradually to perceive the insufficiency
of this path of puritan sectarianism. All the Gospels suggest that
the importance of John the Baptist lies in the fact that it was
through him that Jesus came to recognise the originality of his
own quite different mission, and they dramatise this in the scene
of the baptism of Jesus by John. Jesus' vision and the voice from
heaven which announced his mission to him (Mark 1:9–11 &
par.), despite their legendary form, are undoubtedly the concentrated summary of an experience prepared for many long years.
It can often happen in the lives of future great personalities that
they reach a momentary high point when suddenly there is a

marked emotional break, often accompanied by optical experiences of clarity and beauty and moral catharsis (rather like the sudden transition to the fanfare theme in the third movement of Beethoven's 9th Symphony). It is no accident that a part of Church tradition (in the Orthodox Church) then retained the memory of the significance of this scene in the conviction that at that moment Jesus first 'became' — by divine adoption – God's Son, the one 'in whom the Father was well pleased'. Here, in a legendary form, we are faced with a real experience, such as is known to us from the lives of other significant personalities, in which reverence for one's master suddenly changes into an understanding of one's own higher mission.

The report that then he felt the need for solitude — 'The Spirit immediately drove him out into the wilderness' (Mark 1:12) – is certainly no less significant. Here again we are given a summary account of an indubitably long process, perhaps a stay of several years in the desert. The need for solitude — to clear one's mind, to become aware of one's mission, to concentrate one's spiritual powers — is just as essential for a future great personality as the already mentioned separation from one's former teacher. Moreover, in this period, by means of a moderate asceticism, self-discipline of mind and body and deep concentration, Jesus attained extraordinary powers of control over his nervous system and at the same time acquired the qualities of moral power, personal magnetism, the capacity to draw men to himself with a gesture or a look which are found in one person in a million and without which doctrine alone remains mere words. These qualities, of course, could not be produced by asceticism alone, yet they could not have existed without something of the kind. Without this period of 'wasted time' — for such it must appear at first sight to the majority of modern object-bound men – Jesus could not have later made history. It is especially the twentieth century, endowed with thousands of means of enriching visible human communication, which adopts the onesided and erroneous view that what counts is *what* is said. In reality *who* is speaking is much more important, especially where there is harmony between mature words and a mature person.

But what are we to make of the 'temptation by the devil' with which his stay in the desert apparently comes to an end (Matthew 4:1–11 & par.)? Even though the form of the story is typically legendary, even though similar 'temptations of the just man' by the devil are found in the Old Testament (Job) as well as in non-Jewish religions (in the life of Buddha, Zarathustra and others), and even though the period of forty days is undoubtedly borrowed from the length of time that Moses is alleged to have spent on Mount Sinai (Exodus 34:28), one need not conclude that this story is a mere fable. It is rather the later abbreviated version of a real event in which Jesus gradually became aware of the nature of his future mission and overcame his own reluctance and the possible false paths or satanic 'temptations'. This threefold 'temptation' means ultimately the recognition that what is really important can be found neither in things nor in power nor in concern solely for oneself.

The two episodes – the baptism and the temptation – therefore provide a meaningful prelude to the description of Jesus' public activity. If we compare this account with the lives of other important religious figures or statesmen or artists, we become aware of the far-reaching importance of these events for the whole of Jesus' further activity. Their unquestionably long duration also vindicates the report that by the time Jesus began his public life he was 'about thirty years of age' (Luke 3:23): the profound and rapid effect on his disciples, probably unthinkable at twenty years old, was possible only because the two episodes we have mentioned represent no more than the remnants of information on the long growth to maturity of the hitherto unknown Jesus.

What constituted the commencement of Jesus' public life? Obviously we must not imagine something comparable with the publicity campaigns of today which depend on technical media. They increase the number of people affected, but they also diminish the directly human character of the communication. Jesus' entry into public life was a long-drawn-out and imperceptible process: it consisted in the fact that Jesus shared his thoughts and visions ever more frequently with his fellow men and that in the end listeners, and then actual disciples and admirers, began to gather round him. The undoubtedly authentic episode of his on the whole negative reception in the town of his youth, Nazareth, indicates how long this process too took and that he did not succeed without difficulty. His first attempt among those who remembered his childhood in Nazareth met with no success.

THE MESSAGE OF JESUS

They said: 'Is not this the carpenter, the son of Mary and brother of James and Joses and Judas and Simon, and are not his sisters here with us?' And they took offence at him. And Jesus said to them, 'A prophet is not without honour, except in his own country, and among his own kin, and in his own house.' (Mark 6:3–4)

But his first permanent disciples soon gathered round him. It is not really important whether the one who was to play such a decisive and remarkable role later – Peter – was also one of the first to have followed Jesus; the point is that he was always the 'first' certainly in every other respect, and we shall hear a good deal about him later. The splendid scene which describes the call of the first disciples – 'Follow me and I will make you become fishers of men' (Mark 1:17 & par.) – is certainly a later composition, as are so many other things one reads in the Gospel texts. Simple fishermen of that date would have had not the slightest interest in becoming 'fishers of men', would not even have understood such a phrase and were rather (to continue the fishing metaphor) 'hooked' by the attractiveness of Jesus' personality: yet in spite of later accretions the scene still gives a sense of the extraordinary power Jesus had of attracting people to himself.

The later literary records of the synoptic Gospels, with few exceptions, have not managed to capture this 'personal magic' (but then neither has modern science): all we have is phrases, words. Yet it is clear that in reality it was not only Jesus' teaching which played an important role here, but also, no less notably, the sheer pull of his overwhelming personality, a kind of awe in those he met, more easily expressed in artistic than in historical terms (as in some of the masterly descriptions of Tolstoy, Dostoievski and Thomas Mann). There are only hints of this in the synoptic Gospels. For example people were seized with astonishment that he should teach 'as one who had authority, and not as the scribes' (Mark 1:22 & par.). It comes out too in the sudden exclamation of the easily excitable Peter: 'Depart from me, for I am a sinful man, O Lord' (Luke 5:8). Wonder is a more common theme in the independent tradition of John's Gospel: even though its authenticity may be doubted to a large extent, a few passages reflect, with astonishing persuasiveness, at least an echo of this element of the oldest tradition, for example in the truly emphatic

confession: 'We have beheld his glory, glory as of the only Son
from the Father . . . Grace and truth came through Jesus Christ'
(John 1:14, 17). This is an aspect of the personality of Jesus which
will never be fully clear to us in all details. Reports about his
power to heal the sick also belong here to some extent. Even
though legend-making exaggeration was most at work here, the
narratives on the whole are undoubtedly not without some basis
in reality. However, to exclude them completely from the scope
of a rational interpretation, to limit oneself to Jesus' *thoughts*,
would be the greatest misunderstanding – professors can earn
their living only by 'having ideas', but no prophetic figure, certainly no founder of a new world religion, has confined himself
to 'having ideas'.

I stress this point since there is today a tendency to overlook it.
It has become so deep-rooted that it necessarily makes the whole
of early Christianity very puzzling indeed. One cannot stress suf-
ficiently that it is impossible to find the reason for the powerful
impact of Jesus simply and solely in his 'programme' or 'doctrine': one can in any case find parallels for many of his thoughts
in the Old Testament, the Essenes and John the Baptist, and also
in the Jewish rabbinic tradition, various Hellenic mystical and
philosophical ideas, and especially Gnostic ideas. Modern men,
however, are so alienated from humanity, so much turned into
'things', lost in the fetishes, rites, stereotypes and institutionalised
relationships of over-organised industrial society, that they have
no suspicion of what the spiritual and moral power of a truly
mature personality can mean.

So the fallacy has become deep-rooted that great historical personalities are influential chiefly because of their ideas – which
people today are anyway beginning to treat as objects on a par
with other exchangeable commodities. But thoughts can prove
attractive to people only when they are organically related to the
rest of a man's life. Only a man can act upon other men with the
total power of his mind and activity. 'Ideas' alone, a programme,
doctrine: these are effective only in so far as people experience a
convincing harmony of thought and personality in the other, that
is to say when the one who utters the thoughts is at the same time
the *exemplar of their realisation*. Jesus' 'doctrine' – save the mark! –
sets the world on fire not because of the obvious superiority of his
theoretical programme, but rather because he himself was at one

with the programme, because he himself was the attraction.

Only when that has been emphasised can we move on to analyse some of the alleged thoughts of Jesus contained in the tradition of the New Testament texts, especially the synoptic tradition, that is, the records made some time between the sixties and the nineties of the first century by Mark, Matthew and Luke. Although the composition of these Gospels is late, modern scholarship and especially the school of form criticism (Bultmann, Dibelius, Jeremias and others) has succeeded in distinguishing with a probability bordering on certainty distinct strata in the editorial work of the so-called evangelists, and then again arriving at what could be the most ancient level which comes either from Jesus or from sources close to him. The school of form criticism, as its name suggests, works through a literary critical study of individual shorter or longer 'forms' – apophthegm, controversy, parable, legend, story and so on – and traces the history of their tradition. Today we do not have to be so hypercritical that we must resign ourselves to never reaching the thought of Jesus himself. There can evidently be no certainty on details, any details, but that is not the point. There is no need to be sceptical about the basic lines of Jesus' message, especially if we compare it with that of other similar movements.

It will strike every reader who takes up the New Testament texts without preconceived ideas, led on simply by his desire to know and readiness to understand, that they are characterised by a sense of extreme urgency. They are concerned with something which is seen as of the highest importance, as unique and revolutionary, even though the vast majority of contemporaries took not the slightest interest in it. The early Christians considered their 'cause', their 'truth' – even though it was for the time being accessible only to a minority – to be so urgent because they believed that it drastically revised human concerns and values and because something which would totally transform the situation was happening or about to happen. It is well known that such ideas are always rooted in a profound social crisis: and yet here the response to the causes of this crisis is the firm and unconquerable conviction that the human and social crisis has already reached its high point, that the measure of suffering is already fulfilled and that mankind is on the threshold of universal salvation which will usher in the golden age, God's age, an era of full human prosperity. These texts make such a powerful impact because they derive not from any kind of academic speculation about human or divine realities but from the immeasurable accumulated pain and suffering of the oppressed, the humiliated and the insulted, and their present make-or-break situation. But suffering and pain, 'taking up one's cross' (Mark 8:34 & par.; Matthew 10:38 & par.), never have the last word; they enter into the 'dialectic of the cross', the most fundamental paradox of early Christianity. That means the hope of a complete transformation of circumstances – and not a flight from the world as many have onesidedly or mistakenly imagined. What is at stake is the final positive inversion of the world crisis, which restores the fortunes of the humble, the suffering and the enslaved. The so-called 'denial of the world' that we find in the early Christian texts depends above all upon this expectation of a real upheaval; it is therefore not any absolute denial of the world but simply a judgement passed on the present situation. It is certainly not easy to imagine oneself in the psychological situation of people who in their own estimation were on the threshold of a vast cosmic and historical catastrophe and who thought of it as a necessary transition stage towards the ultimate rehabilitation of all positive human values; nevertheless, in such a situation, human values do not remain unaffected. For when the mind is focussed on the prospect of a profound upheaval, not only are pain and poverty and private property relativised, but family relationships weaken, the responsibility of the son to his parents becomes of secondary importance, and wife and child may be abandoned for the Gospel, for the sake of the Kingdom (Mark 10:29 & par.).

The fundamental idea – or rather the ideal, the hinge of action, the framework of thought, the common factor running through all the parables and reflections, the basis of the logical structure and also of certain internal contradictions of some of the conclusions – is indubitably the idea of the closeness, the immediacy and the exacting claim made upon men by the 'Kingdom of God' or the 'heavenly Kingdom'. It both resembles and differs from what the Jewish prophets had preached for at least 500 years. The idea of a coming 'Kingdom of God' in the sense of a future ideal state of mankind, brought about by supernatural or divine intervention, refers to the same reality which is the chief content of the work of Isaiah in particular. We shall indicate later what was new in Jesus' conception. Meanwhile, it is indisputable that with this central concept of his own, Jesus is solidly in the line of Jewish prophetic tradition. The imperfect, indeed painful, present state of things will soon come to an end, and a wholly new order, a new era, a new Jerusalem will take its place. Here one must note that Jesus makes no fundamental distinction between 'this' world and the 'other' world (and this is true of the Old Testament also) and that therefore it is not stated whether the forthcoming catastrophe is an event of 'this' world or (Jesus himself would not countenance this 'or') the irruption of the 'other' world into the human situation. There are no barriers here between 'natural' and 'supernatural' powers. To construct them after the event means that one has imposed on Jesus the pattern of Greek thought, the categories of monism or dualism. This is precisely what is not true of Jesus. In his idea of the 'coming of the Kingdom of God' there were certainly elements which we *today* should describe as 'supernatural' or mythological or coming from another world. But because Jesus and his first disciples did not draw a line between this world and the 'other' world, the consequences of his reflections about the Kingdom of God concern this world, with its history, politics, social situations, and the real longings of real men for their earthly future.

In this one can trace in Jesus – as opposed to the majority of the prophetic descriptions of the future found in the older traditions – some remarkable changes which are no doubt linked with what is for us one of the most important questions that we can ask: why was it that among so many earlier and contemporary prophetic announcements concerning the 'coming age', this one alone should result in the foundation of a new movement? Or to put it more precisely: why did a vast movement, incomparably broader in scope than anything which had previously emerged from Judaism, and which rapidly and irreversibly transcended the frontiers of Israel, hitherto such an exclusive nation, base itself on an appeal to this man Jesus? One of the most outwardly striking features of Jesus' preaching is that, unlike older prophets and the chiliastic movements, he did not describe in any detail the forthcoming 'heavenly Kingdom'. We are thus faced with the curious fact that this 'Kingdom of God' which attracts millions of people as an ideal state is nowhere even described (apart from one or two uncharacteristic points), let alone painted in any detail. From beginning to end Jesus' ministry is wholly *eschatological,* that is to say that everything in his visions and descriptions is related to the future upheaval, is directed towards it: yet it is not at all *apocalyptic,* it contains no colourful descriptions of the state that will come after the catastrophe. That a group of his disciples should relatively soon begin to feel the need for apocalyptic material is proved by the fact that even the 'Apocalypse of John', which is evidently of rather late origin, was counted among the books of the New Testament even though Jesus does not appear directly in it. Its fantasies, its colourful visions, for example the detailed description of the 'Holy City' (Revelation 21:2ff) where there will be no tears and no mourning, and the description of the terrible end of unbelievers (Revelation 21:8 and elsewhere), make a striking contrast with the synoptic tradition, since there was nothing of the kind in the older levels of tradition which go back to Jesus himself.

But that merely brings us to the problem of *how* Jesus gathered his disciples and supporters: it is certainly not explained by the fact that he avoided apocalyptic statements – his success did not depend on avoiding something. Nor was it simply the notion of the 'Kingdom of God', a mere concept – ordinary people, then as now, are not philosophers who can enthuse over an idea. The 'Kingdom of God' became a central theme only because it must have had something attractive, fascinating, arresting. If it was not the fantasy of apocalyptic visions, what was it?

This takes us to the most important aspect of the message of Jesus, without which we cannot understand him or his effect on the world. We should like to stress that it is a mistake to suggest that Jesus won men to himself by his emphasis on the 'Kingdom of God'. This idea is only slightly false, but it sets one off on a decidedly wrong track. The causes of the remarkable effects of Jesus' preaching cannot be explained by saying that he proclaimed the 'Kingdom of God' as the coming of a future age; that was common to Jesus and to many of his predecessors and contemporaries. What Jesus proclaimed was *the demand which the 'future age' makes on men in the present* – which is something very different. The essence and meaning of his preaching is not: 'The heavenly Kingdom is coming'. It is rather: 'Be changed! Repent! Take yourselves seriously. You stand before God and he speaks to

you. He is close to you and you should be close to him' (cf.
Matthew 4:17). Or as it is put in more developed but certainly
still abbreviated form in Mark: 'The time is fulfilled, and the
kingdom of God is at hand; repent, and believe in the gospel'
(Mark 1:15 and cf. Matthew 4:17).

It is no accident that Mark and Matthew should begin their account of Jesus' public life in this way; the sentences are not intended as sentences like any others – and no doubt that was why
the two evangelists place these words as a sort of epigraph at the
beginning of their work – but express the meaning of Jesus'
preaching, his *entire* preaching, and are the common denominator
of every event, every parable, every simile. The Greek word
metanoeite is traditionally translated as 'do penance'; today this expression arouses churchy or religious associations which did not
exist at the time of Christ. Its philological content and the whole
context make it clear that the phrase would be better understood
if it were translated as 'Change yourselves', 'Change your
minds', 'Become different', 'Look at the inner transformation of
yourselves'. The concept of metanoia (inner transformation) is
also found in Luke (Luke 3:3). John begins Jesus' first theoretical
discussion of his Gospel with a similar concept (the 'new birth',
John 3:3). The Epistles of Paul show the same concern and it is
found in all the books of the New Testament, including that
most famous phrase of the Revelation of John: 'Behold! I make
all things new' (Revelation 21:5).

The most important of these texts, that of Mark, makes it clear
that it is not simply 'any old quotation' from Jesus, something
selected at random to begin the Gospel – it resembles in its very
formulation four headings, four theses, the essence of all that will
follow.

All subsequent details possess authenticity only to the extent
that we understand them as the details of a basic message concerning repentance for the Kingdom of God; this holds whether we
are dealing with the individual examples given in the Sermon on
the Mount or with the complicated moral exhortations of Paul.
The whole New Testament, and indeed the whole Christian
tradition, are summed up in the following splendid expression of
the Sermon on the Mount: 'Seek first God's kingdom and
righteousness, and all these things shall be yours as well'
(Matthew 6:33). This does not mean that one should dismiss

details as trivial; it means simply that one can arrive at a right attitude towards them only through a higher overall perspective. Something similar was expressed by Augustine when he wrote: 'Love – and do what you will.' Even the famous assertion that the Kingdom of God does not come externally, observably, but is rather 'within' (cf. Luke 17:20–1) shows that the main thrust of Jesus' message – as opposed particularly to the apocalyptists – is this demand for inner transformation, not at all a passive waiting for the apocalyptic catastrophe, although in modern times this expression has often been understood incorrectly as a withdrawal into interiority, as an existential programme. Both tendencies were found in the original teaching of Jesus, the inner and the external, the demand for inner transformation and the expectation of a cosmic catastrophe.

What does all this mean? As far as the *content* of his message is concerned, Jesus did *not* attract his disciples by preaching the Kingdom of God or by his teaching about the future. The two doctrines do play an important part, but the *essence* of his personal impact lies in the *opposite* tendency: he led men away from the conventional popular-prophetic picture, from the apocalyptic future which has traditionally attracted the interest and attention of the discontented because it is full of fantastic promises, to the recognition that the future is *your concern* here and now, the business of every human 'I' thus 'addressed'! In that sense Jesus brought the future down from the clouds of heaven and made it the concern of the everyday. He thereby fulfilled that at which the whole Jewish Old Testament tradition, especially the Prophets, had been aiming, and which was also the meaning of the original Mosaic concept of monotheism as a concern of the subject, of the human 'I': the future is not something that 'arrives' – from foreign parts, independently of our own activity, like a change in the weather – but something that *depends on us,* at every moment; it is the claim of the present on us, the challenge to the human ability to use every moment to the full! In modern terminology we should say that Jesus turns a future which is essentially alien to us, an awaited future which might come one day, a future which is part of nature, into an experienced, a human future. It would therefore be possible, once we have set the time-conditioned mythological colouring behind, to translate or rather interpret (and after 2000 years any translation that is not also an interpretation is nonsense) Jesus' message in the following way: 'Get a grip on life, the perfection of humanity is possible. Perfection is near, that is, you can grasp it, you can be morally better, purer, you can be more of a person – through your own action'. In other words: no one ultimately forces you to be mean, vulgar, cowardly, egoistical – to live at a non-human or 'reified' level, as we should say today. Even when the circumstances of life, the 'world', the 'age we live in', personal weakness or cunning calculation lead us to do so, in the end a person is always able, even in chains, to avoid reducing the content of his awareness and conduct to his own needs, to rise above himself, to become different, to transform himself from within, to begin to move by his own efforts towards the 'Kingdom of God' and so to belong to it.

There can be no doubt that Jesus here touches on one of the key problems for the genuinely human character of our life and for the *truthfulness of human existence*. While the Old Testament prophets had pointed out the dimension of the future and so laid the basis for the dynamism of Western history, perhaps even of the history of all mankind (in that through Marxism this dynamically conceived universalism is still penetrating the vast countries of the Far East who until recently had not known it), Jesus gives this future dimension its human character by ridding it of its alienated, apocalyptic and fantastic character and liberating it from the prison of metaphysics. Jesus in this way abolishes the future as something that merely replaces the present, a wretched, lost, squandered future, a future in which the prevailing misery of human reality is met only by empty dreams. Jesus shows not how to escape from the misery of real life but how to overcome one's own moral misery and lowliness.

Yet we must once again emphasise that this idea did not attract the disciples and future enthusiastic apostles because Jesus had somehow thought it out and delivered it as a professor or a rabbi might have done – a thought and no more, an ideal, a 'manifesto' – much less that he had, with Greek or German thoroughness, analysed it down to its last consequences and fully developed it: that would have left everyone quite cold. No, the idea 'worked', attracted disciples, they understood him and believed in him, not because he had thought things out speculatively or put great ideas before them, but because he embodied this lived future with his own being. They saw in him a man who already belonged to this coming Kingdom of God; they saw what it meant to be 'full of grace', what it meant to be not only a preacher but himself the product of his preaching, a child of the future age to the marrow of his bones.

This astonishing orientation towards the future which is not passively awaited as something foreign but is rather experienced as something lived in the present, as the source of meaning for human life, as inner satisfaction, strength and – as they called it – 'faith': this is the basis of early Christianity. It was through this transformation that mere malcontents and dreamers of a chiliastic end to history became the first 'believers' in Jesus. The four basic theses of Mark (the fulness of time, the Kingdom of God, the inner call, joyful faith in the Good News) sum up the whole conceptual horizon of Jesus' first disciples: to recognise and choose the future, in the widest sense, as here and now *my* business and profess it with all my heart and soul in faith! These first disciples did not really believe in *Jesus*: led by him, indeed 'wrenched' by him, they believed in *the Gospel,* in the proclamation of the nearness of the future age and the claims it made on every man.

We can best visualise this non-apocalyptic, non-fantastic, yet radical 'living off the future' if we understand how Jesus taught his disciples to 'pray', that is, to be fully present to oneself in the Mosaic sense mentioned above, to be wholly at one with oneself. If we compare the accounts in Luke and Matthew (Luke 11:2–4; Matthew 6:9–15) with each other and then with the whole character of the synoptic tradition in general, something like the following pattern emerges. *Our Father who art in the future age*: 'heaven' undoubtedly here means neither a spatial nor a spiritual kingdom in the sense of Greek dualism; it refers rather to that awaited future, the 'heavenly Kingdom', which is not a spatial but a temporal concept. *Hallowed be thy echo*: 'name' should not be taken in the sense of a string of syllables possessing magical power, for such an interpretation would go against the whole synoptic tradition, and there is no hint of anything comparable in Jesus' preaching: it means rather that the smallest echo, the least sign of the future Kingdom, must be 'holy', that is, essentially binding. *Thy Kingdom come*: here the future is called very clearly into the present; the future too is our concern! *Thy will be done in this future Kingdom as in our lives now*: the meaning is the same, but there is a slight development: it is no accident that this phrase is missing in Luke, Matthew adds it. *Give us today our bread of tomorrow*: once again it has the same meaning; some corrupt manuscripts, but especially the difficulty of knowing what the superfluous word 'daily' can have meant in the original context, suggest that it was not originally a prayer for bread but rather a prayer that the 'Kingdom' would be as obvious and self-evident as the need for bread. *Forgive us our faults, as we forgive those who have offended against us*: a way of raising one's thoughts above daily weaknesses, a form of the basic teaching: 'Change yourselves'. *And lead us not into the day of corruption, but free us from evil*: the Greek word *peirasmos,* which is relatively infrequent in the texts of the New Testament, was for centuries traditionally translated as 'temptation', Latin *tentatio,* in the sense of *moral* snares and trials; the leading Czech orientalist, Otakar Klíma, made it clear on the basis of newly discovered Manichaean manuscripts that the word originally meant the day of horror and devastation which was to precede the irruption of the Kingdom of God in the eschatological vision; in our opinion this interpretation fits better into the overall original, undoubtedly eschatological meaning of the Our Father, as also the other places in the New Testament which make use of the word *peirasmos* such as 2 Peter 2:9, Revelation 3:10, and especially Mark 14:38 & par.

That is the only *prayer* which Jesus taught his disciples. Jesus places surprisingly little emphasis on prayer, other expressions of worship, and in general meditation on 'divine realities'. In particular one must point out how this 'living off the future' did not lead Jesus to any kind of meditative life in seclusion from the world. When Jesus left John the Baptist, there was no road back to John's way of life, to the Jordan and the rocks round the Dead Sea, near the Essene-Qumran hermits. That would have gone against his conception of the Kingdom of God as a demand made on men here and now. In his expectation of the Kingdom man must not flee as far as he can *out* of this world, but rather shoulder demanding tasks *in* this world; he must bear the future in the present; he must not only *have* 'faith' – the determination to change himself in response to the claims of 'God's Kingdom' – but also *live* faith and therefore spread it, profess it, proclaim it, win others to it.

The point about faith is not that it provides advantages or

security or that it is a comfortable guarantee of 'salvation'; it is rather that a believer must consider the most difficult undertaking in the world as his own: 'Enter by the narrow gate; for the gate is wide and the way is easy that leads to destruction, and those who enter by it are many' (Matthew 7:13). What is asked of the believer is not withdrawal into himself, not introspection, not cultic practices, but *activity*: 'You will know them [false prophets] by their fruits' (Matthew 7:16, cf. Luke 6:43–5); 'Why do you call me "Lord, Lord" and not do what I tell you?' (Luke 6:46; cf. Matthew 7:21). Jesus never asks his disciples to learn any dogmatic formulas; he asks them to act in favour of the Kingdom of heaven. 'Go and do likewise' (Luke 10:37) is how the parable of the Good Samaritan ends; the Samaritan is the prototype of someone with a different faith who nevertheless acts with mercy and really helps the victim. The believer has to be the 'salt of the earth' and the 'light of the world' (Matthew 5:13–14), but that has meaning only when he is salt and light *for others,* for mankind, for the world: 'Let your light so shine before men that they may see your good works and give glory to your father who is in heaven' (Matthew 5:16). One needs to persevere in this effort, without being discouraged or frightened by failure: 'Ask, and it will be given you; seek, and you will find; knock, and it will be opened to you' (Matthew 7:7). If the Kingdom of God is lived out, even though it may be among few people for the moment, it will work like yeast, like a seed (Mark 4:30–2 & par.); in time it will bring about great changes among men. One should remember that the activity enjoined is not just of a transitory nature, due to become superfluous once the Kingdom of God breaks in; it is rather that Jesus brings together both ideas 'in the fulness of time': precisely because of this activity the future age is already here.

Obviously Jesus' teaching cannot be reduced to exhortations to human activity; there is no doubt that Jesus expected the coming of the Kingdom to be brought about also through the decisive intervention of God, or at least through some supernatural powers. We can say that the desired change depended on two factors — the involvement of God *and* simultaneously the conduct of men, their activity or passivity in the face of the coming revolution.

The controversy which has raged off and on for the last century about whether the Kingdom of God in Jesus has a 'future' or

a 'present' reference is in our opinion artificial, basically irrelevant, and founded on a misunderstanding of the very essence of
eschatological thinking, which is the total penetration of the present by the future in the understanding of consistently eschatological people, of whom Jesus was indisputably one. It is interesting and in our opinion not just paradoxical that because of
this – and the essence of Jesus' message is unintelligible otherwise
– many modern Marxists can in some respects evince more understanding of the present than many Christians who find this
longing expectation of the future completely strange. Like all
those who think eschatologically, Jesus was obviously convinced
that the definitive redemptive process had already been inaugurated by his present activity: although he undoubtedly
thought that the culmination of this process still lay in the future,
even if clearly in the immediate future. That is why it is perfectly
logical that we should find alongside each other in the synoptic
tradition expressions such as 'Blessed are the eyes which see what
you see' (Luke 10:23 & par.) and 'Then they will see the Son of
man coming in clouds with great power and glory . . . and he
will gather his elect from the four winds' (Mark 13:26f & par.).
The idea of the 'Kingdom of God' must have had a radical
significance for Jesus' first disciples, in both its present and future
sense; yet it certainly cannot have been easy to make this dialectic
of the concept of the 'Kingdom of God' plain and intelligible to
everyone even in the prophetic-chiliastic milieu of Galilee. Many
of the so-called parables of Jesus can be seen as a way of trying to
make this aspect of his preaching comprehensible. In spite of their
diversity the classical parables are nearly always about a certain
process: ripening (Mark 4:28), growth (Mark 4:30–2), the working of yeast (Matthew 13:33 & par.), spring buds (Mark 13:28–9
& par.), a search (Matthew 18:12–13 & par.). The common factor is that something dramatic is going to happen in the future
but that its seeds have already been sown. And then it is often
stressed that *how long* this process takes is unimportant (Matthew
20:1–16); much less can one speculate on the minimum quantity
of service necessary (Luke 15:11–32; 18:10–14). The Kingdom of
God can shine out in its fulness at any moment, even for
latecomers; it can be like the discovery of a rich pearl which can
come at any time and which overshadows everything else
(Matthew 13:44–6).

If we study the parables of Jesus without any religious or anti-religious prejudices, we shall ultimately realise, we believe, that despite their naturally time-conditioned form they concern something which is in fact remarkable. They make an important contribution to the *dialectic of human existence in time,* to our capacity to exhaust the potentiality of each moment. Man is fully aware that his life takes place in time: this provides the basis for his ability to know, to evaluate and to imagine the future, and so to strive to give meaning to what happens. But this same ability brings with it a danger: man can understand his present simply as a means and so rest satisfied with the present in all its impoverishment, mediocrity, emptiness – with only the haziest expectation of a change in the future. Man becomes accustomed to fight not for life but for mere survival – deep and genuine happiness seems to be merely a promise, yet the present is decided by overwhelmingly pitiful means. When that attitude becomes the basis of a whole life-style, it is the greatest error into which man can fall, for then he turns his back on the challenge of life and makes of it instead a talent buried unused (Matthew 25:14–30 & par.). In the last analysis, a genuinely human existence cannot be attained except through a present which is lived as fully and intensely as possible. Either humanity is the fully humanly lived moment – or it is not realised at all. And each moment has in a sense its own autonomy – it can be squandered or used to the full; the most wretched among us can suddenly come to be and live the Kingdom of God, while the most deserving fail utterly. Each moment is a new opportunity for man, but also a fresh problem. This is the meaning of those sayings of Jesus which, against all moral and religious tradition, devalue those who accumulate profit and in their place stress the opportunity that exists even for social misfits, outcasts and failures – like the humility of the public sinner (Luke 18:10–14), the prodigal son (Luke 15:11–32), the labourers in the vineyard (Matthew 20:1–16), the love of the prostitute (Luke 7:36–50). The point of all these incidents is to illustrate how far-reaching and how transforming the moment of change can be, the one fully lived moment in which all human possibilities are suddenly realised.

As a claim on men in the present, the Kingdom of God determines each situation. On the one hand it enables men to understand that morality is ultimately a matter of each developing situation, but on the other it can then exercise a direct and profound influence on that situation. This is the first and weightiest consequence of Jesus' inversion of what had hitherto been purely prophetic thinking. But is this not mere moonshine? Or an illusory turning away from reality, and therefore a kind of 'opium' – the role of religion? It is true that later it was often interpreted in this way. And there can be no doubt that certain illusions played a part in the thought of Jesus and his disciples: they were convinced, for example, that they would themselves experience the arrival of the 'Kingdom of God' through supernatural intervention. Paul describes this illusion of early Christianity as follows:

> I tell you a mystery. We shall not all sleep, but we shall all be changed, in a moment, in the twinkling of an eye, at the last trumpet. For the trumpet will sound, and the dead will be raised imperishable, and we shall be changed. For this perishable nature must put on the imperishable, and this moral nature must put on immortality. When the perishable puts on the imperishable, and when the mortal puts on immortality, then shall come to pass the saying that is written: 'Death is swallowed up in victory'. 'O death, where is thy victory? O Death, where is thy sting?' (1 Corinthians 15:51–5)

Death and hell were later to show their sting only too clearly, and in Christian history too. Although similar illusions played a part in early Christianity and were later used in typical 'opium' fashion, it would be the gravest of mistakes not to see that the concept of the 'Kingdom of God' as the maximum demand on man and consequently the fulfilment of the present moment is in no way an illusion. Without something of the kind, human life remains pitiful. This discovery is therefore not the drug-like withdrawal of man from reality but on the contrary the path to man's self-discovery, to the possible reality of a responsible life. In the history of man's self-reflection, it represents the finding of a pearl or at least of a possible leaven of humanity, as the previously quoted parables so aptly express it (Matthew 13:33–46 & par.).

Later on, through the influence of what had already become a Hellenistic milieu, the purely spiritual conception of 'salvation of

the soul' came to predominate in Christianity, with the result that
the tradition of the 'Kingdom of God' was interpreted in a
Platonic way as a prediction partly about the religious life of the
Church and partly about the afterlife conceived of as a purely
spiritual form of happiness. It is possible that some aspects of this
interpretation had already had a direct influence on Jesus' circle,
perhaps because of Pharisaic attempts and the utilisation of certain Greek ideas about the soul and its resurrection in Judaism.
But the ordering of the levels of the synoptic tradition makes it
clear that very realistic and almost naturalistic worldly ideas of
the Kingdom of God were characteristic of the most ancient
tradition: 'As my Father appointed a kingdom for me, so do I ap-
point for you that you may eat and drink at my table in the
kingdom, and sit on thrones judging the twelve tribes of Israel'
(Luke 22:29–30). There is no doubt therefore that in the thought
of Jesus himself religious ideas were mingled with a realistic and
often radically naturalistic feeling for contemporary man, his
needs and his desires.

It was not, therefore, any glorification of poverty and suffering
as they are, and not simply the opium of promises that a future
reward would compensate for patience in earthly life, which led
Jesus to apostrophise as 'blessed' – apart from 'believers', that is,
those who had already 'changed their lives', who were already
vibrant with the hope of the spirit of the future – above all the
suffering, the oppressed, the wretched, the unfortunate. In the
greatness of his heart he 'had compassion on the people' (Mark
6:34; cf. 8:2) and tried to help them as far as possible, and as
preacher of the transformation of the present into the Kingdom of
God, he opened it above all to the poor and suffering: 'Blessed
are you poor, for yours is the kingdom of God; blessed are you
that hunger now, for you shall be satisfied; blessed are you that
weep now, for you shall laugh' (Luke 6:20–1). The word 'blessed' currently used in translations has certain cultic associations
which did not exist for those who listened to Jesus; the Greek
word *makarioi* suggests something more like 'Your salvation is
here' or 'You're in luck's way' (cf. Matthew 5:3–12). Jesus'
preaching is not devoted to the glorification of poverty and
deprivation, on the contrary: not only must the poor be helped,
but in the climax of the synoptic tradition Jesus directly identifies
himself for future purposes with every suffering person, who

must be actively helped: 'As you did it to one of the least of these
my brethren, you did it to me' (Matthew 25:40). Action is called
for, real help! With these elements Jesus' message and early
Christianity, even though, as we readily concede, it is not an
aspect placed at the forefront, acquires a social and revolutionary,
world-shaking character. We should not underestimate these
elements, since in the history of Christianity they have often
provided the motivation for revolutionary groups; but it would
be equally wrong to take them out of context and give them an
exaggerated importance as has often happened, no doubt with
the best of intentions, in the socialist movement, as for example
in Karl Kautsky. Teachings which can be interpreted and exploited in a revolutionary way were no more than an organic
part of the structure of Jesus' eschatological thinking, which certainly had other features and which also demanded a renewal
other than the mere social or political one.

Just as poverty is not glorified for its own sake, so wealth as
such is not condemned. There can be no doubt, however, that
the deepest basis of all eschatologico-prophetic and chiliastic
visions of the future is ultimately the simple human sympathy of
the prophets for the suffering, the experience of their misery and
pain, the effort to assist them – a certain identification therefore
with social interests which are then modified by the shape of
their   ideological   expression,   for   example   by
religious-eschatological thought. On the one hand, therefore,
social concerns and class struggles are the historical *basis* of eschatological visions and desires and then have a greater or lesser
social impact and can give rise to more or less strong social
movements; on the other hand, however, the eschatological way
of thinking and the action which flows from it can never be
reduced to the social or material side of human suffering. It must
be concerned with the transformation of the *whole* man, human
distress must be overcome in all its aspects, and not just in the
form of oppression, need, slavery etc. This is why, however
much the poor and hungry are to be helped, the ideal is not simply that there should be abundant wealth and possessions for
everybody; for these can so easily be accompanied by other
manifestations of human weakness: 'How hard it will be for
those who have riches to enter the kingdom of God' (Mark 10:23
& par.). What is the difficulty? The rich are so filled with

worries about things, possessions and pleasures that it is difficult to bring them to accept any idea of change, or to feel the need for that inner transformation which life in the Gospel requires: '. . . the cares of the world, the delight in riches, and the desire for other things, enter in, and choke the word, and it proves unfruitful' (Mark 4:19 & par.; cf. Matthew 6:19–24 & par.). Early Christianity constantly criticised the way things and possessions lead to the dehumanisation of man, even if not to the same extent as, say, Taoism in China.

Yet in all the popular protest movements, from ancient times through the Middle Ages right up to the modern period, it is not only the things and possessions of the wealthy classes that are rejected but also (most explicitly again in Chinese Taoism) cultural forms and current educational customs, to a large extent intellectualism too and the traditional forms of rationality. For if in the eschatological perspective the entire 'old world' is condemned to destruction, and a 'new Jerusalem', a new and wholly different era dawns at last, dreamt of by uneducated, simple people in the Jordanian desert or Galilean hills (here one should note that Jesus is reproached with not being learned like the scribes – John 7:15, a passage which links up with Mark 6:2 & par.), how could such people retain any esteem for the culture and the intellectual values of upper-class schools and the hierarchical caste? Tensions between men of learning and popular dreamers are found in all religions, even though there was never an insuperable barrier between the two and individuals with the spirit of the one involuntarily inspired the others too. In Jesus himself this sort of antagonism is not particularly marked, certainly not so strong as in John the Baptist or in the tension between Taoism and official Confucianism in China. Unlike the majority of the prophets, Jesus often has dealings with representatives of the official establishment. He does not appear to hate them and may really have taken part in the controversies between Sadducees and Pharisees (e.g. Mark 12:18–27 & par.). There are even theories that Jesus' frequent conflicts with the Pharisees belong to a later tradition, and that he himself came from the ranks of the Pharisees. We do not consider that to be credible, but it is certain that opposition to the learned establishment is notably less strong in Jesus than in most prophets from Lao-tse to Muhammad. Nevertheless it is found in Jesus, *perhaps* in the view that faith is the only necessary condition for the performance of a miracle, for the experience that 'your faith has made you well' (Mark 5:34 & par. and cf. Matthew 9:28–9), in the faith that can move mountains (Matthew 17:21; cf. Luke 17:6), but above all in his stress on the *child-like* character of faith, and, connected with that, in the strengthening (with respect to the older Jewish tradition) of the idea of God as *Father*. The importance of the fatherhood of God comes out particularly at the beginning of the only prayer that Jesus taught (Luke 11:2ff cf. above) and also in the way Jesus in his agony addressed God as 'Abba' or 'Daddy' (Mark 14:36 & par.). Later, under the influence of the independent Johannine tradition (cf. John 10:30; 14:6–13; 17:1 and elsewhere) this formed the basis for that specifically Christian dialectic of the Father–Son relationship in the conception of God against which Freud, with his theories on man's subconscious drive to repeat in one's adulthood certain childhood experiences, provided the basic demythologising prophylactic. That, however, is a long way from disposing of the matter.

That a child should be put forward as an example is something quite new in the history of religions and equally new in the history of cultures. Before Jesus, nobody in the world imagined that childhood represented a human value or that it was an exemplar of humanity. Before Jesus, the children who appeared in the literature of Asia or Europe were always humanly unfinished, incomplete, not yet adult, and therefore secondary and of no importance for human values. At the very best the child is understood, in Karel Svoboda's phrase, as 'a serene and moving contrast', never as an example or value. And even when it was recognised, long before Jesus, that not only things but also the average attainments of intellect and civilisation often do no more than alienate man from his humanity (a theme which is found in Chinese Taoism, especially in Chuang-tse), one looked for a contrast, for a path to salvation, either in simple folk (a certain simplicity becomes a value particularly in moments of radical universal danger), or possibly in people of times long past (the 'ancients' or 'seers' of old Chinese, Indian and Slav religions), or in people of the future (as in the Jewish prophetic tradition mentioned above). And if ever older piety unconsciously sublimated and accorded religious status to the real-life human relationships of the lower to the higher classes, it was always – and especially in Jewish tradition prior to Jesus – the relationships of a simple member of the tribe or of the tribe itself to its leading representative, never narrower family relationships.

Certain elements in the synoptic tradition prove that Jesus himself did not start from family experiences of his own, either in the ordinary or in the Freudian sense. His recognition that childhood and youth represent a positive value was certainly based on particular personal experiences and on real contact with children, yet in essence it is really a kind of critique of society, a critical comparison of the forms of experience of children and adults. The very immaturity (so-called) of the young means that they are not already fixed in the attitudes typical of mature but alienated adults. The child is not yet an objectified person, he is not yet lost in the Many, and so the child is in his own way – like women in male-dominated civilisations – capable of the 'one thing necessary': raising oneself above the 'many things' of Luke 10:41–2, above everything that traditionally, and not without justification, came under the religious critique of the process of civilisation. The child is capable of being fascinated by a single thing, just as Jesus asks of his disciples total commitment to the Kingdom of God. This comes out in those absolutely unambiguous words: 'Truly, I say to you, unless you turn and become like children, you will never enter the kingdom of heaven' (Matthew 18:3). The Kingdom of the future age, however, belongs to children also because, like all weak creatures, they must be cherished and cared for since they cannot care for themselves; and so 'whoever receives one such child in my name receives me' (Mark 9:37 & par.).

This human characteristic of Jesus which won the admiration of so radical a critic of Christianity as Karl Marx, evident in his not at all sentimental love of children, in his essential need for contact with them, in the identification of himself with children (a trait which in spite of the distance in time from the Gospels is also found in men like Francis of Assisi and in the Czech visionaries of the eighteenth and nineteenth centuries who called themselves 'Children of the Pure Life') – this trait was so powerful and effective not because it was the result of speculative theories on the 'non-alienated' nature of children, but because Jesus *lived it out*, like the other signs of the future age, to the full. Otherwise it would simply have been a flourish, an oddity, self-

indulgence. It worked only because Jesus was perfectly at one
with his 'word', because he was himself his 'word', the human
embodiment of his own teaching (cf. John 1:14). That is why in
spite of the centuries that have elapsed we too can feel the immediacy and sincerity of the words, 'Let the children come to
me' (Mark 10:14). And that is why later opponents of Christianity felt that this was not simply a concern for defenceless children,
but that it expressed the need of every really mature person to
rise up against the destructive tendencies of egoistical class interests and fetishised civilisation, the need too, therefore, for the
truly revolutionary spirit which does not abandon the struggle
even after the second or third failure. There are other indirect
echoes of Jesus' real love for children in a number of other
passages in the evangelical tradition, as for example in the legend
which has come down to us only in a much later version, that the
'beloved disciple' was very young, unlike the others (the legend
is associated with John: cf. John 20:2–3; 21:23), and certainly in
the Christmas narratives, to which we shall return.

The exaltation of childhood in Jesus' teaching is linked with
those moments when he wishes to stress the innocence of the
dove, the helplessness of the lamb among wolves (Matthew
10:16) and similar themes, and with those features of his personality on account of which he himself is seen as a 'lamb' (1
Corinthians 5:7; 1 Peter 1:19; John 1:29; Revelation 5:8–15).
Now this concept is ambiguous. In our present context,
however, there can be no doubt that it includes the simplicity
and freedom from 'things', from immersion in the Many, from
the cares of worldly life, which is found in all great religious
systems and which plays an important part not only in the lives of
saints and monks like Benedict and Francis of Assisi, but also in
the lives of men like Tolstoy and Gandhi. This aspect is not so
fully developed in Jesus himself as among those we have mentioned, and it even seems that Jesus substitutes for self-denial, for
which he, unlike John the Baptist, seems to have a certain mistrust, the need to imitate the simplicity of children. Jesus certainly
counsels self-denial although he does so relatively infrequently.
There can be no doubt, for example, that one of the great
moments in the Sermon on the Mount and one which certainly
goes back to the source Q, is a polemic against worrying about
life and the means of life: 'Look at the birds of the air' (Matthew

6:26 & par.) and 'Consider the lilies of the field, how they grow' (Matthew 6:28). These poetic exhortations undoubtedly contain such counsel. But if we look more closely at the whole context we eventually notice that the real point of these texts is rather that we should strive for the 'dialectic of the present moment': the conclusion of the text demands that we should carry the future age in our hearts – yet for that very reason concern for tomorrow is condemned (Matthew 6:34), evidently on the lines of the polemic against the 'postponement' of human existence and the demand to live fully for the moment. And the real power of these images lies here, not in self-denial. Despite all the aesthetic beauty of these sayings, despite the relative accuracy of the criticism directed at an objectified life-style concerned with outward things, worries and cares, and which was valid even in that age, one must nevertheless observe that such a critique of civilisation – whether found in the ancient Chinese sages or in Gandhi – cannot lead us out of tragic impasses and contradictions of the work process. This is because they divert attention away from work, which is necessary to the human condition, and direct it towards the untroubled beauty of nature; but this does not solve the problems of the work process in the process itself. If Christianity was later to become the religion of a continent which has a dynamic approach to work, this is certainly not because world-denying tendencies are present in Jesus' teaching, but on the contrary because they are weaker in him than in comparable movements.

Yet even the more important 'child' and 'Father-Son' relationships in Jesus' message have to be correctly understood. On the one hand they contribute to man's paternalistic self-reflection and strengthen the agreeable feeling of being at home in the universe which is the house of the Father and in which, in the end, warmth, goodness and protection will prevail. Certain elements in the synoptic tradition, for example the saying, 'But even the hairs of your head are all numbered' (Matthew 10:30 & par.), involuntarily prepared the ground for the later fusion of the early Christian tradition with the Stoic and Neo-platonic view of providence and thereby also the questionable ability to discover a meaning in everything, to explain and justify everything. Then when, at the time of the discovery of the expanding universe, modern critical and sceptical tendencies began to make themselves increasingly felt, nourished both by scientific rationalism and by experiences of every kind culminating in Auschwitz, the paternalistic and providentialistic view of man, of good and evil, of the meaning of life and ethical values entered a crisis which can annihilate everything in modern man's self-understanding since it arouses feelings of rootlessness, emptiness, uselessness and meaninglessness. This prompts us to question those splendid, childlike experiences of the good Father who 'knows what you need' (Matthew 6:8); they made life more bearable, less desperate, for millions, which in itself would be no bad thing, but they fed and enhanced, by the principle of the supposed fatherly basis of being and especially of human existence, certain infantile features of human self-understanding which are no doubt beautiful and to some extent necessary in childhood but which, continued into maturity, make one incapable of bearing the hard blows of fate, the 'slings and arrows of outrageous fortune', and of fighting back and committing oneself when life no longer seems like one's father's house.

On the other hand, however, this esteem for childhood as a value and for children as fully human is an important part of the history of humanism, the history not of alienation but of man's humanistic self-discovery – not only because Jesus' teaching has provided the basis of the tradition by which the weak are to be protected, without which humanism becomes an arrogant path to gradual self-destruction, but also because certain aspects of childhood and youth remain of positive value even for adults. Adults who have retained from childhood a certain capacity for openness, directness, innocence, concentration, even the naiveness appropriate to those who are not yet completely absorbed by inhuman social organisations and specialised achievements, are the only ones capable of allying the 'cunning of the serpent' to the 'innocence of the dove' (cf. Matthew 10:16). They are the only ones who have grown up in a truly human way.

We can avoid the absurdities and endless controversies of contradictory interpretations only when we inquire into the relation which these details bear to the basic thought of Jesus. We cannot emphasise this too much, since throughout the centuries so many errors in this matter have been based on the chance quotation of passages torn from their context. This is especially important for a certain number of quotations which have become 'household words': there are many for example in the Sermon on the Mount (Matthew 5–7; cf. Luke 6:20–49 and elsewhere) because of which, according to Marx, every moment of life convicted the Christian community of hypocrisy. When for example in the Sermon on the Mount, which many generations have regarded as the quintessence of Jesus' teaching and loftiest 'ideals' (though we know by now how inadequate these two terms really are), we are told that not only murder but even an angry word against one's brother will be punished, that not only adultery and rape but looking on a woman with desire are condemned, that oaths are rejected and replaced by a plain 'yes' or 'no' (Matthew 5:21–37), clearly one is not dealing with any kind of moral--juridical casuistry for everyday matters. In any case Jesus could use very sharp language; thus for example he abuses the Pharisees as fools and vipers (Matthew 23:17–33). The Sermon on the Mount is something other than a code for gentlemen. It makes clear the demands that must be met if one embarks on the conversion required by the Kingdom of God. Let us recall once more the conclusion to the Sermon on the Mount: 'Seek first his kingdom and his righteousness, and all these things shall be yours as well' (Matthew 6:33).

The authenticity of Jesus' teaching flows from the fact that everything is subordinated to the all-encompassing and powerful idea of the Kingdom of God with its demands of inner conversion; individual moral principles, the moral-juridical and ritual demands of the Mosaic Law are all tested by this norm. According to the synoptic tradition it was only in this way that one could free the old Mosaic prescriptions from routine, habit, from a mechanical and therefore often purely formalistic fulfilment. Only in this way could one find their original and vital meaning; and then the commands that at the start were simple and uncomplicated can be freed from all compromise and made even more rigorous in their consequences. Only where a positive and thorough-going eschatological way of thinking has developed (that means not simply a negative vision of general catastrophe but rather the encouragement of positive human values), can commands and prohibitions find a justification in morality too. That is why in eschatological teaching we often meet opposition to those who cultivate individual virtues, pious habits and rituals

– evidently without the basic conversion in eschatological faith. Jesus' famous saying, 'Leave the dead to bury their own dead' (Matthew 8:22 & par.), which certainly comes from the oldest level of the synoptic tradition, is addressed to the devout and the pious. An analysis of it would contribute much towards the understanding of Jesus' preaching. It is perfectly logical, then, that his preaching should be directed not to the 'pious' or the 'devout' who are falsely complacent and therefore satisfied with the *status quo,* but rather to the disinherited of this world, to those on the edge of society, the prostitutes, tramps, the rejects, 'sinners', since these people are ready for faith and the demands of the Kingdom. That is why Jesus says: 'Those who are well have no need of a physician, but those who are sick; I came not to call the righteous, but sinners' (Mark 2:17 & par.).

One must understand in a similar light those important elements in Jesus' message which traditionally – although essentially mistakenly in our view – have been regarded as key passages for his 'ethic' such as his teaching on the love of one's neighbour, pacifism, radical forgiveness and the rejection of vengeance. In view of their importance let us quote the most famous texts, although by no means the only ones applicable to the problem: 'You have heard that it was said, "An eye for an eye and a tooth for a tooth". But I say to you, Do not reply to the evil man in kind'. (It transpires from the context that the traditional translation 'do not resist one who is evil' does not bring out the dual meaning of the Greek: *mè antistēnai tō ponerō.*) 'If any one strikes you on the right cheek, turn to him the other also . . . Give to him who begs from you, and do not refuse him who would borrow from you. You have heard that it was said, "You shall love your neighbour and hate your enemy". But I say to you, Love your enemies and pray for those that persecute you . . . Beware of practising your piety before men in order to be seen by them . . . When you give alms, do not let your left hand know what your right hand is doing' (Matthew 5:38 – 6:3 and cf. Luke 5:28 – 6:36). It is perfectly clear that we are here dealing with something that is unique in the history of the Jewish prophetic movement, and unique in the history of ethics: an attempt to tackle in a new way the age-old problems of human enmity, mutual violence, the use of force, etc. It was not long, however, before there was controversy in early Christianity about what these assertions really meant for human action and decision in concrete cases. Indeed, it is probable that the controversy already existed, that Jesus put forward his teaching as his personal answer to a problem that had already been raised.

The problem of force, especially when it is political force, that is, when it takes the form either of repression or of revolution, had already been posed by the Roman occupation of Israel. Revolutionary resistance had already begun before the time of Jesus, and after his death it led to the two great rebellions which brought about the utter destruction of the Jewish state. That there should be so soon after the time of Jesus an attempt at revolution, an intransigent challenge to those who held power even at the cost of what Jews like Flavius Josephus regarded as the tragic end of the Jews, suggests that the legitimacy or illegitimacy of the use of force to liberate and save the country must already have been discussed, at least in principle. Because Judaism began to witness the rise of a special attitude to this problem, which at the time of the later Jewish wars was on the sideline, as it were, or even out of the picture altogether but which ultimately proved capable of surviving that period and of triumphantly gaining widespread recognition, it would have been remarkable if Jesus had not had a personal position on force and the occupying power, on hatred and the use of weapons. The synoptic tradition as a whole clearly suggests that there were many more direct references to the use of violence and arms than those contained in the Sermon on the Mount. This comes out most clearly in the story of Jesus' arrest, which certainly reflects an armed struggle or an attempt to fight and in which Jesus himself ostensibly forbade his friends to continue their armed resistance, 'for all who take the sword will perish by the sword' (Matthew 26:52). It is also evident that in circles close to Jesus there were some who did not reject the use of force; and that makes it all the more likely that he must have foreseen this problem. Moreover, the existing situation contained a flagrant contradiction: the best elements in the Jewish Old Testament tradition were never narrowly nationalistic, still less chauvinistic — in the end Yahweh was the God of all peoples. The Roman occupation, however, had led this small, proud and now deeply humiliated people to hatred and nationalism. This raised a difficult problem, since outwardly the Roman occupation forces showed none of the primitive brutality that the

Assyrian or Babylonian occupiers had shown; but then precisely because of the conciliatory and indulgent attitude of this incomparably more powerful empire, which could not be fought with the methods of David and the Maccabees, the hatred of the 'sons of light' for the 'sons of darkness' had to take on other forms which admittedly could not destroy the enemy but which would at least preserve intact all that was valuable, great and unconquerable in the Jewish tradition. So it came about that the greatest Jewish prophet of the century – and this is what always happens with prophets – took up an essentially new point of view. In order that everything 'divine' and human in Judaism might be saved, it all had to be renewed.

Jesus' teaching on the love of enemies, on generous forgiveness, on the renunciation of vengeance and force etc., was for a long time considered a sort of 'ethic' of Jesus or the basis for a 'Christian morality' and described, sometimes even by those who had grasped the eschatological core of Jesus' thinking, at least as a 'transitional ethic' or (in the words of Albert Schweitzer) as an 'interim ethic'. Neither expression seems to us to be particularly happy, since both involuntarily carry ancient Greek or modernistic ideas on ethics into eschatological thinking. It is worth pointing out (against current ideas of 'Christian morality', sometimes found even among Christians and almost invariably among their opponents who often compete with Christians in their ignorance) that the commands to 'love God with all one's heart' (Deuteronomy 6:5) and to 'love your neighbour as yourself' (Leviticus 19:18) are found word for word in the Old Testament, go back to Moses and appear in the synoptic Gospels as direct quotations (Mark 12:29–31). What is new and original here is the extent to which this commandment goes: it includes the command to love *enemies*. One must be careful to avoid arbitrariness in understanding and interpreting this passage: the only correct basis of interpretation indubitably poses the question of the place which these expressions from the Sermon on the Mount occupied – could only have occupied! – in the thought of Jesus taken as a whole, in more concrete terms, the question of what part they play in the context of that need for conversion with which the eschatological vision of the future age became the total claim on the 'inner change' mentioned above. It is a question of providing not casuistic rules for everyday life but ex-

108   A MARXIST LOOKS AT JESUS

amples of the total claim made on possible human activity. It is,
then, an exacting demand made on the 'I' of the 'believer', the
man who is entirely possessed by the Kingdom.

Consequently it would be entirely wrong to understand the
charge 'not to resist one who is evil' or to 'forgive one's enemies'
as passivity, as a charge to let murderers murder, tyrants oppress,
swindlers grow rich; it does not mean that one should not do
what one can, that one should literally 'not resist one who is evil'
in the sense of submitting to his power. That is completely opposed to the evangelical tradition; Jesus himself uncom-
promisingly resisted evil wherever he found it. The controversy
between Jesus and the Zealot resistance fighters, as also, evidently, between Jesus and the majority of his fellow Jews, was *not*
about whether one ought to resist evil – that was acknowledged
by everyone: the controversy was rather about *how* one should
fight evil, about the most effective means (even if that is rather a
modern formulation). It corresponds better to the structure and
meaning of Jesus' message if we say that the controversy was
about what action – in the field of human relationships generally
and especially when they take the form of conflict – is suitable
for the man who is possessed by the ideal of the future age and is
striving to bring about the transformation of his own existence.
Our activity should be *pacific*. Now pacifism does not mean
passivity. It does not mean lack of interest, indifference or giving
in to evil and the powers of evil – all that contradicts essential
elements in the synoptic tradition. Similarly, forgiveness does not
derive from weakness, contempt or pride. To love one's enemy
does not mean to reconcile oneself to the hatred which prompts
his action, nor does it mean adopting his ideas, still less shirking
all conflict. These would be defective interpretations of words
taken out of the context of the synoptic traditions and could give
rise only to the greatest misunderstanding.

From the whole of the synoptic tradition it is clear that we are
dealing with activity, with conduct, which is imperative, with a
missionary endeavour and therefore with an interest in the other
person, in his future, in his 'conversion' and capacity for 'faith'. It
is therefore a question of seeing the other – one's neighbour, even
if he is an enemy, a stranger, a social outcast, of a different creed,
guilty of something – not only as he is now but already in the
'prism of the Kingdom', in the prism of the radical, total change

that is to come: not only as he is, therefore, but as he could and as he will be. The enemy must be resisted in so far as he serves the power of darkness, although it would be better to say that the power of darkness should be resisted rather than the enemy. He should be seen not as the servant of darkness but as someone who is capable of a future conversion. Therefore, though he uses evil means – despotism, the sword, force, darkness – one must not answer him with these same means. If one answered him in kind, with lies, deceit, violence and force, one would be denying oneself and him the future and the possibility of change, one would be perpetuating the kingdom of evil. The principles of pacificism and forgiveness of the enemy cannot, of course, be applied to every possible situation in human life; but in general the task of the man who is gripped by the ideal of a renewed future is that he should always and in all circumstances look for better moral means than the other, including his enemy, is now using. This approximates to Jesus' own explanation of these ideas, in other words to the injunction not to reply in kind to enemies (Matthew 5:43–8). Hence too the demand for a 'higher righteousness' (cf. Matthew 5:20) as a general legal norm.

Just as Gandhi was later to realise that true pacifism (*ahimsa*) must not be passivity, giving in to the power of evil and oppression, but makes sense only as an organic part of the search for truth (*satyagraha*), the same is true of the problem in the synoptic tradition. There too it is not primarily a matter of negative, passive pacifism (*mè antistēnai*) but of living in the positive spirit recommended in the parable of the Good Samaritan (Luke 10:37). Then pacifism appears neither as flight nor as capitulation but as a form of total responsibility for others, including enemies. It is a question not of 'non-activity' in the Buddhist manner, but of the introduction of a higher form of moral behaviour which would also be capable of attracting others.

Even though this teaching on pacific action has undoubtedly important consequences for the history of humanism and the anthropological self-understanding of man, one has also to point out that Jesus' attitude is quite unlike that of Seneca, for example; it does not depend on the relationship and therefore the necessary sympathy of all members of the human race, or on the sentimentality of many who are 'humanists' perhaps because they cannot bear the sight of blood. Jesus and his time saw only too much blood! 'Love of one's neighbour' has nothing to do with sentimentality, nothing to do with the 'faint hearts' or the Epicurean or *petit bourgeois* attempt to remain aloof from events. 'Love of one's neighbour' in Jesus' teaching is the fruit of patience and an extremely hard life. It is not, then, so much a 'compassion' in Schopenhauer's sense or a sensitivity to the weakness of others, as a *severe and uncompromising demand on oneself,* an undertaking to commit oneself for others to the utmost and to prefer to suffer injustice and violence rather than to be their cause. But that is not an end in itself, as though it were some kind of Stoic training of the personality, nor is it the Faustian ideal of being dynamic in a dynamic world and crashing down with that world when it collapses. It is more a matter of laying hold on the Kingdom of God by accepting its demands and the new meaning it gives to life.

If we recall the Beatitudes of Luke in which the poor, the suffering, the hungry and the persecuted are said to be 'blessed' (Luke 6:20–3) and compare them with the fuller text in Matthew, the additions fit in with the whole of the synoptic tradition at its deepest levels. 'Blessed are the meek, for they shall inherit the earth . . . Blessed are the merciful for they shall obtain mercy . . . Blessed are the peace-makers, for they shall be called sons of God' (Matthew 5:5–9): these words are based on Jesus' eschatological vision and form an organic part of this concept of the future age, and they show what human society must be if it is to be worth living in: it will be a society not of violent people but of gentle people, not of warmongers but of peace-lovers.

This principle of the eschatological claim made on oneself is the only way we can explain the paradox that on the one hand Jesus has left behind extremely *radical demands,* that on the other there are reports of extremely *liberal, compliant behaviour* on his part, and this towards people who were a far cry from his vision of Israel's and humanity's salvation and from the absolute claim on self! Let us not be afraid to say openly what ecclesiastical tradition out of embarrassment has not translated or only half-translated: Jesus' dealings with 'tax-gatherers and sinners' really meant – no matter how much this shocks the pious – that Jesus did not hesitate to sit down at table with prostitutes and collaborators (cf. Mark 2:15 & par.), that he had dealings with officials of the Roman administration (Matthew 8:10 & par.), that he put himself on the same level as Magdalen who originally belonged to the world's oldest profession and who, what is more, was probably hysterical, that he expelled seven demons from her (Luke 8:2) and that he calmly said of a public sinner, 'Her sins, which are many, are forgiven her, for she loved much' (Luke 7:47) – although the context makes it clear what kind of love this was. This is only an apparent contradiction, and in reality the two attitudes are two aspects of the same eschatological claim: one who already lives the 'faith', that is the change (metanoia) in view of the Kingdom, makes the greatest possible demands *on himself*, but for that very reason gives to others 'without pay' (Matthew 10:8), even gives 'good measure, pressed down, shaken together, running over' (Luke 6:38), does not condemn others, is patient and indulgent with them, and does not convict them for their weaknesses: 'Judge not, and you will not be judged' (Luke 6:37). One must commit oneself totally to win others and yet not condemn them when one fails.

The message of Jesus, then, is not contradictory but absolutely unequivocal: the most stringent demands are made on oneself – and not for purposes of display or showing off but as an inner moral requirement – and *therefore* one must have the greatest respect for and patience with others. 'Why do you seek the speck that is in your brother's eye, but do not notice the log that is in your own eye?' (Matthew 7:3).

Even though, then, the contrary has often been true in the praxis of 2000 years of Christianity, though men with the words of Jesus on their lips have made and make the harshest demands on others while absolving themselves, though the principle of the 'speck in the eye of the brother' was one of the reasons which led Marx to accuse Jesus' followers of hypocrisy, doubledealing and Pharisaism, one must nevertheless acknowledge that something immeasurably great and important entered human history through the message of Jesus. It comes from the depths of the Jewish tradition in the greatest upheaval of its history. Unlike the great religious systems of India and China and in particular contrast with the Persian religion of Zarathustra and with Manichaeism (whose disciples for a time competed with Christians for the leading role in European history), and also unlike the Qumran-Essene sect and a series of later sects, Christianity is at its heart, as a consequence of this combination of radicalism and leniency in Jesus, *exacting but not esoteric,* that is, not exclusively for the 'elect', the 'chosen ones' or any kind of élite. This is why Jesus' demand for change, his conception of the eschatological call to conversion, could for centuries be the basis for the intellectual history of the West from St Augustine to Leibniz and Hegel, as well as for future democratic, humanistic and social-revolutionary movements, from the Donatists, Waldensians, Jan Hus and the American Declaration of Rights, down to socialism and Marxism, with which a new chapter begins in the history of the Western world opening up new horizons similar to those of the time in which Paul, full of enthusiasm for Jesus, began his wanderings round the Roman Empire.

Just as today there is both a fundamental upheaval – a revolutionary change in human relationships and in human hearts – and a preservation of the original bases of culture, of the pillars of humanity forged by millennial effort (and in fact these aspects merge: the revolution is itself the only possible basis for the preservation of culture and the human race), a similar polarity must have emerged in primitive Christianity in relation to Jewish Old Testament traditions and values. This must now be the last problem area in our analysis of Jesus' message: his relationship to the Jewish tradition and its representatives. Did Jesus make the Mosaic Law more stringent or did he weaken it? It is no accident that for centuries there have been controversies on this point, and one can bring forward good arguments for both positions. The revolutionary contrasts of our own age, which in so many ways is comparable to the time of Jesus, may help us to avoid the inappropriate either/or of this question. The well-known passage in Matthew's Gospel which asserts that Jesus did not come to destroy the Law but to fulfil it and the accompanying explanatory material (Matthew 5:17–20) can scarcely be authentic since it is found only in Matthew and fits in altogether too neatly with his emphasis on Jesus as the one who fulfilled the Jewish Law, the one in whom long-awaited events happen 'according to the scriptures'. But even if we leave aside this passage, there are elements in the synoptic tradition which interpret the Mosaic Law even more strictly – one has only to think of the phrase repeated in the Sermon on the Mount: 'It was said to the men of old, but I say to you . . .' (Matthew 5:22, 28, 32, 34, 39, 44 etc.).

THE MESSAGE OF JESUS

Obviously we must also take into account Jesus' undermining of individual prescriptions of the Law, which undoubtedly gave rise to the tendency already present in Jesus and explicitly stated by Paul: 'The written code kills, but the Spirit gives life' (2 Corinthians 3:6), which in the end exempted Christians from any obligation to keep the Mosaic Law. The explanation of this apparent paradox lies not in the mere enumeration of statements for or against the Law, but only – as in everything else – in an examination of the peculiarity of the eschatological orientation in Jesus: one who lives in the spirit of the Kingdom of God must necessarily make stricter demands on himself than those imposed by the Law and juridical tradition, conversely one who does not live in the 'spirit of renewal' in no way profits by fulfilling the Law however strictly, since the formalistic fulfilment of the Law is against its very essence.

From this point of view it is psychologically very interesting to see how Jesus, who is almost aggressively generous in his attitude towards prostitutes, tax-gatherers and others who were traditionally despised, attacks so vigorously and perhaps onesidedly those who were consciously and explicitly the 'devout' of his time: the Pharisees, firmly entrenched in law and order. Resorting to *polemic* – the systematic dissociation from another prominent person whose ideological alignment is essentially different – in the process of clarifying one's person and aims, seems to be something even the greatest personalities need. Jesus first became certain of his own mission in his youth, in gradual dissociation from the movement of John the Baptist. One can explain why the synoptic tradition gives us only a few indirect hints on this question by the lack of historical interest of the early Christians, to which we referred earlier. Yet this explanation would in all probability not apply to the period of Jesus' *public* activity: perhaps because of Jesus' esteem for John, perhaps because some of John's disciples came over to Jesus after John's execution. At the time of Jesus' public ministry, the main recipients of his polemical jibes were the Pharisees; but whether the butt of his acid criticisms was in fact typical of the historical Pharisaic movement is a question which need not especially interest us in our present context. What is certain and does matter to us is that Jesus frequently inveighed against a characteristic – clearly present in people who, judged by externals alone, were not the worst — which then, because of his influence, passed into Christian tradition as the phenomenon of so-called 'Pharisaism'.

When an eminent and essentially deeply positive thinker is prompted to such frequent, striking and violent polemic as Jesus was by Pharisaism, the explanation must without exception be sought in *inner* causes, that is, it is closely connected with what is most decisive in the person concerned. Pharisaism as Jesus saw it presented *negatively* the heart of his own message. If Jesus directed the attention of thousands who already believed in the future radical upheaval to its claim on oneself, to the need for inner change, he attacked 'Pharisaism' so vehemently only because it was, in regard to *this,* not only the public opposite but even a kind of persiflage or caricature. That Jesus was so critical not of the clearly conservative Saducees or of the pagans but of the liberal and reformist Pharisees, is an instance of a paradoxical and yet in its way psychologically understandable phenomenon, characteristic of the history of religion and politics, according to which those who believe differently are attacked with more energy than those who believe nothing.

The Pharisees too were concerned with moral renewal; they were ready to assimilate and utilise everything contemporary — including Jesus. Yet basically — according to Jesus — even when the Pharisee aspired to reform, he was smug and self-satisfied. 'God, I thank thee that I am not like other men' (Luke 18:11) is Jesus' witty parody of the basis of every Pharisaic prayer, of every Pharisaic concern for reform. 'You are those who justify yourselves before men' (Luke 16:15) is Jesus' accusation against these men who were equally far removed from the great prophetic yearning for the future and from any radical demand for change or conquest of their present 'I'. That is the essence of Pharisaism, and everything else — 'Pharisaic hypocrisy', superficiality, formalism, display of their own virtues, love of praise, coveting titles, grasping for success (Matthew 23:5–28 & par.) — is merely a consequence. Another important consequence is that man as understood by Pharisaism is able to accept all true doctrines but incapable of acting according to them (Matthew 23:1–4).

There is no need to stress that Pharisaism has been found among Christians throughout the centuries, and that it is also widespread among our contemporaries, especially in the form of a typically intellectualist and pseudo-revolutionary self-satisfaction. The synoptic tradition's polemic against Pharisaism – and evidently Jesus' own polemic – had as their object not so much the real historical class of Pharisees as a certain universally human phenomenon of 'Pharisaism'. One can deduce that from the simple fact that the critique in the synoptic tradition includes a large number of characteristcs which could scarcely be found in the same group of men. The stress on the strict fulfilment of the Law, on the formalistic carrying out of regulations, on blind observance of the sabbath, on the past and on the cult of ancestors (Matthew 23:29–39 & par.; cf. Luke 6:6–11 & par.) – this the synoptic non-Palestinian tradition, no longer in direct touch, falsely transferred from the Sadducees to the Pharisees. It was the Sadducees who at the time of Jesus represented the type of the 'religious bureaucrat'. Every age and every school has this type of person who busies himself (or herself) exclusively with the already established structure and, while preserving the original *form,* loses touch with the original *meaning.* Anyone, therefore, who has a real feel for older values must appear to them as a trouble-maker and a revolutionary.

That comes out most clearly in the polemic of Jesus whenever the meaning of sabbath observance is discussed. For Jesus and his disciples the sabbath is what it originally was, a day of rest serving man's relaxation and recreation. All the multifarious ritual regulations which a millennial tradition prior to Jesus had gradually concentrated on that day of the week were meaningless, once the feel for the essence of the sabbath rest was lost. Jesus emphasised that one may do anything on the sabbath which helps one's fellow men or gets them out of a disagreeable or damaging situation, without bothering with the formal prescriptions of the Law. The structure has meaning only in so far as it helps the living to preserve the content. Ultimately Jesus' words can be understood as applying to all cultic and religious prescriptions: 'The sabbath was made for man, not man for the sabbath, so the Son of man is lord even of the sabbath' (Mark 2:27–8). In such passages Jesus' eschatological vision, which is a constant factor to be borne in mind, appears once more: for if the awaited judgment is concerned solely with the sincerity of the human claim on self, the original relation between form and content, between cult and its human meaning, is restored. These aspects too of Jesus' disturbing message have remained painfully relevant, not only for those who were the direct object of his attack, the Jewish formalists, ritualists, bureaucrats and those whom the Talmud rightly calls 'the just who have gone mad', but also for those who accept Jesus and confess him. The same types began to emerge among Christians, and indeed to predominate. As in the time of Jesus himself, there was an ever-increasing contrast between dogmatic churchy people and 'heretical', 'worldly' people basically open to change.

The example of my own country illustrates the point. The whole centuries-old Czech tradition, the tradition of a country at the crossroads of Europe which, like Israel, is exposed to influences from all corners of the world, has produced a particularly sharp antithesis of this type, sharper than in most European countries; an antithesis, in other words, between the legalistic-formalistic and the 'open' conception of tradition, and between the prophetic-eschatological and the Pharisaic concept of the claim on self.

The work of the leading pioneers of the Hussite renewal movement, especially Matěj von Janov and Jan Hus, can in some sense be considered a critique of the 'Pharisaism' of their time and of their ecclesiastical superiors. In Matěj von Janov we read the same complaint in hundreds of different versions: 'They have pangs of conscience if they eat liver-sausage on Fridays, but to oppress the poor does not disturb them' – all applications of Jesus' critique of Pharisaism and of formalistic fidelity to the Law. What we know, from countless unambiguous documents of the fourteenth and fifteenth centuries, of the inflammatory impact this type of critique had at that time greatly helps us to understand the dialectic in Jesus' attitude and the significance of his behaviour in his time.

We have now dealt with the first part of the original evangelical preaching: *the message of Jesus*. The second part which is no less important for the history of Christianity concerns *the preaching about Jesus*. That will be the subject of the next chapter. And even if the conclusions of the next chapter in some ways alter what we have already established, we can already say that something extraordinary and of incalculable importance entered history with the message of Jesus: whatever value we put on this or that detail, we cannot deny that the problem itself, whether one can live off the claim of the future or not, whether man can, by his own efforts, shape himself, change his whole behaviour, or not, is of decisive significance.

Related questions are whether childlike simplicity can be exemplary for adults, whether there exists a morally higher form of activity than the use of violence, whether we can have moral influence on the will of one's enemies. Scarcely anyone — especially since science, and particularly social science, began to play a qualitatively more important role than in the time of Jesus — can categorically maintain that these questions are solved in the synoptic texts. But the fact that these questions were raised, not in an academic but in an existential way, so much so that Jesus and thousands of his followers have been ready to defend these truths with their own blood and their own lives, is of enormous importance. If not everyone — since there are millions to whom personally nothing of human importance is at stake — then at least those for whom something humanly significant and true is at stake can readily discern that in the bewildering abundance of the late accounts of the synoptic tradition a whole series of ostensible sayings of Jesus are the fruit of subsequent legend-mongering and yet that a large number of other words of Jesus cannot be, because they bear the distinctive seal of the living personality of Jesus of Nazareth, compared with whom the most eminent figures of early Christianity — not excluding Peter and Paul — were, in their own estimation, mere novices. These authentic sayings are not primarily those of particular theological notoriety or the classical 'wingèd words', but those which, though less striking, less proclaimed in Christian tradition, speak directly to the heart and betray something not expressible in legends. We could give a host of examples — but here one only suffices. In it we can feel a mind both alive with the conviction, indeed certainty, that it announces something of huge significance and yet filled with a kind of longing for something earth-shaking, something in the future which also implies the human uncertainty over the fate of this announcement, unknown yesterday and therefore perhaps to be destroyed tomorrow: 'Every one to whom much is given, of him much will be required; and of him to whom men commit much they will demand the more. I came to cast fire upon the earth, and would that it were already kindled!' (Luke 12:48–9).

Similar words could be spoken yesterday, today or tomorrow by anyone concerned with things of human importance. Yet Jesus was a man of his time and environment, and therefore his mental patterns were based on age-old Jewish traditions, which were then being shaken by a new social crisis. These traditions contained an idea of the future which not only was still operative after 1000 years and valid for all human history but also bore the signs of the times, for example, by often being associated with belief in an extraordinary personage possessing strength and power. There were dozens of prophets, yet there arose the idea of someone more powerful than mere prophets. Thus, even though it was amongst the people rather than in the official classes of Judaism, the memory of the David who was past and belief in a David who was to come – a future 'anointed' hero – lived on, and the idea of the mysterious 'Son of Man' lived on too. That was to be Jesus' destiny.

CHAPTER V

The Christ

And between the throne and the four living creatures and among the elders, I saw a lamb standing, as though it had been slain ... and I heard around the throne and the living creatures and the elders the voice of many angels, numbering myriads of myriads and thousands of thousands, saying with a loud voice: Worthy is the lamb who was slain, to receive power and wealth and wisdom and might and honour and glory and blessing! (Revelation 5:6, 11–12)

All that we have said in the last chapter about Jesus' thought shows not only that he was a great man but that he was concerned with the real problems of real men who try to ponder the meaning of their existence in the world. The central point in his teaching, that emphasis on the future which makes a binding claim on man in his present, summed up by Jesus in the words, 'Repent, for the kingdom of heaven is at hand' (Matthew 4:17 & par.), is not remotely fantastic or mythological. On the contrary it represents a deep experience of every honest 'philosophy of man'. It says in substance that a man can become truly human and live to the full extent of his powers only through his personal, irreplaceable, demanding commitment to the fulness of the present; and yet that this fulness of experience is possible only on condition that the present is not viewed as an end in itself but is open to the positive and far-reaching vision of the future. Someone who is prepared to defend any current fad or tell opportunistic lies can have a certain superficial social and personal success in any age; but only the man who gives himself in his present to something important and meaningful can have true success.

Yet at the same time — and it cannot be otherwise for any thinking man — Jesus was strongly affected by the ideas of his time and milieu, and this does not mean simply ideas from the immediate social crisis that the country was going through in his lifetime; he was also deeply rooted in the centuries-old traditions of his country and people. In a development which lasted over 1000 years and which is essentially different from that of other cultures of the same period, the Jewish people and the Old Testament traditions created values which are of importance for the whole of mankind; and the questions which they raise are not out-of-date even today. Judaism was incomparably better than other ancient traditions at grasping the reality which myth contained and conveyed; and yet even the basic traditions of Jewish history do not get away entirely from the mythical. It crops up even in the central idea that the Kingdom of salvation is 'close at hand' and is within the grasp of the individual's own efforts, an idea which is one of the most important discoveries along the road to man's true self-understanding and self-discovery. From this important recognition that the fulness of human existence is 'near', that 'true humanity' is within the reach of personal activity, that a real chance is given to every man to lead a fulfilled life, it was only a step to the mythological idea that 'man', the new future man, 'the Son of Man' is really coming and not just in any metaphorical sense expressing the goal of human endeavour, but in reality, accompanied by a great demonstration of power and glory.

This brings us to the biggest problem of New Testament studies and the biggest problem posed by the figure of Jesus: what is the relationship in the synoptic tradition between the historical Jesus and this long-awaited and mysterious being, the 'Son of Man'? For almost a hundred years New Testament scholarship has known that this is one of the most difficult and at the same time most important problems in considering the person and influence of the Master from Galilee. It is obviously linked with the basis of the announcement of the Kingdom of God, as for example the following emphatic words show: 'For as the lightning flashes and lights up the sky from one side to the other, so will the Son of man be in his day' (Luke 17:24). That is clear enough. But we shall soon see that it raises great difficulties.

Let us first of all summarise the facts that are not in dispute. Though the idea of 'Son of Man' is beyond doubt of Old Testament origin, it plays only a small part in the tradition of the Old

Testament as a whole. The expression 'Son of Man' occurs several times, but with one exception it is a simple synonym of 'man' without any special emphasis (cf. Psalms 8:4 and 80:17); in Semitic languages the use of the euphemism 'son' is traditional, just as we, for example, say 'human being' or 'human creature'. Even in the sole Old Testament text in which the term 'Son of Man' occurs — and then in a rather obscure way — in the context of the awaited apocalyptic catastrophe, and in a similar context to that of the synoptic tradition and particularly of images of New Testament revelation, the term originally bore the current, quite unprophetic meaning. There is reference to a being 'like a son of man' (Daniel 7:13), that is a being who was not human but like a man — and who in some mysterious way would achieve power and glory and hold eternal sway over all peoples. Because of the fixed literary formulation of this text and its rather confused context, the reference acquired a certain autonomy in later exegesis: that is, instead of being simply a euphemistic synonym for 'man', it became an independent idea, a 'name' for the originally unnamed and mysterious being. Whether this happened for the first time with Jesus, or whether between Daniel and Jesus a group or sect existed which already used the expression in this sense but left no literary documents behind, we do not know. It is not important.

On the other hand, in the New Testament, and especially the synoptic tradition, the expression 'Son of Man' is one of the most frequent and, in terms of content, one of the most central of all. Yet a close study of the synoptic tradition shows irrefutably that this term must have been somewhat controversial, as we can see from a certain fluctuation in its use and non-use. For this there were certain readily intelligible rules of which the authors and editors of the synoptic tradition were not aware but which precisely for that reason give us an insight into their deeper intentions. This judgment is based on the following facts.

(1) Among the sayings in the synoptic gospels which use the term 'Son of Man', there is a group of words which Mark, Matthew and Luke undoubtedly used but which are clearly not the result of their own literary workmanship. A comparison shows that the words come from the oldest strata, which go back to the lost source Q (Q being earlier than Mark) — to the real words of Jesus which then become an alternative source to Mark

for Matthew and Luke. Now throughout this source the coming of the 'Son of Man' is spoken of in the future, and always in the third person. These expressions must have become somewhat rigid in the Christian collections, for we notice no tendency in the editors to remodel them. That too is a sign of their antiquity and of the importance they had for the first three or four Christian generations.

(2) Apart from this, there are considerable variations, but even these present certain noticeable characteristics. Thus one can trace in particular the editors' concern to insert the term 'Son of Man' into sayings where it was not originally found, mainly to strengthen the identification of this concept with the first person in Jesus' sayings. For example if we compare Mark: 'Whom do men say that I am?' (Mark 8:27, a scene also included by Luke, 9:18) with Matthew, we find that literally translated the question becomes, 'Whom do men say that the *Son of man* is?' (Matthew 16:13). Further comparison reveals that in a perfectly simple passage of Mark's in which the evangelist uses the term 'Son of Man' in the older sense of 'man' in general (Mark 3:28–30) Matthew and Luke have added the phrase 'Son of Man', even though it makes the context much more obscure (Matthew 12:31–2; Luke 12:10). We can also note how the coming of the 'Son of Man' is mentioned at the start of Matthew's description of the last judgment, and yet in the narrative itself, without any apparent reason and in contrast with the rest of the synoptic tradition, the idea of 'king' is used (Matthew 25:31, 34–40). Clearly this was originally a parable in which the king rewarded and punished, which was then later rather ineptly linked with ideas about the coming of the Son of Man. We realise, then, that in certain sayings, even though the synoptics uniformly record them as 'Son of Man' sayings, the simple term 'man' conveys the meaning better. One example is Matthew 8:20 & par. and probably also the saying, 'The Son of man is Lord over the Sabbath' (Mark 2:28 & par.).

(3) When one has become aware of this fluctuation between the first and the third person, it becomes even more striking that the synoptic tradition and indeed the New Testament tradition as a whole does not include a single passage in which the term 'Son of Man' is used in the second person. In other words there is no indication in the oldest tradition that Jesus was ever addressed as

'Son of Man' or that the editors ever thought of introducing this usage, even though they were sensitive to the implications of the use of the first and third persons.

What conclusions can we draw? Above all, we must be careful to avoid the tempting but over-hasty conclusion that Jesus of Nazareth never identified himself at all with the 'Son of Man', and that this entire identification is perhaps the work of a later theological tradition, which therefore 'falsified' the evidence. From the three points that we have made, certain more modest conclusions can be drawn:

(1) that there is a certain difficulty, a certain problem, in the simple identification of Jesus with 'the Son of Man';

(2) that considerable thought had already been given to this problem, long before the editing of the synoptic texts, and that tradition, even before Mark and Matthew, had 'worked' on it, perhaps even before the lost source Q was put together;

(3) that we must be extremely prudent and careful in picking our way back through the synoptic traditions to the historical Jesus – and this observation will hold for every aspect of our question. In fact one needs to be much more cautious here than in the previous discussions on Jesus' own message about the 'Kingdom' and 'conversion', the authenticity of which is evident;

(4) that we can move on relatively sure ground in this question only if we confine ourselves to those sayings which speak of a *future* coming of the Son of Man, since these are the earliest sayings.

We shall begin then from these demonstrably old texts of the synoptic tradition. The Son of Man preached by Jesus will come 'in glory' (Mark 8:38 & par.), 'with great power and glory' (Mark 13:26 & par.): in the synoptic tradition this is a fixed and almost untouchable form of expression which later editors unconsciously transfer to other places in the accepted and extended tradition. Plainly it was deeply rooted in the consciousness of the Christian communities of the first century and had immense importance for them, perhaps central importance. The coming of the Son of Man transforms the eschatological catastrophe into the 'Kingdom of God' which is proclaimed by Jesus. It will be preceded by certain cosmic disasters – and this is the only tiny hint of apocalyptic thinking in the synoptic tradition – but then the age of justice will come (Mark 13:1–32 & par.; cf. Luke

21:27–8 & par.); later on, these passages were conceived of as integral parts of the so-called 'Last Judgment', which is really secondary since it is only Matthew who gives it, and he shapes it by refashioning what was originally a parable (Matthew 25:31–46). The synoptic tradition as a whole makes it plain that there was originally no question of a judgment, at the most of a constitutive part of the general catastrophe; and in particular that there was nothing 'last' or final' about it, since it inaugurated the longed for beginning of the Kingdom of the future age. 'But I tell you, hereafter you will see the Son of man seated at the right hand of Power, and coming on the clouds of heaven' (Matthew 26:64 & par.): that sounds more like a jubilant fanfare announcing future joy than the proclamation of a catastrophic end.

We can compare these words with the words of Stephen, the first martyr, shortly before his execution: 'Behold, I see the heavens opened, and the Son of man standing at the right hand of God' (Acts 7:56). Wherever we come across the term the 'Son of Man' in the New Testament we are faced with the same apparent paradox: the stock of concepts which early Christianity uses in this context is remarkably small, there is endless repetition, as though people had undergone some dogmatic schooling; yet the emotional content of all these passages is without exception extremely strong, despite a certain clumsiness of expression. This contrast between the poverty of the images and the wealth of feeling can be explained only by the fact that we are dealing here with something of central importance, which once aroused the deepest emotion only partially hinted at in the surviving texts, but which for some reason lost much of its significance at a relatively early date. A few stereotyped images and expressions remain, but the creative spirit has moved on elsewhere.

Originally the idea of the 'Son of Man' was probably one of the most effective elements in the various prophetic discourses of Jesus; this also explains why third-person statements on a future 'Son of Man' had become so fixed in the minds and hearts of the first preachers of Christianity that later editors probably could not take it on themselves to remodel them. When, at a later stage, Jesus was directly identified with this long-awaited hero of the future, and this process may already have begun during his lifetime (we shall have to come back to this point later) and certainly went on after Calvary under the influence of the Easter faith, this expression had to be used, at least for some time, and the various traditions had to be brought into at least relative harmony with each other. Then came the remodelling of a few sayings which we have already described. In other words, the redactors transformed the 'Son of Man' image, and the result of their efforts is the synoptic text as we know it today. Thereby, however – and this is one of the most astonishing things in the bimillenary history of Christianity, and clearly too the key to certain riddles – the history of the 'Son of Man' image was at an end. Of course the Church could retain and continue to use the few sayings on the 'Son of Man', but it contributed nothing further in the direction of the previous development: it never celebrated or proclaimed Jesus as the 'Son of Man' – although it was otherwise downright lavish with his titles! One can explain this only by the fact that in the first century this concept was closely linked with that of parousia, that is with the belief in an imminent, real and miraculous upheaval, and when the latter did not take place, the idea of the 'Son of Man' died together with the expectation of the parousia.

This brings us to one of the most important and difficult questions in New Testament research: whom did men think Jesus really was, and what did he think of himself? It is beyond doubt, irrefutable, demonstrable and at the same time fairly obvious that many of his hearers, having heard him speak and perhaps begun to understand his message, thought that he was one of the prophets; he was often thought to belong to the ranks of the more popular prophets like Elijah and John the Baptist: 'Who do men say that I am? And they told him, John the Baptist; and others say, Elijah; and others one of the prophets' (Mark 8:27–8 & par.). For a long time after his death and after the formulation and diffusion of the Easter faith, a similar idea lived on among those who had known him and who now worshipped him. One can see this particularly in the fact that according to the synoptic tradition, especially Mark – and its universally stereotyped formulas (Mark 1:34 & par.; 1:44 & par.; 3:12 & par.; 7:36) – Jesus forbids his disciples to tell the people about his mission and his miracles (which led M. Dibelius to remark that Mark is the Gospel of 'secret epiphanies', a paradoxical and yet apt phrase), even though this prohibition sometimes had no meaning at all in the more or less public setting in which it is given (cf. Mark

5:38–43 in particular).

This feature of the Mark-tradition – which is plainly older than the editorial work of Mark – can be explained only by the fact that as faith in the messianic nature of Jesus spread (owing partly to the support of the redactors), it had to compete not only with hostile traditions but also with contemporaries who had known Jesus in his lifetime but who had previously heard nothing of his messianic status. Some explanation of why nothing had been heard about this earlier had to be given. In this matter the editors went so far that they presented even well-known parables (the Sower, the Prodigal Son, the Wise Virgins, the Rich Man and Lazarus), which in Jesus' preaching were without a shadow of doubt intended to *explain* the idea of the Kingdom of God, as a form intended to *conceal* a merely esoteric revelation: 'so that they may indeed see but not perceive, and may indeed hear but not understand' (Mark 4:12) – which contradicts the whole spirit of the New Testament proclamation. There can be no doubt therefore that the disciples' answer given above to the question of whom the people took Jesus to be was wholly accurate: for the vast majority of people, Jesus was in his life-time, and long afterwards in their memories, no more than a typically prophetic figure.

More important, however, is what those closest to him thought and what he thought about himself. Although beyond any doubt he announced a certain eschatological process, the question remains: what part did he assign himself in it? In a sense he undoubtedly cast himself in a prophetic role – even the synoptic tradition records sayings in which Jesus does not hesitate to describe himself as a prophet (cf. Mark 6:4 & par.). But that is only a very vague description, and perhaps an adaptation to the ideas of a wider circle of hearers. The question is whether he gave himself any role over and above that of preaching and prophecy. Here we touch on the difficult problem of Jesus' self-understanding and what those closest to him thought about him.

The idea soon began to take shape and predominate among those close to Jesus, even in his own lifetime, that he was more than a prophetic figure, more than a simple preacher, that he had a definite mysterious mission in the eschatological events he proclaimed, that he was therefore a messianic figure. This group then began .o put forward the opinion to those who were not so close that to themselves alone was it given 'to understand the mystery of the kingdom of God' (cf. Mark 4:11 & par.) and not to those 'who saw but did not perceive, heard but did not understand'. It is clear that this opinion was in the first instance that of a minority; otherwise the events of the passion and all that followed would be absolutely inexplicable. A number of scholars today consider it more than probable that advocacy of this opinion was above all the work of Peter, the most outstanding of Jesus' disciples. The famous scene at Caesarea Philippi which reaches its climax in Peter's confession of faith, 'You are the Christ' (Mark 8:29), is no doubt – like the scenes of Jesus' baptism by John and the temptations in the desert which we mentioned earlier – the dramatic and abbreviated presentation of what was a long process leading up to an important event. The editors of the synoptic traditions were not writing history but setting down for the Christian community the doctrines of the faith. As we have seen, the term 'Son of Man' is puzzling, and there is no less difficulty and obscurity in the use of the concept 'Messiah' – but this time for almost the opposite reasons. We saw that the 'Son of Man' is never found in the second person – and in fact 'You are the Son of Man' sounds absurd – but in the case of 'Messiah' exactly the contrary happens. It is particularly striking that Jesus, who speaks so convincingly of the 'Son of Man', never uses the concept of 'Messiah' at all, and in the synoptic tradition it is not Jesus who tells Peter about his messianic mission, but rather Peter who announces it to Jesus! It is true that the synoptics know of a few occasions on which Jesus does not reject, or even actually commends, similar confessions of faith when they are made by those close to him; yet he never makes such claims himself. The single instance in the New Testament where Jesus says *egó eimi,* 'I am', in reply to a question whether he is the Christ (Mark 14:62 & par.) is isolated and untypical compared with the rest of the synoptic tradition; in any case it appears in the parallel texts as 'You have said so' (Matthew 26:64) and 'You say that I am' (Luke 22:70). This is clearly something rather different, and it fits in better with other passages in John and in the synoptic tradition where it is those close to Jesus, not Jesus himself, who use this concept. It therefore almost seems as though a group of Jesus' disciples, above all the energetic and independent-minded Peter and perhaps 'his own' or 'those who were with him' (Mark 1:36; Luke 9:32) – phrases used by the synoptic tradition to indicate a smaller group within the apostles – had come to the opinion that Jesus was the Messiah, and that it was then Peter and the others who, in exchanges with Jesus, aroused the latter's messianic awareness!

Just as all genuinely mature human life is based on dialogue, and unrelating monologue is a sure sign of failure, Jesus' so-called 'messianic awareness' too was a fruit of dialogue. It was constituted, clarified, and confirmed in dialogue with those closest to him who at first had been incredulous, had not identified themselves with the essence of his prophetic and eschatological preaching, but who then came to 'believe' – that is, in the Good News as Jesus announced it – and were filled with enthusiasm. The result was that they began to turn the preacher into the object of the preaching. How could it have been otherwise? Every 'revelation' is always a 'revelation' *for* someone: it does not simply enter men's heads, as a comet does the solar system, but takes gradual possession of their understanding and feelings, their moral sense and will. But as soon as faith has seized the will, the one of whom faith was asked himself begins to ask for faith; the one to whom something was revealed himself becomes the revealer. This happened in the case of Jesus too. The famous scene at Caesarea Philippi reflects in a compressed form the origin of Jesus' messianic awareness in his dialogue with Peter. Although Peter here represents all those who were close to Jesus, it is clear from the whole synoptic tradition that Peter's was in one way an exceptional, a unique, role not comparable with that of the other apostles and disciples. We might even allow ourselves the hypothesis that to the two most difficult problems of synoptic research already mentioned (the mystery of the 'Son of Man' and the 'secret epiphanies') we should add a third similar 'mystery' which has remained obscure hitherto. We refer to the 'mystery of Peter', that is, his role – relatively scantily recorded, indeed rather concealed than revealed, in the synoptic tradition – as a 'partner in dialogue', in a certain sense even as a co-founder or co-preacher of Christianity. Of course Peter had reasons for making the same judgment on himself as John the Baptist before him (so we are told): 'He must increase, but I must decrease' (John 3:30). This impatient, impulsive, contradictory and highly active man, Peter, was not at all 'lamb-like' but was much more inclined to 'care for the flock' (John 21:15, 17), as the unanimous evidence of the entire synoptic and Johannine traditions makes clear. However, even if there is something authentic in the late (and evidently legendary) report that Jesus loved John more (John 13:23 and elsewhere), there is still more evidence for the fact that conversely Peter 'loved the Lord' (John 21:15 & par.); and it is well-known that the subject of love, not the object which can continue in passivity, performs prodigies of activity, that the loving not the loved person necessarily possesses the force which can mould the human will.

At the time of Jesus, there was no clear distinction between the conception of Jesus as a mere 'prophet', as Judaism and Islam honour him, and the conviction of his 'messianism'. If we trace the semantic changes of the term *maschiah* (= 'Messiah'), the Hebrew for 'the Anointed One', in the Old Testament in greater detail, we discover that unlike 'Son of Man', a term found and taken in an apocalyptic sense only in Daniel, the category of 'Anointed One' was very diversely understood in the Old Testament tradition and could be applied to several quite different figures who were all, whatever their special mission, men of flesh and blood. It was not only King David who was understood to be 'anointed' and so honoured (2 Samuel 5:3) – although the term has obviously been connected with the practice of anointing the king for a long time, and only later took on the meaning of 'saviour', 'liberator', 'redeemer' – but also the Persian king Cyrus, who freed the Jews from the Babylonian captivity (Isaiah 45:1); and later still the Roman Emperor Vespasian, and even the revolutionary leader Bar Kochba, were also called messiah for similar reasons.

Prophets too could be called 'anointed' (1 Kings 19:16; Isaiah 61:1), but the Jewish tradition had as yet no concept of 'Messiah' in the sense of some kind of metaphysical-gnostic, divine, super-natural being. The 'Anointed Ones' were very real heroes of the tribe, kings or prophets, whether of the past or of the future; as such they were certainly the recipients of God's favour, but within the bounds of human possibility, not in any 'supernatural' way. In the pre-Hellenistic and non-Hellenistic milieux, it would never have occurred to anyone that Yahweh, the 'God of Israel', could in any sense have 'an eternal son'. The idea of 'Son of God' is not found in the Old Testament texts; it comes from Hellenistic sources. And since there had been several messianic figures in the past (Joseph of Egypt, Moses, David), there could still be more in the future and they would be of various types. Alongside the prophet Moses was his brother, Aaron the priest. And every people honours not only those who have led it to victory but all those who have courageously shed their blood. In the time of Jesus to say of him that he was '*maschiah*' was therefore almost equivalent in the Palestinian milieu to saying that he was a 'great prophet' or that he was 'called to greatness'.

At the time of Jesus, therefore, the conviction that he was a *messianic* figure could quite easily gain currency without in any way contradicting the general feeling of wider circles that he was a *prophetic* one. At that time, however – and this must be stressed – it did not necessarily mean (in fact it could not have done) that Jesus was the same as the mysterious 'Son of Man'. Whether the conviction of Jesus' messianism developed after Calvary or began in his lifetime is not very important; however, we think that in his lifetime there must have been at least certain foundations laid, even if only in the smaller group round Peter, because otherwise certain further facts would scarcely be explicable.

In our opinion, to ask whether Jesus was considered (and considered himself) a prophet *or* the Messiah is on the whole a misleading question; it does not correspond to the situation at the time of Jesus. The real and relevant question is rather what sort of revolutionary, hope-arousing and therefore messianic figure he was or could be considered to be and considered himself to be. We have already said that these ideas developed over centuries, nourished by the constant catastrophes of Jewish history and the people's longing for some escape from oppression. For centuries the 'messianic problem' coincided with the perfectly customary desire of an oppressed people for liberation. This explains why it grew stronger every time there were crises in society. If we follow the whole series of messianic figures who appeared among the ordinary people of Israel down the centuries, we understand that the real dispute was concerned with how freedom was to be brought about, with what type of man was needed to save and liberate the Israelite people.

It is on the whole understandable that as Jesus' movement began, the oldest, primitive idea of a kingly 'Anointed One' should begin to arouse the hopes and aspirations of the masses.

The latter thought of a Messiah along the lines of King David, who would embody and be the leading figure in a predominantly political liberation movement. The Davidic-messianic ideas, which were certainly associated with, amongst others, the person of the Galilean preacher of radical renewal, were partly satisfied by historical memories of this most famous leader in Jewish history as they were preserved in the biblical books of Samuel and Kings, but also by those sublimated religious and cultic moments intended to bridge the gap between history and hope, to set past and future in relation with each other so that historical memory could initiate present action. This can be seen particularly in some of the Psalms, which for centuries had sustained the Davidic-messianic hope (cf. especially Psalms 2, 24, 45, 72, 89, 110 and 132):

> May he defend the cause of the poor of the people,
>   give deliverance to the needy, and crush the oppressor!
> May he live while the sun endures,
>   and as long as the moon, throughout all generations!
> May he be like rain that falls on mown grass,
>   like showers that water the earth!
> In his days may righteousness flourish,
>   and peace abound, till the moon be no more!
> May he have dominion from sea to sea,
>   and from the River to the ends of the earth!
> May his foes bow down before him,
>   and his enemies lick the dust!
> May the kings of Tarshish and of the isles render him tribute,
>   may the kings of Sheba and Seba bring gifts!
> (Psalm 72:4–10)

How easy and imperceptible is the transition here from social-revolutionary to imperial hopes! But if by Jesus' time the first aspect has prevailed, undoubtedly with regard to the Roman occupation, the more thoughtful students of Jewish history might already have wondered to what extent the second aspect lurked behind the first. We read in the following typical Davidic-messianic psalm: 'Ask of me, and I will make the nations your heritage, and the ends of the earth your possession' (Psalm 2:8). But we must remember that in the Synoptic tradition it is the tempter in the desert and not God who speaks like this to Jesus (Matthew 4:9).

We cannot say on the basis of the synoptic tradition what those closest to Jesus thought about this Davidic idea of the Messiah, but it is quite clear that many of his followers among the people thought of him as in the line of David. In so far as they associated Jesus with the messianic concept, they obviously looked to him for the future political leader, the one who would free them from the power of Rome, renew the Jewish empire and be the future 'Jewish king'. The clearest sign of this tendency in the synoptic tradition is found in the Marcan version of Jesus' entry into Jerusalem, when those greeting him allegedly cried out: 'Blessed is the kingdom of our father David that is coming! Hosannah in the highest!' (Mark 11:10). Otherwise Jesus is called 'Son of David', especially in Matthew, only by strangers, usually in paying homage (Matthew 9:27; 12:23; 15:22; 20:30–1 & par.; 21:9; 21:15; 22:42 & par.), never by those of his own circle; and as a self-characterisation the phrase would sound quite absurd. Either Jesus and his intimate circle of friends did not have this concept of the Davidic Messiah at all, or it was found only among some who were not the most influential of his disciples. Jesus certainly did not dream about being a political liberator: we have already seen that his ambitions were vaster and more profound. Later on Jesus was perhaps really condemned by the Roman procurator as 'King of the Jews' (Mark 15:26) and therefore as a revolutionary and traitor. A Roman official who was not very well informed about Jewish religious and eschatological questions could well have imagined that Jesus wanted to be some sort of king, though there is another version of events in which the reason for the title was that the Roman procurator wanted to teach the Jewish authorities a lesson and get his own back on them for forcing him to go through with an execution he did not really want (cf. Mark 15:16–19). But none of this indicates any real political claim on the part of Jesus (as especially Carmichael recently thought), only a cunning way of imputing guilt to Jesus or of actually convicting him at a level intelligible to a Roman official. To some extent the accusation and judgment were a kind of preventive measure, so that Jesus should not actually become what the great mass of the people wanted him to become. Political reprisals often strike at potential rather than actual tendencies (Tacitus has described tyrants' fear and harassment of those to whom it might even occur to step out of line); in this sense the borderline between an 'act of justice' and a judicial murder is always blurred, difficult to trace. On the other hand Jesus' preaching of the 'Kingdom of God' implied at least a certain part of the Davidic concept of the Messiah, especially where it touched on freedom. If we carefully consider the synoptic traditions in their entirety, it seems that Jesus did not reject the Davidic idea of the Messiah but refused to allow that his mission and message could be reduced to this purely political level.

Long before Jesus, however, there had developed in Judaism other, non-Davidic concepts of the Messiah. It happens in the history of all countries and peoples that there are on the one hand successes, victories, fame and fortune, and on the other failures, defeats, catastrophes and sufferings. And at the beginning of the life of a hero it is not at all clear whether his way will bring him to the throne or the gallows, whether his ideas will be honoured or mocked – and by whom. Thus there was in Jewish history the basis for a Messiah who would not be of the Davidic type. The experience of suffering gave rise to the idea of a suffering Messiah who would redeem his people, by freely taking upon himself their suffering and thus opening the way to redemption as the patient 'Servant of the Lord' (Hebrew = *ebed Yahweh*). The idea of a suffering and dying Messiah refers back to some extent to earlier ideas which, as in all religions, stress the positive meaning of suffering, and consequently to a question which is not only of strictly religious significance but also one of the most difficult problems of human existence as a whole. In primitive, less developed forms of religion, there are always ideas about a reconciliatory sacrifice, often very crude, depending on an anthropomorphic view of a god who has human passions and weaknesses. People believed for example that one could avert disaster of the tribe or family by sacrificing something 'representative' in advance: wine (among the Greeks), animals (early Jewish religion), enemies (executed by many primitive peoples), selected virgins, etc. It was also thought that one's own guilt and sins could be atoned for in this way, indirectly and conveniently.

This is a very ancient religious archetype which is apparent in a particular way in Jesus' movement and in his own self-understanding, but which not only in Jesus' thought but also before him took on more complex and sublime forms. Apart from the cruel meaninglessness of offering a beautiful maiden to the sun-god, as the Incas did, all peoples learned through their battles and sufferings that a person's self-sacrifice could indeed save the lives of others, if only in the sense that the heroic bearing of pain before death could be a source of moral inspiration to others. But in the history of all peoples there is also meaningless suffering, absurd struggles, superfluous sacrifices, blood shed in error. Yet one may ask whether the search for life's meaning, for a truly human history would be at all possible without meaningless suffering; and whether therefore mistaken, meaningless, even absurd sacrifices do not have some kind of meaning after all . . .

Long before man came on to the scene and without his help nature was full of violence and bloodshed. Although human history too is full of them, it is man and man alone who, as a rational being capable of compassion, can set himself the goal of preventing the shedding of blood and the use of violence; history also shows, however, that it is easier to proclaim such an ideal than to be faithful to it in reality. Where and when these ideas of sacrifice and the meaning of suffering are combined with certain metaphysical claims, religious concepts and political goals, one of two things can happen: either the original primitive conceptions can be overcome or brought to a level appropriate to man as a cultural and responsible being; or through them age-old masochistic and sadistic archetypes can be realised which lead to the murder not only of a virgin but of thousands and millions of people. On the one hand, with the total break with anthropomorphism under Moses and the prophetic discovery of the dimension of the future, the Old Testament tradition made the primitive magical concept of sacrifice impossible; on the other hand, however, the inveterate animal instinct for killing and the primitive sense of 'sacrifice' can intrude into the realisation of the most human intentions. After the experiences of this century there is no need to emphasise that the problem of violence is as far from a solution today as ever. Those belonging to the people from which Jesus came have been exterminated in such a terrible way that in comparison the Egyptian and Babylonian captivities seem like an idyll.

It is not surprising, however, that a people which already 1000 years before Christ had fashioned a religion so fundamentally

different from that of other tribes and peoples could and must
have come to deeper answers to the question of the meaning of
suffering and sacrifice in human life, and to special solutions to
the problems of good and evil, redemption and salvation. Here
more than elsewhere there was a conflict between the idea of
God and the real situation of the world. Here more than
elsewhere suffering became a crying problem:

> Again I saw all the oppressions that are practised under the
> sun. And behold, the tears of the oppressed, and they had no
> one to comfort them! On the side of their oppressors there was
> power, and there was no one to comfort them. And I thought
> the dead who are already dead more fortunate than the living
> who are still alive; but better than both is he who has not yet
> been, and has not seen the evil deeds that are done under the
> sun. (Ecclesiastes 4:1–3)

The Book of Job in particular provided the basis for the reflection
of many generations on the possible meaning of the suffering of
the just man; Job's 'contending with God' (Job 9:3) centres on
the question of how it is possible to combine faith in God with
the search for a meaningful life, given such terrible and absurd
cases of suffering – a suffering which cannot imaginably be
reduced to any such meaning-giving concepts as 'testing' or
'punishment'. It was also recognised, however, that the positive
human values of health, satisfaction and happiness do not mean
simply freedom from pain and suffering, but that a certain
measure of pain and suffering can have positive meaning, not for
their own sake but if they are borne for the sake of these values.
The question automatically arose – as if the early primitive pagan
ideas of sacrifice were returning at a higher level – whether suffering must not precede future salvation (we must remember that
in chiliastic-eschatological thought the future Kingdom of
freedom is always preceded by a terrible catastrophe and incalculable suffering), and whether the voluntary acceptance of
suffering might not contribute to the advent of salvation.
   This leads us to the genesis of the idea of the 'suffering Messiah'
which differs essentially from the Davidic conceptions, although
it is found frequently in the Psalms and the prophetic books (cf.
especially Psalms 22; 31; 38; 69; 142; Isaiah 53). Whereas in the

Psalms and a number of other Old Testament texts there is a general description of the man who suffers and overcomes pain which is not (at least in the authors' own intentions) given a messianic interpretation, we can see in Isaiah or whoever was the author of the second part of the book of Isaiah (known as Deutero-Isaiah) that this 'man of sorrows' (Isaiah 53:3) is certainly at a turning-point in history, that his suffering has a certain universal and representative character: 'Surely he has borne our griefs and carried our sorrows' (Isaiah 53:4). He freely accepts his terrible death as in some sense necessary: 'He was like a lamb that is led to the slaughter . . . he opened not his mouth' (Isaiah 53:7). That is something completely new. Although the term Messiah is not explicitly used in this passage, the text begins to take on a messianic and redemptive meaning when it says that 'with his stripes we are healed' (Isaiah 53:5). It could be linked with the Davidic tradition of the Messiah as a variant. For his suffering is no longer an end in itself or merely the courageous bearing of pain; rather it has begun to have a meaning in the eschatological process of salvation. Thus we come to the phenomenon, of immeasurable importance for the understanding of Jesus and his environment, that the perfectly sound observation that man can achieve nothing truly great without exertion, suffering and sacrifice is combined with certain age-old religious archetypes on the redemptive and representative meaning of human sacrifice. In association with the eschatological proclamation of the coming Kingdom and in an extremely critical political situation in which everything was ready to explode, all this was bound to bear remarkable moral and intellectual fruit.

In the first century, faith in the coming of a Messiah was deeply rooted in the idea that the messianic upheaval would come at the highest pitch of suffering. One can think of two comparable phenomena outside Christianity. The Talmud, for example, says that the Messiah will come when the face of the age is the face of a dog, when men will seek in vain even for a fish for the sick to eat, when there is universal decline. At the very moment at which all is apparently lost, the supernatural redemption starts and the Messiah comes. (In Hinduism there is a similar idea in that Vishnu always comes to save the world only in moments of continuing decline.) The idea closest in time and content to that of Jesus, however, is found in Flavius Josephus' description of the final phase of the first Jewish-Roman war: when humanly speaking all was already lost, the Jewish warriors fought on to the last drop of blood and clearly expected to descend to the very depth of suffering so that the messianic turning-point could materialise. According to Josephus, it appeared as if they reproached God for still hesitating to punish his enemies. It is difficult for us today to think ourselves into this heroism, but indirectly this, too, can help us to understand the dialectic of suffering and victory, death and redemption, in early Christianity.

During his public life did Jesus have any clear idea of his coming suffering? Did he go towards death consciously? Or to put this more tersely: was he fully aware that he was a Messiah, as Isaiah had described him? If older theological tradition – up to the nineteenth-century – uncritically accepted all the prophecies of Jesus about his forthcoming passion and resurrection (cf. Mark 8:31 & par.; 9:31 & par.; 10:33 & par.; and elsewhere) and did not puzzle its brains over the various problems to which they gave rise, modern critical scholarship considers these predictions of Jesus to be retrospective statements, that is to be sayings which were attributed to Jesus only later, after Calvary and the Easter experience. We think that this second extreme position is equally incorrect and leads to the same illogical conclusions, because it does not pay sufficient attention to the psychology of prophetic figures. Even if the formulation of the passion predictions as preserved for us in tradition is plainly and in every case post-Easter, that does not mean that such thoughts played no part in Jesus' life. Indeed, it would be astonishing if they did not, at a time when executions of popular heroes and leaders of every possible opposition movement were everyday events. Even today people who embark on a public career risk their lives because they are exposed to the attentions of those in power and to all manner of assailants and psychopaths: how could the leading prophetic personalities of the past not have had this possibility constantly before their eyes? Hundreds of cases from history and from their own time confirmed the truth of the saying, 'O Jerusalem, Jerusalem, killing the prophets and stoning those who are sent to you' (Matthew 23:37); and the fate of John the Baptist was a constant reminder to Jesus of this possibility. It is perfectly understandable and obvious that he must have thought about these matters and spoken about them with at least some of his dis-

ciples. Furthermore in the synoptic tradition the first of Jesus'
predictions of his own suffering all follow the accounts of the execution of John the Baptist. It is also natural that those who loved
him should fear this possibility and that Peter should try to dis-
suade him from such thoughts (cf. Mark 8:32 & par.). Jesus'
dialogue with Peter on this subject (Matthew 16: 21–3) is also,
therefore, in its psychology and pertinence, perfectly justified
and credible, and it is by no means illogical that Jesus on the one
hand should entrust his flock to Peter and give him authority but
then, on the other, immediately afterwards call him 'Satan'.
Anyone who does not see this does not understand human nature,
the logic of love, the doubts and anxieties which flow from it.

The idea of sacrificing one's life for others is found in all ages,
obviously not in established circles, for whom nothing of vital
importance is at stake and who are therefore incapable of asking
themselves the question of the significance of death, but among
all popular opposition movements, whether they are religious or
revolutionary in inspiration (there is always an interchange
between the two). The main reason for this is undoubtedly that
its partisans are convinced of the magnitude, extent and importance of the cause in question, and this inevitably in their eyes
throws individual human life into the shade. There is, however,
another factor at work: in all opposition, sectarian, oppressed
human groups, the urgently and imminently felt danger from
without leads to humanly closer, firmer relationships *within* the
group; there comes into being a much deeper mutual love and
solidarity than among the wealthy and ruling classes. Jesus' words
apply to every oppressed movement: 'Where two or three are
gathered in my name, there am I in the midst of them' (Matthew
18:20); and the later and already somewhat stylised words hold
true, if not in their precise formulation at least as far as their
meaning goes: 'This is my commandment, that you love one
another as I have loved you. Greater love has no man than this,
that a man lay down his life for his friends' (John 15:12–13). It
belongs to the logic of human nature that the more deeply one
loves life, the 'cause' and one's brothers in the cause, the more
one is determined to stake even one's life.

However, it was also part of the logic of eschatological
preaching that Jesus confirmed his mission and message with his
own suffering and life: this is always the case with the truly great,

especially among prophetic figures (we Czechs think of Jan Hus). If Jesus sent his disciples out as 'sheep in the midst of wolves' (Matthew 10:16 & par.), if he demanded total commitment, perseverance, fearlessness, the courage to confess him openly before men (Matthew 10:32 & par.), the courage to bear mockery and persecution for the sake of him and his preaching (Matthew 5:11 & par.; 10:22; 10:38–9 & par.), he could hope to encourage them not with mere words and invitations but only with his readiness to precede them with his own example. And so the idea of possible suffering and death on his part must beyond any doubt have played an important part in Jesus' life. The words which the Johannine tradition ascribes to Jesus: 'I am the good shepherd, the good shepherd lays down his life for his sheep' (John 10:11), were never spoken by Jesus in this form, since they contradict the form of the synoptic tradition too strongly, yet Jesus must often have felt within himself something corresponding to them; otherwise their appearance in the Gospels would be quite inexplicable.

The question, then, is not whether Jesus had or had not some inkling of his forthcoming sufferings – that seems to us to be beyond dispute – but rather whether he ascribed to his future suffering a purely moral significance, like any great and loving person who is prepared to sacrifice himself for his brothers, or a certain eschatological significance as well; and finally to what extent in his thinking his death had a certain eschatological 'replacement value', whether, for example, inspired by Isaiah and the social situation of his own time, he regarded a painful death as a possible or even necessary passage to the 'Kingdom of God', which was the central theme of his preaching. Without wishing to assume that Jesus had a perfectly rationally thought-out plan – a man does not think in this way of his own death, and the idea of a 'plan' corresponds only approximately to the structure of eschatological thinking – we do assume that it would contradict the whole spirit of Jesus' 'proclamation' if he understood his death in purely 'moral' terms, that is, without any connection with the awaited eschatological upheavals, to which he was undoubtedly committed with his whole soul, heart and will, and therefore, too, with that part of his mind which began to occupy itself with envisaging his own death.

After the concept of the real future advent of the 'Son of Man

in all his glory' which we verified earlier, we have now encountered the second markedly mythological feature in Jesus'
thought: the idea that his own suffering and death would have
metaphysical value as the necessary condition for the full physical
realisation of the 'Kingdom of God', for the transition from a
position in which it was 'near at hand' to its actual concrete
presence, and therefore for the 'salvation of mankind'. What is
involved here is a certain enhancement of that eschatological
archetype which we have already noted in connection with the
Jewish revolutionaries in so far as they risk their lives in the conviction that in this way they are hastening on a better future. We
do not need to devote space here to demonstrating that these are
only superficial analogies. The fact remains that the eschatological concept of suffering has a basic reference to the
wholly real and proper universal meaning of bravery, suffering
and sacrifice for the sake of one's brothers, for truth, for the
better life, for freedom, and that it does not deny the reality of
these things. On the other hand one cannot dispute that not only
does this natural, moving and inspiring readiness to lay down
one's life for a conviction or friend, to suffer for a cause or for the
truth (as we find it in some of the martyrs of scientific progress
but most frequently in the heroes of revolutionary and national
freedom movements) here receive a certain mythological colouring – this was frequently the case elsewhere, for example among
political martyrs – but that mythology here constitutes the very
heart of the problem. What is at issue here is not just a general
understanding of the possible meaning of pain, sacrifice and
death, but the very precise idea that a particular concrete death –
that of Jesus of Nazareth – would usher in a particular cosmic upheaval. One can question today whether Jesus was right or
whether he suffered simply from a tragic illusion; but if one is
familiar with the mythological structures in human history, one
can scarcely doubt that such ideas are a typical component of all
mythological thinking. Conversely, however, precisely because
we know the myths of other peoples, from the Indian to the German and the Slav, we become aware of how ephemeral are the
traces of reality found, for example, in Greek mythology compared with the proportion of humanly important matter
associated with the myth of Jesus of Nazareth. The picture of Andromeda, her hands chained to the rocks and abandoned to a

terrible death, likewise as a sacrifice for the guilt of others, has inspired dozens of painters; but history has been shaped only by the picture of Jesus hanging with pierced hands on his cross, because the 'cause' for which he suffered was so much more human, because he *really* died in torment: no Perseus came to save him.

We must distinguish two levels of the problem. The first is how the idea of the 'suffering Messiah' originated and spread; on the whole this is a simple and obvious question, and we have already discussed it. The second is how this idea of the 'suffering Messiah' came to be associated with Jesus of Nazareth; this is a problem which has divided, and still divides, scholars according to their religious denomination, and today even within the same denomination. It is understandable that the whole further development of Christianity, starting with the redaction of the synoptic texts, was at pains to present this identification of Jesus with the suffering Messiah as absolutely self-evident from the very beginning, that is, clear at least to Jesus himself, though not at first to his closest friends. However, because there were sayings, firmly anchored in tradition, in which Jesus had clearly predicted his suffering and the messianic significance of his death (Mark 8:31 & par.; 9:31 & par.; 10:33 & par.; 14:21 & par.; 14:41 & par.; and elsewhere), something of a puzzle arose: because these words must have been spoken to someone, someone must have preserved them from the road to Jerusalem to the time of Pentecost: but why in that case were the disciples so confused and distressed in Jerusalem? Why did they flee to Galilee? Why was there this hiatus between Calvary and Pentecost? Why did they flee the place of horror – and at the same time carefully preserve the words which gave messianic meaning to this horror? The editors of the tradition were well aware of this contradiction and tried to resolve it by suggesting that the disciples had not understood these predictions: 'But they understood none of these things: this saying was hid from them, and they did not grasp what was said' (Luke 18:34); 'But they did not understand the saying, and they were afraid to ask him' (Mark 9:32). It is certainly remarkable that somebody should faithfully transmit texts the meaning of which he did not understand; it is even more remarkable that the perpetrators of this paradox were those to whom Jesus had 'given the secret of the Kingdom of God' (Mark 4:11 & par.); and most remarkable of all is that the very same

tradition should also report how at least Peter had discussed these
matters with Jesus (Matthew 16: 22 & par.; Luke 22:33 & par.) –
and this at the heart of the Gospel, which brings out both Jesus'
messianism and Peter's personal mission! How *could* Peter fail to
understand that Jesus was determined to suffer? Nor were the
other disciples quite so impercipient as the synoptic tradition
sometimes depicts them. True, there is no reason why they
should have understood everything straightaway, and there is no
reason to doubt the credibility of the story that naive squabbles
arose among some of them in which they shared out posts in the
coming Kingdom of God (Luke 22:24; Matthew 20:25–8). Yet
anyone who had been with Jesus on earth for any length of time
could not have directed his thoughts in totally the wrong direction; he must have understood something of Jesus' preaching and
personality, must have been attracted and enthused by
something. Once we have seen how unthinkable it is that Jesus
did not ponder the meaning of his suffering long before Calvary
and speak about it to his closest companions – it is equally unthinkable that Peter and the other disciples should not have understood this. If there was something they had not understood
and their incomprehension produced such great confusion among
them after Calvary, it was something other than the fact of suffering. If even Peter, who is presented in the synoptic tradition as
the discoverer of Jesus' messianism (Matthew 16:13–23 & par.)
and to whom Jesus in his reply (doubtless in a conversation of
months' duration) explains the messianic conception, failed to
understand something and therefore needed to 'turn again' after
Calvary (Luke 22:32), it could not remotely have been Jesus' suffering. Anyone who accepts this would have to set aside the
whole of the synoptic tradition. Thus we reach the following
conclusion. If the disciples fled headlong to Galilee (Mark 14:28
& par.; 16:17 & par.; Matthew 28:10 & 16), in other words
home, as most people do when faced with an emotional distur-
bance or a disaster, it was not because Jesus had never spoken to
them of the suffering that awaited him or because his arrest, torture and execution had come as a surprise to them. The real
reason for their surprise and panic must be sought elsewhere.
There is only one explanation which does not force us to remove
essential sections of the synoptic Gospels, especially the frequent
'predictions' of the passion: they were expecting something else

to happen and it did not happen, or at least not immediately and in the way they had imagined; hence the panic, hence the later 'explanation' that they had failed to understand something essential in their conversations with Jesus. However, before we discuss the passion itself, we must resolve a number of other difficulties.

Suffering – and by that is meant the fulfilment of the mission of Isaiah's 'suffering Messiah', the 'suffering Servant' – evidently could not itself exhaust the significance of that mission; it was only the first stage in the messianic process. For all eschatological thinkers before and after Jesus it is self-evident that after the suffering come glory, victory, the start of a new era. That must have been true for Jesus too and for all those closest to him. Quarrels, obscurities, expectations, disappointments, fresh hopes, etc. – these could affect not the essence of this eschatological archetype (which persists, incidentally, in the movements of the Middle Ages and the modern period), but only the manner in which this two-stage messianic process would come about and who would have what place in it. This is the only subject that Jesus could have discussed with Peter: there was no controversy over the principle of suffering and subsequent victory. Jesus was hailed by Peter and his companions as the messianic figure, and he himself stressed the necessity of suffering, but that does not mean that Jesus must necessarily thereby have been identified with that coming mysterious and victorious 'Son of Man' whom he preached. On the other hand, this identification was not excluded, just as David had started life in poverty before he was 'anointed', so the future David could suffer before gaining the victory. Let us therefore consider now the question of the identification of the suffering Messiah with the victorious hero of eschatology.

The fact that there were several types of Messiah in the imagination of the Jewish popular movements (although in the end they could be reduced to two, the suffering and the conquering) and especially the fact that the eschatological process was to have two phases or stages – suffering and victory – could be taken to mean *either* that the Messiah had a double task *or* that there would be two successive messianic figures. Both variants existed at the time of Jesus singly and in combination. The idea of a single Messiah was more common, and yet there is a certain amount of evidence for the theory of two Messiahs.

In the Qumran documents the idea of the two Messiahs occurs as a distinction between the so-called Messiah of Israel and the Messiah of Aaron. As opposed to the political, national hero of Israel, the priestly Messiah of the Essenes (after Moses' brother, the High Priest Aaron) could have been responsible for diverting Jesus' attention from the Davidic-political to the spiritual-reformative interpretation of the messianic process. Some of the salient features of the 'priestly' concept of messianism are found especially in the Epistle to the Hebrews, but there are hints too in the Pauline Epistles and in the synoptics, especially where Jesus is depicted as forgiving sins, a typically priestly act. Even so, this concept does not appear to have had any more emphatic influence on the actual eschatological conceptions of the New Testament, and in particular of the synoptic tradition, than that.

What is more important for us is the distinction which is made only very much later, in Jewish texts from the second century onwards, between the awaited 'Messiah, son of Joseph' and the 'Messiah, son of David'. While the first dies in the messianic battle, the second reaps the victory. We do not know whether the name of Joseph, which is also found in the story of Jesus, is used by chance here or whether there is a link with the synoptic tradition. Nor do we know whether these ideas are earlier than the synoptic tradition. There are marked contrasts: for example, the Son of Joseph here has more the characteristics of a political leader while the Son of David is a more supernatural figure, but this is not important in our present context. What matters is only that the idea of a messianic pair is found in Jewish history before as well as after Jesus, and that it could therefore also have played a definite role in the genesis of his personality and in the thinking of Jesus and his disciples.

Does the idea of a double Messiah appear in the New Testament texts even if in a veiled manner? We have previously noted that the mysterious figure of the awaited 'Son of Man' for a while played an important and indeed a key role in Jesus' preaching, and this can be seen in the depth of feeling aroused each time that he is mentioned. This means that the Gospels had already identified Jesus with the 'Son of Man', but at the same time it is clear there were certain problems and difficulties in this identification which we have already mentioned. If we further recall that even Peter's confession of faith did not necessarily in-

volve identification with the eschatological figure of the 'Son of
Man', it is obvious that we can at least concede as a hypothesis
that perhaps the archetype of two Messiahs entered into Jesus'
thinking, and that subjectively he could have thought of himself
as the suffering Messiah distinct from the future 'Son of Man', the
conquering Messiah. Jesus would then have found himself both
announcing and fulfilling the *first* stage of the eschatological
process. This would explain the sayings about the 'Son of Man'
in the third person and also the difficulties experienced by the
synoptic tradition in identifying the two figures. Then too the independent Johannine tradition, which contains some far from
clear hints that after Jesus' death another figure is to be expected
(John 14:16, 26; 15:26; 16:7), would not indicate a purely
spiritual coming: the obscure designation '*Parakletos*' ('Com-
forter') would originally have meant another messianic figure.

Another hypothesis is possible which in our opinion is the only
one that enables us to interpret the entire New Testament tradition, including all the difficulties and 'mysteries' already mentioned, and it has the added advantage of offering the basis for
the best and clearest understanding of what happened on Calvary
and subsequently; it is the hypothesis that Jesus *originally* appeared
as the magnetic preacher of the 'Kingdom of God', of radical
conversion and of the coming of the 'Son of Man', and *only later*
appropriated the idea of his *future* identification with the coming
'Son of Man' in his glory, to which suffering was a necessary
transitional phase. If we interpret Jesus' self-understanding in
consistently eschatological terms, the difficulties of identifying
him with the 'Son of Man' are removed altogether. If we are
dealing with a purely eschatological future identification, we can
readily understand why there are no sayings about the 'Son of
Man' in the second person and why the sayings which are given
in the surviving texts in the first person are rather suspect: Jesus
evidently did not identify himself in the present with the 'Son of
Man', even when towards the end of his public life he allowed
others to make a future identification. Then when, in conjunc-
tion with the development of belief in the resurrection,
everything which their memories had retained of Jesus' life was
seen in a new light, there was no longer any reason to maintain
the idea of a double Messiah, and thus Jesus was fully identified
with the 'Son of Man', although the principal sayings remained

in the third person because that was the form in which they had been handed down.

This further helps to explain a second group of sayings with a fixed literary form, those concerned with the future suffering and death of the Son of Man, which clearly and unmistakably refer to Jesus himself. Just as none of the synoptic writers has any sayings of the type 'until I come . . .' but only sayings like 'until the Son of Man comes', none of them has sayings which take the form 'until I suffer . . .', but only 'until the Son of Man suffers . . .' (cf. Mark 8:31 & par.; 9:31 & par.; 10:33 & par. 14:21 & par; 14:41 & par.); and even though it is perfectly clear that these words refer to Jesus, they are never transposed into the first person. And conversely, no matter how frequently the synoptics speak of Jesus' doings and miracles, no matter how frequently they recount the addresses and discourses of Jesus, the term 'Son of Man' is hardly to be met and is not found at all in the parables or Sermon on the Mount. This evidence too shows clearly and on the whole irrefutably the secret of the identification referred to. It was of uniquely future reference; Jesus therefore does not exclude his future transformation into the Son of Man, but it is not something which directly affects the present. That is why to address him as 'you, Son of Man' would be as absurd as addressing someone today as 'you man of the twenty-first century'. The sayings about suffering and death, on the other hand, are entirely concerned with the 'Son of Man', and they derive from Jesus himself, at least in certain basic features. In the eschatological thinking before the passion, the formula 'the Son of Man must suffer . . .' originally meant something like 'one becomes the Son of Man through suffering . . .' or 'the Son of Man will appear only after the necessary suffering', and again some time could elapse before this was interpreted as 'only after the necessary suffering on *my* part'.

In our opinion the case is much the same with the other great difficulty of synoptic research which led to countless controversies among scholars in the last century: the question of whether Jesus considered himself to be the Messiah or not. Was the opinion that Jesus was the Messiah the fruit of Jesus' own cogitations, or was it only at the back of his mind as a possibility ('you have said so', Mark 15:2 & par.), Peter being the first to voice it explicitly? In our opinion this way of putting the question is mistaken, uneschatological, and therefore inapplicable to Jesus. It corresponds to the approach of later theology which, under the influence especially of the Greeks, lost any real feeling for involvement in time and the dynamism of eschatology, and defined messianism in Platonic and Aristotelian terms as a kind of quality that one either has or has not, or in any case as something given in advance. But this way of thinking is out of harmony with Jewish tradition and the milieu in which Jesus and Peter lived. The idea that someone was already born Saviour of the world, that he 'was' the Messiah even as a child, could arise only in a Hellenic or Roman context. To people educated exclusively to the messianic conceptions of David, Daniel and Isaiah, to the Galilean revolutionaries and idealists, to the Jordanian prophets and even to the learned circles of official orthodoxy in Jerusalem, the notion of a Messiah from birth, a Messiah in this sense fully fledged, would have made no sense whatever. According to the unequivocal tradition of Judaism, the Messiah could only *come*, could only appear in the midst of events, he could not be *already there* in swaddling clothes surrounded by a mother's tenderness.

In Jewish and also early Christian tradition (before its Hellenisation) the test of messianism is not a human quality, psychological or moral for example, or ontological in the christological sense. The decisive criterion is exclusively the messianic event, the bringing of salvation, the ushering in of the real political or eschatological upheaval. Consequently, to 'be the Messiah' would not make much sense for Jesus and Peter and the disciples; what would make sense for them was to 'become the Messiah', that is to inaugurate the messianic event even though through suffering. If Peter really said to Jesus once or several times, 'You are the Christ' (Mark 8:29 & par.), he could not have meant that Jesus possessed the messiahship as some kind of intrinsic quality. For that would go against the whole of the Jewish prophetic tradition and particularly Jesus' own proclamation of the future age. It could only mean: 'You are called to undertake the messianic task!' Admittedly anyone who is called to future greatness already *is* in some sense the one that he will become. But there can be no doubt that the indicative 'You are' was originally more a kind of imperative: 'Become the Messiah', 'Fulfil the messianic hopes', 'Bring about the messianic change', etc. Only in this way does it make sense. Jesus was hailed, at least by those closest to him, as one called to a messianic mission and entrusted with the task of introducing the eschatological event. Plainly already convinced of his vocation to inaugurate the messianic event, he goes finally to Jerusalem, to the centre of Jewish conservative orthodoxy and the Roman administration. It was certainly not just an ordinary missionary journey, like the journeys in Galilee and Judaea, nor was it the ordinary Jewish pilgrimage. 'Behold, we are going up to Jerusalem, and everything that is written of the Son of man by the prophets will be accomplished' (Luke 18:31 & par.). (Jerusalem lies on a rocky hill, and furthermore Jesus and his disciples were approaching it from the East, from Jericho, from the great basin: hence the 'going up to Jerusalem'.) But what did this 'all' mean in Jesus' thinking at that time, somewhere on the Jordan? What was it that the disciples apparently did not understand (Luke 18:34)? In other words, how far did they have other ideas about the journey to Jerusalem, how far were they disappointed, confused and shocked by what really happened there?

Jesus went up to Jerusalem shortly before the beginning of the Paschal feast, at which the faithful streamed into Jerusalem from all directions to celebrate the greatest of Jewish feasts, the commemoration of the Exodus from Egypt, that first redemptive event which for all prophetic-eschatological hopes of Jesus' time was the greatest 'prototype' of the expected salvific event of the near future. And now, contrary to all his previous practice, Jesus does not avoid the applause of the crowd or violent polemics with the defenders of Jewish orthodoxy in the Temple (Mark 11:11–12:37 & par.). Nor does he hesitate to address 'the crowds' directly (Matthew 23:1 & par.) and deliver his sharpest polemical attacks on those who 'sit on Moses' seat', 'bind heavy burdens, hard to bear, and lay them on man's shoulders' (Matthew 23:2–4). If Jesus really concluded his speeches to the pilgrim crowds with a description of the religious leaders as 'whitewashed tombs' (Matthew 23:27) and as notorious murderers of just men (Matthew 23:32–6 & par.) – one cannot be certain of the genuineness of these speeches but they seem probable – such invective would have been enough to get him arrested in any period of history, above all at a time when occupied Jerusalem was in the grip of revolutionary ferments. But did Jesus come to Jerusalem simply to indulge in vituperation? That would be a

contradiction of everything that we already know of him. There
can be no doubt about it: he went up to Jerusalem with a higher
purpose in mind than controversy and criticism.

The famous scene of Jesus' entry into Jerusalem (Mark 11:1–10
& par.) is the record of a misunderstanding. It expresses the
political and revolutionary aspirations of the people and the
hopes they pinned on this prophet from Galilee, whose teachings
must have already been known to some of the inhabitants of
Jerusalem but who was only a vague figure for the majority of
them. Precisely because of this misunderstanding, there can be no
doubt about the credibility of this incident, for legends do not invent misunderstandings. The people of Jerusalem regarded Jesus
as a new David and expected speedy and effective action from
him; so it is easy to understand how they could turn against him
in their disappointment and cry out so soon afterwards to the
Roman procurator, 'Crucify him' (Mark 15:13 & par.). Later
legend-mongering could scarcely have made up the scene of the
'Last Supper of the Lord' either (Mark 14:22–5 & par.), even if,
as in a series of other similar cases, it is a condensed account of
several such meals shared in a spirit of love, understanding and
brotherhood. It provides us, however, with one of the most
remarkable sayings of Jesus: 'From now on I shall not drink of
the fruit of the vine until the kingdom of God comes' (Luke
22:18). That suggests a very optimistic idea and the hope of a
rapid victory for his own cause.

A few days after Jesus' arrival in Jerusalem, there was a kind of
public clash in the Temple, which the synoptic tradition presents
as Jesus' attempt to clear the buyers and sellers out of the Temple
(Mark 11:15–17 & par.). A few scholars have understood this
scene to be the echo of an attempt by Jesus' disciples to take over
the Temple at Jerusalem (Kautsky, Carmichael and others) and
suggested that this was the real reason for the arrest and trial of
Jesus. That cannot be completely excluded, for the
Qumran-Essene sect as well as the radical revolutionary Zealots
were opposed to the Temple at Jerusalem and very critical of the
priestly hiearchy, and that could have had some influence on the
circle of Jesus' closest acquaintances which, as we know, included
men from such radical groups. This theory is confirmed by the
fact that the two witnesses who gave evidence against Jesus attached importance to the Temple of Jerusalem, even though what

they were trying to say is not very clear (Mark 14:58 & par.). However, this purely political interpretation of the reasons for the arrest of Jesus is founded on too narrow and vague a basis, and it contradicts the whole essence of the message of Jesus which forms the heart of the synoptic tradition. It also fails to explain how Jesus could stay with his disciples at Bethany in the days before Easter without being arrested – for Bethany was only an hour away to the East of Jerusalem; moreover he seems to have been able to go to Jerusalem daily (Mark 11:11–12 & par.; and elsewhere), crossing the deep valley of the Kedron and going through the Garden of Gethsemane, once again without being arrested. All that suggests that the reason for his arrest was not political activity but the violent debates in the Temple.

The reports on the last days of Jesus are rather uncertain; we know for sure only that he was arrested, swiftly condemned, and then rapidly and discreetly executed. The disciples scattered and fled in their confusion. They had gone home to Galilee in the North. None of his own disciples was present at any of the judicial proceedings, at least according to the reports that have survived – which considerably diminishes their credibility. But at his execution 'there were women looking on from afar' (Mark 15:40); in Matthew this becomes 'many women' (Matthew 27:55), while Luke has 'all his acquaintances and the women' (Luke 23:49). When John for his part adds that 'many of the Jews' were present (John 19:20), this gradual 'escalation' suggests that in this case only Mark can really be relied on.

Although therefore everything which happens after Jesus' arrest is relatively uncertain (we have here really only one source, Mark, on whom the others depend), and although the legend-building impulse was later at work here more actively than elsewhere, and the critical scholar must therefore regard as hypothetical everything which goes further than Mark, there are nevertheless parts of the narrative that can be considered with a high degree of probability to be trustworthy. They are in conformity not with the ideas and wishes of the scholars but with the basic tendencies of Jesus' teaching as we have so far traced them and established them as proven. For example the treachery and suicide of Judas, 'one of the twelve' (Mark 14:10 & par.), can hardly be wholly legendary. It was indeed an astonishing betrayal, which seems to meet with the silent approval of Jesus and even to fit into his plans. We must decidedly exclude love of money as motive for the betrayal, although it is suggested by Matthew (Matthew 26:14–16), since it does not convincingly account for his suicide and probably comes from a later tradition. Part of the motive could have been disappointment, perhaps deriving from the collapse of his religious and political hopes – although once more that would have made his suicide slightly remarkable. On the other hand there is something to be said for the theory that Judas acted in the best of intentions, as Goethe, incidentally, without making any special study of the matter, had intuitively felt; the suggestion is that he was not betraying Jesus or giving him away by a kiss (Mark 14:43–5 and par.), but that he was more worried about what seemed like the betrayal of the messianic hopes by Jesus and Peter, and this led him to try to hasten on the eschatological process by forcing a situation in which it would no longer be possible to dodge the issue or delay a decision: either Jesus or the Jewish authorities would have to make up their minds and act. Then the suicide of Judas would have precisely the same cause as the panic-stricken flight of the other disciples to Galilee: 'I will strike the shepherd, and the sheep will be scattered' (Mark 14:27). But the events of Calvary led not merely to Judas' *disillusionment* but to the total collapse of everything for which he had lived, including his hope of bringing his 'meaningless' life (as he saw it) to a triumphant conclusion by trying to force the redemption through his 'betrayal'. Judas had to commit suicide after the failure of all his hopes. The image, then, of Judas the 'traitor' is quite meaningless. If there were anything like a re-encounter with Jesus after death, the Galilean prophet would certainly have welcomed his friend Judas, and in preference to others, as he had said goodbye to him for the last time in the Garden of Gethsemane: with an embrace . . . (Mark 14:45 & par.).

To some extent the same may be said of the trial before the Jewish Supreme Council (or 'Sanhedrin'), the highest organ of Jewish orthodoxy (at that time under the chairmanship of the High Priest Caiaphas), which is alleged to have followed the betrayal. Nothing, of course, is proved with complete historical certainty, not even the fact that they held a session of the Sanhedrin; but the reports do not contradict what we have indicated as Jesus' principal concern, which assuredly did not coincide with what the Council could have regarded as Jewish orthodoxy at that time and which had been the real reason for his journey to Jerusalem. The priestly hierarchy could in the end have only two basic objections against Jesus; first, that his activity had given rise to a certain unrest, possibly also of a political nature, and second — and this would have carried more weight — that he incited the people against themselves, that therefore he disturbed the peace: in the tense situation under the Roman occupation this was to act against the interests of Judaism. To some of the Sanhedrin he might have appeared as a congenial though rather extreme 'patriot'. But for the majority of the unsentimental, conservative members of the Jewish Supreme Council, Jesus was at the very best only a dreamer or visionary, but a dangerous person because of his influence on the public, an insurgent who was playing with fire and who could therefore drag the whole country into danger. That was quite enough to lead to execution even in calmer times. From their point of view they had to condemn him, so as to avoid still worse consequences. It is indisputable that this motivation played a part, even though it is given little prominence in the synoptic tradition, which mentions it for example as an argument put by the Council to the Roman governor, Pilate, to the effect that Jesus was 'perverting the nation' (Luke 23:2) and urging the citizens to disobedience. For Pilate this brought the case clearly into the political arena, as did the alleged claim of Jesus to be the 'king of the Jews' (Mark 15:2 & par.).

More controversial, although better grounded in the synoptic tradition, is the question whether the Sanhedrin openly dealt with the second aspect of Jesus' activity which must have concerned them as guardians of religious orthodoxy: his messianic mission and his conviction that the messianic event was imminent. 'If you are the Christ' — which means after our earlier analysis: If you are to become the Christ — 'then tell us' (Luke 22:67 & par.). Whether this question was so phrased or not, there can be no doubt that the highest religious authority in Judaism had the right, indeed the duty, to ask such a question, since it had been the key problem in the Jewish prophetic tradition for at least 500 years. And if the same problem was at the heart of Jesus' ministry, if only in its later stage, especially on the way to Jerusalem where he then appeared only for a number of days, it is likely that news about him had reached many of the leaders of the hierarchy, even without Judas' 'betrayal'. One must also add that the members of the Sanhedrin, with perhaps a few exceptions (cf. Luke 23:50–1 & par.), could have little sympathy for Jesus: representatives of orthodoxy, hardened in dogmatism, are disinclined to welcome 'reformists' and 'heretics' who bring new life and vivid social relevance at a time when old structures prevail. But if we take into account the duty of the guardians of Jewish orthodoxy to preserve the purity of faith in Yahweh and the integrity of the Mosaic Law, they behaved perfectly correctly and according to the letter of the Law, which had protected Judaism from various false prophets and claimants to a divine mission. There are clear words on this in the Old Testament: 'But the prophet who presumes to speak a word in my name which I have not commanded him to speak, or who speaks in the name of other gods, that same prophet shall die' (Deuteronomy 18:20). The Jewish high priests must have considered with great earnestness whether Jesus was a true prophet or a false one who would have to be punished with death. But it is absolute nonsense to lay the blame for Jesus' death on Judaism as a whole, as generations did for centuries. The unfortunate words of Matthew's Gospel, 'His blood be on us and on our children' (Matthew 27:25), almost certainly unauthentic since they are found only in Matthew and fit in with his personal theological ideas, have for centuries provided the perfect basis for one of the greatest aberrations not only of Christianity but of human history generally, which culminated in Auschwitz. The history of those who confess Jesus includes not only the noble ideals of the Sermon on the Mount but also words which animate the old dark passions from the age of blood vengeance, among them the frightful conviction that a people who had 'murdered God' must be punished for this arch-sin until the end of the world. It is only in modern theology and since Pope John XXIII that there has been a serious effort to make a radical break with this tradition in the liturgy and Christian praxis.

The synoptic tradition concerning the guilt (or partial guilt) of the Roman occupying forces in the execution of Jesus is particularly doubtful. It is true that all the surviving texts describe the guilt of the Romans as minimal, indeed purely formal, in comparison with the allegedly terrible sin of the Jewish hierarchy, and present the Roman Procurator, Pontius Pilate (known from other sources to have been a cruel ruler) as a thoughtful Epicurean who, although he had no understanding of the thought of Jesus, which was bound to seem strange to him, nevertheless showed a certain human sympathy for the victim of torture and sought to save his life: 'What evil has he done?' (Mark 15:14 & par.). Obviously this cannot be ruled out altogether, but it is more probable that this 'magnanimity' of Pilate was introduced into the text at a period when there was an increasing differentiation between Judaism and early Christianity, and that this piece of editing expresses growing hostility to Judaism, whose basically negative attitude to Jesus seemed to the early Christian communities to be the cause of all the suffering and tragedy of the people from the time of the destruction of Jerusalem. It is unlikely that the Roman administration at the time of Jesus would have understood any popular opposition movement as a purely religious or purely Jewish matter; and they were scarcely in a position to understand the originality of Jesus' thinking. It is possible that the participation of the Roman authorities in the execution of Jesus was no less great, indeed was considerably greater than that of the conservative Jewish hierarchy. It is obviously impossible to prove this now; but in one way or another, the formal responsibility for the execution of Jesus must be borne by the Roman Procurator and therefore indirectly by the Roman imperial power. From this point of view, there is a certain historical justice (which occurs here and there in the torrent of history's absurdities) that it should be in the end heathen Rome and not Judaism that became the victim of victorious Christianity.

Roman responsibility also appears in the manner of the execution, crucifixion: the soldiers lead the condemned man outside the city walls where he is stripped, his hands are tied or nailed to a cross-beam which is then raised up on to a short vertical beam to which finally the feet are tied or nailed. The torments accompanying the death agony in this form of execution were extreme. It had originally been used by the Romans only for slaves who were guilty of crimes or who had tried to escape, but then it came to be used in the colonies on insurgents of any kind. It usually took several hours before death came from increasing cramps which eventually affected the respiratory muscles.

Depending on the way they were hanged, the victims might linger on for days, raving, gnawed away by insects, until finally they died of thirst and respiratory failure. Sometimes the executioner would shorten the agony of those who aroused his compassion by breaking their limbs. This prevented them from raising themselves to release the pressure on the chest from the sagging body and thus accelerated paralysis of the respiratory organs. It was in the interests of the authorities to hasten Jesus' death as much as possible. We may perhaps be allowed to hope that the immense agony of the man who did more than anyone else before him to introduce into human history the idea of love for one's fellow-men — because he himself evinced such love — did not last long.

If we are critical in our approach to the sources, we know nothing at all of the details of the 'Way of the Cross', of Jesus' last moments or of his burial. A great deal of what twentieth-century man still thinks he knows about the passion and without which the meditations of the greatest and noblest minds in Europe on pain, suffering and death would be unthinkable (we have in mind not only works like Michelangelo's *Pietà* and Dvořák's *Stabat Mater,* not only great geniuses like Dostoievski but also the countless simple people who in humble village churches lift up their eyes to the figure on the cross — in vain?) is pure legend, dating from even before the Gospels were committed to writing, including the famous 'Seven Last Words' from the cross. There is here a complete lack of historically reliable documents. This, however, does not depreciate the human reality of the experiences which all who approach in faith but not necessarily with strict regard for historical truth have had when contemplating this death — from the author of the legend who thought himself into what the mother of Jesus (who was certainly still alive) might have felt as she later recounted the death of this her very special son and saw herself again under the cross (John 19:25–7) to those moderns, often atheists or free-thinkers, who allow themselves to be moved by Jesus' suffering and death. Humanity does not need verifiable details in order to be touched by the encounter with suffering.

Yet we believe we have found, beneath the surface of the legendary or altered and interpolated details, something small, apparently only a trivial thing, that could well be a historical fact, because in the synoptic tradition it was concealed rather than supported by legendary reshaping. When we put it in relation with certain inconspicuous passages in the synoptic tradition which are often ignored or misunderstood, it perhaps sheds a new light on Jesus' whole life from the standpoint of the cross. We must first of all recall that in practice the whole of the previous exegetical and hermeneutical tradition, fascinated by the astonishing and therefore, it would seem, extremely plausible cry of Jesus on the cross: 'My God, my God, why hast thou forsaken me? *Eloi, Eloi, lama sabachthani*? (Mark 15:34; Matthew 27:46), argued only about whether this was a cry of despair, of disillusionment – wrung from Jesus by his terrible sufferings, of course, but also by his disappointment that his awaited transformation into the 'Son of Man' had not materialised (as the predominantly hostile, 'heretical', interpreters indebted to humanism, existentialism and socialism maintain) – or whether it was simply a quotation from Psalm 22 which begins in this way and which Jesus prayed on the cross, and therefore not remotely an expression of abandonment, despair or loss of faith, as the text in isolation might suggest, but rather the expression of the deepest piety and self-abandonment, as the meaning and conclusion of the Psalm suggest and as Luke cleverly tried to interpret it by correcting the cry to, 'Father, into thy hands I commend my spirit' (Luke 23:46). Neither of these traditional interpretations seems to us entirely satisfactory.

Should we not recall here one of the basic rules of textual criticism: where possible to take as one's starting point the obscure passages concealed by the logic of the context, hidden in material which the writer wishes to emphasise – in a word, to read between the lines? We assume this and further offer the hypothesis that what those gathered at the foot of the cross really heard (as distinct from what theologians later thought they heard) can be inferred from the following text, to which sufficient attention is never paid: 'Some of the bystanders hearing it said, "Behold, he is calling Elijah" ' (Mark 15:35; Matthew 27:47). That they in fact heard Jesus calling Elijah transpires even more clearly from the words which follow: 'Let us see whether Elijah will come to take him down' (Mark 15:36; Matthew 27:49). Who were these bystanders? A few Roman soldiers – who doubtless understood nothing at all; perhaps a few members of the Sanhedrin, who clearly heard it; perhaps also Simon of Cyrene with his sons (Mark 15: 21 & par.); and of the disciples perhaps only some women and they, we are told, saw everything *from afar*' (Mark 15:40). Now who would be a better witness to what Jesus really said – the Jews who mocked him at the crucifixion or the first Christians who later meditated on these events? All things considered, the passage as a whole seems to us to provide evidence to the effect that by the time the Gospels came to be written down, there was still extant a tradition that Jesus on the cross had called on Elijah. Otherwise this reference to the (allegedly false) Jewish interpretation that he called not on God but on Elijah would be superfluous, would make no sense, would be a stupid and tasteless jibe at such a solemn moment.

Did Jesus really call on Elijah? Would it make sense? In other words, could his appeal to Elijah have a deeper relationship to the essence of what we have so far said about the thoughts, feelings and intentions of Jesus? Is the calling on Elijah more probable than the cry 'My God, my God, why hast thou forsaken me'? We must retrace our steps a little and recall another apparently obscure event that has always puzzled the exegetes; some regard it as a simple product of Peter's imagination, others as one of the Easter legends retrospectively projected into Jesus' real life. This is the scene known as the 'Transfiguration' in which on Mount Tabor in Galilee, their home country, Peter, James and John are said to have seen Jesus in power and glory speaking with Moses and Elijah (Mark 9:2–8 & par.; Mark here quite untraditionally puts Elijah before Moses!). The Transfiguration therefore, from the Gospel account, took the form of a dream or vision. Now Moses and Elijah have one thing in common which, with Enoch, distinguishes them from all the other figures of the Old Testament: they did not die an ordinary death. 'No one knows the place of Moses' burial to this day' (Deuteronomy 34:6), the reason being, as non-biblical records in Jewish popular tradition frequently testify, that Moses died by God's breath and was taken up to heaven; Elijah too 'went up by a whirlwind into heaven in a chariot of fire' (2 Kings 2:11). If Jesus' 'Transfiguration' in the glory of the 'Son of Man' was expected at the zenith of his suffering, this encounter with Moses and Elijah in their 'transfiguration' was no accidental remnant of it in the synoptic tradition. And if Jesus himself, as he went up to

Jerusalem in the hope that 'everything would be accomplished' (Luke 18:31), and even on the cross, still expected his transfiguration, his glorification, his entry into the 'Kingdom of God', the beginning of the Kingdom of the future, his appeal to Elijah was not accidental, he still had Elijah's 'parousia' in mind. That is much more natural and logical than the existentialistic, melancholy cry, 'My God, my God, why hast thou forsaken me?' Jesus died as the son of his people, as the greatest Jewish prophet in the tradition of Moses and Elijah — not as a sort of first century Kierkegaard.

If this is true, however, all those passages in the synoptic tradition in which we are told that people considered Jesus to be the prophet Elijah (Mark 8:28 & par.; and elsewhere) take on a new and deeper meaning; it seems that this might have had a meaning for Jesus himself, that it reflected something real in his self-understanding. Particularly noteworthy is the passage which in Mark and Matthew occurs during the descent from Mount Tabor after the 'Transfiguration', when, without any obvious link with the remarkable event on the mountain, it is said that according to the teachings of Holy Scripture Elijah has to return to the world before the Son of Man can come (Mark 9:11 & par.). The obvious reference is to a tradition stemming from the prophet Malachi, according to which Elijah will reappear 'before the great and terrible day of the Lord comes' (Malachi 4:5). Why, however, should this be mentioned precisely as the party were coming down from Mount Tabor? Why should Matthew be at such pains to assure us at the conclusion of this episode that 'the disciples understood that he was speaking to them of John the Baptist' (Matthew 17:13), although John the Baptist was already dead? Is it not more reasonable to assume that the original point of this scene was to interpret the events which had just taken place on the mountain, and that Elijah was mentioned in connection with Jesus, not with John the Baptist? If we then compare all the passages in the synoptic gospels where Elijah is mentioned, the conclusion emerges that it was not only the hearers of Jesus — there is ample evidence for this in the text — but also Jesus himself, in an admittedly obscure way, who stressed the connection with Elijah, and that in some sense Jesus evidently considered himself to be a similar prophet, a figure like Elijah. This does not mean that there was any kind of identification between a living person and the long dead prophet, but it concerned a key problem of Jesus' preaching and personal fate: the belief in his own future identification with the 'Son of Man in all his glory'. Jesus assumed that in the deepest suffering, at the moment of death, he would be saved in a wonderful manner like Elijah, transfigured into the Son of Man who could inaugurate a new age, the Kingdom of God. This explains why Peter and some others placed Jesus even in his lifetime on the same level as Moses and Elijah; it in no way contradicted Peter's confession of Jesus' messianism, but on the contrary enabled the disciples to understand Jesus as an 'anointed', messianic figure, that is, as a figure predestined to future 'transfiguration' like Elijah.

That appeal to Elijah on Calvary (not one of the 'Seven Last Words' established by later tradition and in fact obscured by that tradition) can therefore confirm the interpretations and hypotheses mentioned above and expose the underlying logic; what is at first puzzling thus becomes clear and intelligible in the end – and no less fascinating. The expectation of transfiguration at the acme of suffering to some extent approximates Jesus psychologically to the Jewish freedom fighters who fought in the Roman wars to the last drop of blood because they expected salvation to come only out of the depths of suffering. That, however, is by the by. It is more important that it is now clearer how Isaiah's 'Man of Sorrows' could fulfil the mission of redeemer-liberator, and above all how the puzzling future identification with the 'Son of Man' was intended. It also becomes clearer, not why the 'Son of Man' could speak in sermons and parables, but why the oldest stratum of tradition has preserved sayings about him in the third person which describe not only his future coming in glory but his future suffering. The optimistic outlook of Jesus and his disciples on the way to Jerusalem, even though only partially preserved in the Gospel text, becomes clear and meaningful. Most of all, however, the supposed enigma of why the disciples who had many times been instructed by Jesus about his future suffering should nevertheless have fled in fear and confusion, becomes lucid and perfectly intelligible: it was not the fact of Jesus' suffering that puzzled them; no, they were perplexed and distressed by what did *not* happen on Calvary: the suffering Jesus was not transfigured into the Son of Man, he called on Elijah in vain.

For the disciples, then, Calvary really was a catastrophe – not because Jesus suffered, but because he died. Not even Peter, the one closest to Jesus' hopes and fears, expected that. They had expected suffering, but only as a prelude to the glorification and transfiguration which were immediately to follow it. That is why they fled in perplexity and despair; we may recall how even later Easter legends were still fighting the memories of this grief (Luke 24: 17)! They went home to their native Galilee, just as children do when things go ill. Their whole world collapsed. Some of the women, perhaps led by Mary Magdalen, stayed behind in Jerusalem. This detail too makes sense: these women loved Jesus as women have always loved, with an unconditional, non-ideological love; that is, they did not put so much value on his message about the Kingdom of God, the 'transfiguration', etc., but loved – and this is especially true of Mary Magdalen – a great, pure, magnetic personality. When men, on the other hand, love, they usually do so conditionally, with an eye to social relationships and ideologies; they want results and proofs. Men too were certainly drawn to Jesus; but what counted for them was his preaching, his faith in the future victory, his appearance as the Son of Man. For all of them, including Peter, Calvary was therefore a terrible and tragically disappointing experience. Hence the significance of the words: 'You will all fall away' (Mark 14:27 & par.). They were certainly more bewildered, took more scandal and offence, than the synoptic tradition allows.

This brings us to the most remarkable chapter not only in the history of Jesus but in Christian history generally: after what must have been quite some time (as we know, tradition often compresses into a few weeks what probably took much longer), Jesus' companions returned to Jerusalem, fully convinced that Calvary was not the last word. They saw Jesus as victorious, glorified, alive. What was the cause of this metamorphosis? Peter played the leading, decisive part in it. Even though later levels of the synoptic tradition attempt to cover up and play down Peter's role in this connection for reasons not entirely clear to us (for example by suppressing the original conclusion of Mark's Gospel, which must have concerned visions in Galilee – otherwise Jesus' words: 'I will go before you to Galilee' (Mark 14:28 & par.) would be unintelligible, and by adding the later legends of Mary Magdalen's visions and the empty tomb in Mark 16: 11–18 &

par.), the oldest credible witnesses still evidently concern Peter. The evidence of Paul (1 Corinthians 15:5) who knew nothing of Mary Magdalen, the story of the Emmaus disciples (Luke 24:35) and the whole logic of the subsequent event lead to the following conclusion: the first and principal preacher of the glorified, transfigured, exalted and risen Jesus was Peter, the others were led by him gradually and not without difficulty. Even that part of the synoptic tradition which tried, for whatever reason, not to emphasise his role, in fact to overlay it with something else, does not quite succeed in its aim. Thus, for example, Mary Magdalen is told to 'tell his disciples and Peter' (Mark 16:7), which gives the impression that Peter received news of the resurrection from Magdalen. But Peter, who had proclaimed Jesus' messianic mission, also proclaimed his exaltation, his resurrection, and it was through him that the disciples of Jesus, who in his lifetime had formed a kind of adventist sect within Judaism, became the community of those who believed in Jesus. Early Christianity was born.

The later tradition of the Roman Catholic Church derived the jurisdiction and authority, the teaching and hierarchical primacy of the Roman popes, as Peter's successors, from the so-called 'primacy of Peter', and perhaps because this tradition relied on the description of Peter's role in the New Testament texts, the attention of scholars has concentrated on the question of whether this is biblically justified or not (the main bone of contention between Catholic and Protestant scholars). In biblical research, therefore, little consideration has been given to the specific reason for Peter's unique position among the disciples. There has been no attempt to evaluate and interpret what we must regard as a contradiction: on the one hand the whole of New Testament literature acknowledges the fact of Peter's special role among Jesus' disciples, but on the other it does not reveal, indeed sometimes conceals, the precise nature of that role. In other words, we admit that Peter played a prominent part in the organisation of the first Christian community, as the New Testament describes (Acts 1–5), but the question is, on what basis, in the name of what, Peter carried on this work. The uniqueness of his role must therefore be sought in the precise reasons for his (undisputed) primacy, not in whether the 'primacy' was actually entrusted to him or not.

To its own detriment, Petrine scholarship has concentrated almost exclusively on the famous passage in Matthew's Gospel in which Jesus answers Peter's emphatic confession of faith. If we translate this reply from the terminology in which the Church later fixed it, into a language which corresponds better to Jesus and his message, we get something like this: 'You are Peter, and on this rock (Greek *petra*) I shall set my community, which the gates of the kingdom of death will not overcome; I shall give you the keys of the future age' (Matthew 16:18–19 & par.). It is possible that this passage, which has been one of the most used in the whole of the Bible, was the creation of post-Easter tradition, intended to legitimate Peter's de facto leading role in the early Christian community. But in so far as Peter had already proclaimed Jesus' messianic mission in his lifetime and, as seems well proven, had discussed the meaning of the messiahship with him, it seems likely that as soon as Jesus had determined to accept suffering he would have said something to Peter about the latter's role in the forthcoming event. This could not have been too specific because, if Jesus assumed that the age of the victorious 'Son of Man' would begin after his suffering, it could hardly have occurred to him to draw up a last will and testament and to make Peter his executor and successor. Thus all considerations of whether by his 'community' Jesus could have meant the future Church or of what 'on this rock' could mean are more or less irrelevant. Peter's possible role, in so far as it was certain in Jesus' lifetime, could be intended only eschatologically, which means – as in the question of Jesus' messianism – that it could have been not a matter of any permanent moral or psychological (not to say magical) quality possessed by Peter but only an activity, a role in the messianic event. Onesided emphasis on the dialogue between Jesus and Peter would not have been so irrelevant if scholars had considered the parallel passages. The Johannine parallel, for example, even though of late composition, could have given them a deeper understanding of the passage in Matthew's Gospel. There, Jesus says to Peter: 'Feed my sheep' (John 21:16–17), and this clearly points to an activity.

The Lucan parallel, however, so often forgotten and underestimated, can tell us much more (as far as some short passages and sayings but not events and overall construction are concerned, Luke of all the redactors has preserved the most important element in the old strata of the synoptic tradition). It reads: 'But I have prayed for you that your faith may not fail; and when you have turned again, strengthen your brethren' (Luke 22:32). This passage, one of the most important for our understanding of the passion and also of the 'mystery of Peter' we mentioned earlier, in the form we have it comes from the post-Easter period; but it certainly refers to something ancient, primitive, a certain confidence which Jesus placed in Peter. It also indicates, however, that there was a certain danger that Peter's faith in Jesus might falter. The synoptic tradition has preserved this fact, even if in a later and naive form, in the account of Peter's denial of Jesus (Mark 14:66–72 & par.); if it had really been only such a trivial episode – Peter refusing to tell a serving maid who he was – it would certainly not have passed into tradition. The fact that it is carefully recorded by all the evangelists can mean only that it papered over older reports of a much more serious 'denial'. Without any doubt that denial concerned the Calvary experience, the most difficult crisis of faith. Yet Peter 'turned again' (Luke 22:32) – perhaps the most important clue for understanding Calvary and what happened subsequently! Peter's 'turning again' undoubtedly refers to the fact that he was the first to assimilate the tragedy and absurdity of a Calvary without a parousia and a they-lived-happily-ever-after ending and to realise that Jesus' crucifixion *was* his victory. Peter was then able to 'strengthen his brethren', to restore their faith in Jesus and his preaching which had been so shaken because all had 'fallen away' (cf. Mark 14:27 & par.). This made Peter's role in early Christianity so extraordinary. This was how he soon reached the privileged position which even those who were not specially fond of him – and the New Testament several times hints at their existence – conceded. It seems that Peter did not have the charismatic power by which Jesus drew men to himself, that 'magic' which could make heroes out of weak men; but his energy and his capacity to 'strengthen the brethren' were all the greater. The man who proclaimed Jesus' messianism now proclaimed Jesus' 'exaltation'. Thus he took over the leading role and turned a sect into early Christianity.

It was Peter who drew the dividing line which marked off the early Christians from those round about them. He did not, of course, win over all Jesus' hearers, not even all those who had been attracted by his preaching of a coming age and inner transformation. Many of them remained outside Christianity. And the dividing line is to be sought in their attitude to the events of Calvary. Some of them saw the passion as the end, the great tragedy and scandal, and however much they dreamt of a future age and the future upheaval they remained outside Christianity. To be considered a Christian, a believer in Jesus, one had, with Peter, to believe in his 'exaltation', to regard Calvary not as the end but as the transition to victory and exaltation. The former were soon overtaken by events – especially after the two fruitless uprisings of Jews who thought eschatologically and longed for the upheaval, which both ended in catastrophe – and disappeared from history. But the latter inaugurated Christian history.

At first – and second – sight it is somewhat remarkable that the 'cause' of Jesus did not come to an end with his tragic death on the cross and that his disciples did not simply scatter and vanish without trace like the supporters of all the many other rebels, prophets, preachers of doom, reformists, insurgents and revolutionaries who have fallen victim to the state's concern for law and order. Further, if people had expected that the Kingdom of God would soon break into human history and that the suffering on Calvary would end with Jesus' celebrated 'transfiguration', the appearance of the Son of Man in all his power and splendour, how was it that the supporters of Jesus, or at least those who formed Peter's group, were able to surmount this terrible disappointment, this 'scandal of the cross', and indeed to turn it into a victorious event? How was it that a prophet whose predictions had not been fulfilled should be at the origin of the greatest of world religions? Generations of historians and theologians have pondered and still ponder these and suchlike questions.

Apart from a few details which need separate treatment, on the whole it is clear – and this must be our starting-point – that the psychological and moral basis for this fresh start was Peter's preaching of faith in the exalted Jesus. The death on Calvary was mastered by faith in the conquest of death (1 Corinthians 15:51); faith in the victory of Jesus led to the hope that his resurrection was only a beginning, and that everything else in Jesus' preaching about the Kingdom of God would come to pass later. It was undoubtedly above all through this faith in the resurrection that Christianity, more than any other great religious system, came to be a religion of paradox, as for example Albert Schweitzer stressed, that is a religion in which the inexorable laws of the logic of life and death are transcended.

Resurrection . . . If we have so far seen so many real problems of human life in Jesus' preaching and despite the fact that the hope in the wonderful appearance of the Son of Man was at first understood by Jesus' supporters excessively naturalistically, how could such a remarkable belief take root? Was it really able to rally Jesus' shocked disciples? How could Peter take a handful of scattered men and not only unite them but make them more active, more convinced, more courageous and even, as far as effect is considered, more successful than before? The interpretation spread by the enemies of Christianity even before the redaction of the synoptic texts (Matthew 27:64; 28:15) and revived in the modern period, especially by the proponents of eighteenth-century Enlightenment, that the disciples stole the body and fabricated the story of the resurrection, or – as variations on the same theme – that Jesus was only apparently dead, or that Simon of Cyrene who had helped Jesus to carry his cross (Mark 15:21 & par.) allowed himself to be executed in his place we consider to be absurd. Jesus' disciples are said to have stolen the corpse – and then to have proceeded heroically to conquer the world, to have carried the Good News about Jesus to everyone (cf. Matthew 10:27 & par.), and to have allowed themselves to be beaten and persecuted in his name (Matthew 10:22 and elsewhere). Frauds could have done none of that. It needed true faith and profound conviction to preach Jesus as victorious in spite of the scandal of his death on Calvary. Only genuine faith could be the starting-point for the Christian mission.

Is it sufficient to explain the origin of the so-called 'Easter faith', that is faith in the resurrection of Jesus, with the 'appearances' to Peter and a few other followers of Jesus, and thus with dreams and hallucinations? Peter was indeed that way inclined (cf. Mark 9:2–8 & par.; Acts 10–12; Matthew 14:28–31). But could visions bridge the gaping contradiction between their recent realistic, indeed naturalistic, ideas about the coming of the Son of Man's Kingdom and Jesus' real transformation into the creator of a new age on the one hand, and their sense of despair and emptiness after his death on the other? An affirmative answer to this question cannot be excluded, but we should consider it to be at the very best an inadequate explanation.

We think that visions alone could not have played such a part: at the very least they would have to have been linked with a faith which already existed on some other basis. If they were an extraneous, sudden, unconstitutive element compared with the original nature of Jesus' movement, they would have electrified a small group but they could not have overcome their despair and preserved the continuity of the movement. In other words, the Easter faith was able to unite and galvanise Jesus' shocked admirers only in so far as it had an organic connection with this message. The vision of the risen exalted Jesus was remarkable in its effect precisely because it provided a new interpretation of what had been discussed long before Calvary, if not as early as Jesus' first conversation with the future 'fishers of men' (Mark 1:16–20 & par.) then at least after Caesarea Philippi (Mark 8:27–33 & par.). Peter and his 'party', by which we mean the most discerning group from among the disciples, had been fully aware from the beginning of Jesus' inner struggles, of his preaching and proclamation of the Kingdom of God, but they did not have at all a clear picture of Jesus' own role in the future age; they confessed that he was called to participate in the messianic event, but Jesus had not clarified his exact part in it (although another tradition would willingly have it that he did!). If this is true, the vision of the risen Jesus suddenly provided a new interpretation (which has been more or less normative ever since) of some of the essential points of Jesus' preaching before Calvary. If belief in the resurrection surmounted psychologically this disillusionment of their eschatological expectation and later, from the second century, even excluded the idea of the glory of the Son of Man in practice and replaced it with the image of the risen Jesus as Christ, Redeemer of the world, this was only because this image, too, could be organically incorporated into certain basic components of Jesus' eschatological preaching.

We must recall that what was new in Jesus' preaching and influence was not that he announced the Kingdom of God, the future age, the radical upheaval – a whole popular-prophetic tradition had already done this right up to John the Baptist – but

that he approached every person there and then, at that and at
every moment, with that total summons of the future radical
cosmic renovation, and that in this sense he not only continued
Jewish prophetic tradition, the proclamation of the future, but
also insisted on inner conversion and exemplified it in his own
life. We have already shown that 'faith', as Jesus understood it,
was not remotely a Gnostic speculative opinion about the future
but a radical demand made on man as he stands here and now.
For the disciples of Jesus, faith in the resurrection could replace
the failed parousia of the Son of Man, could provide an organic
basis for the new life and urgency of Jesus' preaching only
because from the start it was concerned not simply with the
Kingdom of the future (basileia) but also with inner conversion
(metanoia). Moreover, since the purely Davidic tendency, the effort to bring about purely secular change and the subjection of all
the peoples of the earth, had been rejected by Jesus as a temptation of the devil (Matthew 4:8–10 & par.), since therefore there
was a preference for interiority over politics, one can understand
why Calvary must have been so shattering, scandalous and
destructive of their naturalistic hopes for the coming of the Son
of Man and the Kingdom of God, and yet it in no way negated
the preaching of the Kingdom itself. Peter therefore found points
of contact to tie in his own preaching of the risen Jesus with those
older elements in Jesus' preaching. He, and through him the rest
of the nascent movement, understood that cosmic miracles were
not needed on Calvary, and that in this respect they had misunderstood Jesus. That is why we find the almost stereotyped formula in the synoptic tradition according to which, whenever
Jesus speaks of the future and allegedly of the resurrection, there
is a clause which explains that his disciples did not understand
him (Mark 9:32 & par.; Luke 18:34 and elsewhere). What was it
that they failed to understand? If Jesus had really spoken of the
resurrection, which is a much clearer idea than that of the coming of the Son of Man and the beginning of the future age, they
would have understood him only too well and would not have
fled from Jerusalem to Galilee. But he was speaking of something
else; that is why they did not understand him.

The resurrection was not preached in a purely materialistic
way, as though it were the reanimation of a corpse. It was not by
chance that part of the early Christian tradition preferred to

speak of 'exaltation' and 'glorification' rather than 'resurrection', and these terms were closer to the older preaching of the glory of the Son of Man. In the understanding of Peter's circle, this way of looking at the exalted Jesus was not very different from how already during his life-time they had imagined him 'transfigured' (Mark 9:2 & par.), that is, in his future identification with the 'Son of Man'. That is why they did not bother greatly with the tomb and the corpse; none of them really knew where the Roman soldiers had buried Jesus, it might even have been in a grave with other condemned men. The details about Joseph of Arimathea, the tomb in the rock, and all the rest (Mark 15:42–7 & par.) are explicable only as a later legend, not directly a fruit of the Easter faith, but a fruit of later controversy about the resurrection. That the disciples had no idea where Jesus was buried is indicated by the careful observation in Mark that 'Mary Magdalen and Mary the mother of Jesus saw where he was laid' (Mark 15:47 & par.). This also proves indirectly that Peter and the others were already on the way to Galilee at the time of the burial. All the other 'eschatological events', the origin of the Easter faith and the time needed for Peter to gather the little community together again (traditionally the time between Easter and Pentecost, though in reality much longer) again took place in Galilee. Thus in the early period of their new belief that Jesus had been 'exalted', it would not even have occurred to them to look for the grave in Jerusalem; and when eventually they returned to Jerusalem, it was already too late. However inconvenient that may be for history, it was all the better for the growth of legends about, for example, Mary Magdalen's vision of the angels (Mark 16:1–8 & par.). But even Paul does not raise questions about these events when many years later he came to Jerusalem to consult Peter and other contemporaries of Jesus, and he is plainly concerned with quite different matters (Galatians 1:18–2:14). Clearly Paul, who gave the resurrection such central importance (1 Corinthians 15:1–58) based his faith on grounds other than the fate of the body and the story of the grave hewn out of the rock.

In fact Paul says: 'If Christ has not been raised, then our preaching is in vain and your faith is in vain' (1 Corinthians 15:14); this already points to a new situation in which the resurrection has begun to take up a central place in the structure

of early Christian thinking and to displace the idea of the 'Son of
Man in all his glory'. Even though Paul and his entire generation
clearly still understood the resurrection as the beginning of the
general resurrection (1 Corinthians 15:51–8), the idea of the
resurrection increasingly replaces that of the 'Kingdom of God',
the Kingdom of the future age. That Peter, Paul and their
colleagues could bring about this change of emphasis in a
relatively short time is partly explained by the shift in the theatre
of operations; some time between the forties and fifties
Christianity crossed the boundaries of Palestine and put down its
first roots in the Hellenistic world, probably first of all in the
nearest important centres like Antioch and Alexandria where
there was little understanding of the typically Jewish
prophetic-eschatological way of thinking, while on the other
hand the influence of Platonism, Gnosticism and oriental myths
provided a better background for a reinterpretation of Jesus than
Israel alone could provide.

   One cannot fully explain the relatively rapid spread of the idea
of the resurrection in early Christianity either by the visions of
Peter and others or by the already mentioned tendency to fuse
the resurrection with the original preaching of Jesus, and these
are especially inadequate to explain how the prophetic orientation towards the future was turned into a demand for inner
reform. The success of the new idea – and the echoes it awakes in
human self-reflection – can be fully explained only when one in-
troduces a third factor. Whereas from Isaiah to Jesus the
prophetic preaching of radical renewal and the future Kingdom,
however mythological, had been able to express certain popular
socio-political aspirations for a transformation of the social situation, and the individual's need constantly to transcend his present
position, the idea of the resurrection or 'awakening' evokes in
mythological form a different set of human problems and desires.
There is, for example, the question of one's own death, which is
much more difficult for a being endowed with consciousness
than for inferior creatures. The problem of the meaning of death
and related questions concerned with the transiency of things, the
mystery of time and of what is indestructible in the universe: all
these questions become more and more urgent as soon as a man
leaves the secure membership of race and tribe and becomes an
individual being capable – perhaps! – of seeing himself as the

focus of cosmic events.

Perhaps because tribal unity was especially strong among the Jews of the Old Testament, this idea remains relatively un-developed despite progress in dealing with other questions. It is true that in the Old Testament there are occasional hints about a kingdom of the dead (*sheol*), but it is not emphasised at all. The meaning of human life clearly lay in its fulfilment here below and consisted in a long life, prosperity, the family, and in sharing in the destiny and serving the cause of the people of Israel through fidelity to the covenant with Yahweh. No one seems to have bothered his head with what happened to individuals after death; in so far as there were any ideas at all of an afterlife, they were rather of a kind of shadowy existence which certainly did not sound very desirable. The few cases that are mentioned where there is reanimation of the dead (2 Kings 8:1; 13:21) are understood as miracles, and not as the ordinary rule or as ex-amples of the transition to 'eternal life'. When the idea emerged of a general resurrection of all the dead at the end of time (Ezekiel 37) it was more a matter of the prophetic-eschatological view of the future than a solution to the problem of individual death. The concepts of 'soul' and 'immortality' were still un-known, at least in the sense that Christianity and Islam were later to use them. In the pre-Christian era, the problem of death and the human desire to escape one's fate was really better understood in certain Eastern religions, for example in the myths of the death and reawakening of Osiris, Tammuz and, in India, of Shiva, the creator and destroyer. It is highly improbable that any of this directly or indirectly had any influence on Peter in Galilee after Calvary; but there can be no doubt that it had prepared the ground in the Greek world by the time Paul and his companions began their great missionary journeys to diffuse knowledge of the risen Redeemer. The tradition of Platonic dualism also helped. It would be naive to try to put on the same level the resurrection of Christ and Egyptian or Babylonian myths on dying and rising divinities. The latter were clearly natural myths which expressed the hopes and desires of natural man; but in Christianity the idea of the reawakening was associated with the radically social problematic of redemption. The very fact that the idea of a victor over death merged into the idea of the Christ, that is, the Messiah, the Redeemer, opened up much deeper moral and anthropological realms – all the more since this idea was connected with Jesus' preaching on the 'Kingdom' and the need for 'conversion'.

This brings us now to the beginning of the development of early Christianity proper. It was primarily based not on Jesus' preaching of the future age and the need for radical inner conversion but on faith in Jesus the victorious Christ, the conqueror of death and evil, the bearer of salvation, a faith substantiated by Peter, Paul and others. The two do not of course exclude each other logically, but psychologically they are not the same, and the latter prevailed not simply as a complement to the former but also at the expense of its intensity. The original purely eschatological preaching of Jesus was summed up in the phrase, 'Behold, I make all things new' (Revelation 21:5), the characteristic formulation of Paul is rather, 'If anyone is in Christ, he is a new creation' (2 Corinthians 5:17). The two assertions are logically in perfect harmony with each other, but in the mind of the believer they have diametrically opposed effects depending on which one stresses, whether one says that all things shall be new tomorrow, or that all things were made new yesterday. A movement which saw its radical renewal somewhere ahead in the future became gradually and unobtrusively the community of those who believed in a Conqueror who had already made all things new. There are various hints given in the New Testament that the early Christian communities had some inkling of this apparently insignificant but in fact far-reaching change (e.g. 1 Corinthians 1:10–16), but the actual transition was probably much more dramatic than these hints would suggest.

The Christian 'Easter' grew out of Pentecost, when this fundamental change occurred as the apostles under Peter's leadership, 'filled with the Holy Spirit' for the first time (Acts 2:4), saw Jesus' ministry in a new light; in other words, the vision of the risen Jesus was relocated in the *past,* three days after the crucifixion. This so-called 'Easter faith' determined all subsequent development. As soon as the teaching about the risen Christ had spread and gained a foothold, it must have influenced the entire tradition concerning Jesus; all the stories about Jesus began to be re-evaluated and restructured in the light of the Easter faith. Some elements could obviously remain untouched: thus the parables and certain brief sayings about ethics were left

as they were. On the other hand passages concerned with the
messianic question and the Son of Man were obviously directly
influenced and rapidly remodelled by the Easter faith. None of
this implies conscious falsification, deception, concealment or
touching-up of the truth: it all happened with the best of intentions and in the conviction that it was only now for the first time
that these passages were really understood (Luke 9:45 and
elsewhere). Full understanding replaced partial understanding.
Despite this, there lingered on for many years memories of Jesus
which had not been filtered through the sieve of the Easter faith,
mostly oral but sometimes written traditions about Jesus'
teaching, his sayings and parables. Thus the source Q – 'Sayings
of Jesus', a scriptory source (German: *Quelle*) for Matthew and
Luke – which literary criticism can reconstruct, contained only
Jesus' purely eschatological preaching of the Kingdom of God
and the need for inner conversion and did not give an account of
the resurrection. Paul and Mark assumed that their readers were
familiar with the material in Q, and so, except in a few instances,
did not make much direct use of it themselves. But when
Matthew and Luke, each in his own way, extended their Gospels
of Jesus, which culminated in the resurrection, by including these
'Sayings', the source Q came to seem superfluous and dispensable
and so was soon forgotten. Yet its presumed content can be at
least approximately reconstructed by studying the texts that are
common to Matthew and Luke but which are not found in
Mark; thus Q is of considerable value in the attempt to reach
back to the oldest and pre-Easter layers of the synoptic tradition
– and so to Jesus himself.

In the texts, however, which have survived and which are later
than Q, everything is already refracted through the prism of the
Easter preaching, so that in every case one must distinguish
carefully between what can be considered as belonging to the
tradition from the time of Jesus and what is the result of the new
and distorting tradition. Sometimes the distinction is easy to
make. For example, predictions about the suffering of the Son of
Man are concluded by predictions about this resurrection,
although the context reveals that the latter predictions were not
part of the original tradition: thus Peter, who is supposed to have
heard them, nevertheless reproaches Jesus. If Jesus really had
spoken about his resurrection, then Peter's reproaches would

have been groundless (Mark 8:32 & par.; cf. Matthew 17:23).
This process of reinterpretation probably began before the year
40, and thus long before the first written version of the synoptic
tradition.

Paul brought in important changes which make him after Peter
the most important, the most influential and the most successful
of the apostles. It was he who shaped the Christian message for
the non-Jewish and predominantly Hellenistic world, and so he
became the third and last founding figure of Christianity. Paul
came from diaspora Judaism, and this prepared him to address the
non-Jewish world exclusively, as he finally did. It is astonishing
and almost incredible how little the great 'Apostle of the Gentiles' bothered with the details of his Master's life; modern
theologians know much more about Jesus than Paul did – and
that is presented as a fact, not as irony. Paul was interested in a
certain theological and ethical problem: the question of redemption, the fact that Jesus had inaugurated a process of redemption,
justification and renewal. He meditated on these matters. But he
showed no interest in *how* this process began somewhere in
Galilee. It would of course be wrong to reduce the thought and
preaching activity of Paul simply to what we can gather from his
surviving letters; there can be no doubt that he knew a collection
of sayings and stories about Jesus (perhaps the lost source Q that
we have already mentioned) which he used and took for granted,
and therefore (like Mark after him) did not repeat. What interested Paul above all was not Jesus of Nazareth but Christ, the
ground of faith, the Redeemer, the One Proclaimed, Christ as the
object of faith and norm of the believer's moral behaviour. Over
and above that he analysed the practical problems of daily life in
the Christian communities; he knew their needs and warded off
dangers to their faith and new-found justification. We learn
nothing at all from Paul about Jesus as a man. Faith for him – or
so it seems – does not need many facts. Few have been able to
compare with Paul in the enthusiasm of his faith. It was natural
that the first two generations should not have been very interested in Jesus' past life and on the whole could not be, and so it
would never have occurred to any of them to write books about
him. No one who has really surrendered – as Jesus preached and
intended – to the eschatological hope, to belief in the radical
collapse of everything which existed and in the beginning of a

completely new age, a new world, a new Jerusalem, is going to indulge in historical scholarship or seek some form of literary expression. It is not surprising, then, that few sources should have survived; it is rather surprising that such relatively full sources have in fact come down to us.

It is incontrovertible that Paul through his practical and theoretical activity broke open the older narrower conception of Christianity as a reform movement within Judaism in such a way as first to isolate the so-called Judaeo-Christian trend and then to replace it altogether. This trend was represented most notably by the so-called Ebionites (from the Hebrew *ebjon,* poor) who did preserve certain features of radicalism and were perhaps even influenced by the puritanism and asceticism of the Qumran-Essene sects but who still considered Jesus to be a Messiah of a purely Jewish type, a reformer of Judaism who had come only for Jews. Against them – and to some extent against Peter himself (Galatians 2:14) – Paul successfully asserted faith in Jesus as the universal Redeemer of all peoples and therefore a concept of Christianity not simply as a reform of the synagogue, a reform of the people of the 'old covenant', but as the beginning of a 'new covenant', a 'new testament', a religion which did not complete Judaism but which deprived it of its special place before God and the world. In Paul's view it was no longer a matter of fulfilling the Law (Matthew 5:17), but of freeing oneself from the prescriptions of the Mosaic Law: 'But now we are discharged from the law, dead to that which held us captive, so that we serve not under the old written code but in the new life of the Spirit' (Romans 7:6 and elsewhere).

Historically it was Paul who spread the good news about Jesus through the world and for the world as a radically universalist ideal uniting people across the barriers of nation and language, tradition and custom. One cannot rate too highly the significance of this for the last 2000 years of history. Even though the Catholic Church later understood this universality predominantly in an institutional sense, the idea of universality survived and inspired the finest minds of Europe from Jan Hus and Leibniz to Marx. Our question here, however, is whether the Pauline theology of Jesus was appropriate to Jesus or whether it was in contradiction to him. It is not clear whether and to what extent Jesus had this universal openness to all mankind. The three or four sayings in the synoptic tradition which open the preaching of the 'Good News' to all peoples (Mark 14:9 & par.; Matthew 28:19 and elsewhere) are extremely suspect, and there is not the slightest reason for supposing that they come from the oldest levels of the synoptic tradition which go back to Jesus. Nor is the saying found in Matthew very credible, in view of Matthew's well-known tendencies to 'Judaise': 'I was sent only to the lost sheep of the house of Israel' (Matthew 15:24). The most important of the sayings which express a certain universalism and which come from the earliest period is this: 'Many will come from east and west and sit at table with Abraham, Isaac and Jacob in the kingdom of heaven' (Matthew 8:11 & par.). Jesus – like all Jewish tradition – spontaneously and without needing to think about it very much felt that Israel was to be the setting of his work for the Kingdom of God; but this did not exclude a universalistic openness towards non-Jewish peoples. One needs only to recall Jesus' friendly attitude towards the Samaritan people and indeed towards Roman officials (Luke 7:1–10). Certain contradictions in the synoptic tradition in this respect reflect the contradiction in Jesus' own attitude towards non-Jewish peoples during his ministry – the universalist element gradually became stronger. In the prophetic tradition Israel was to be the focus or theatre of the eschatological upheaval, and yet the latter's effects were to reach out to all mankind. The same tension certainly existed in Jesus' own mind. There was therefore no contradiction between Jesus' message and Paul's turning to the pagans, because it was only through Paul's theoretical and practical work that Jesus in fact became the 'Saviour of the Gentiles'. The next development was then logical: Christ became 'Pantocrator', the Lord of the world and of all things. The basis of the swift and extensive diffusion of the new faith was primarily the social crisis of the Roman Empire which – especially after the disappointment of illusions of political salvation – favoured the development of a new, strong, inspiring religion of redemption, the diffusion of the cult of the 'Saviour of the world'.

After Paul the next most important step was the composition of systematic 'Gospels' as a kind of quasi-biographical complete account of Jesus' activity. The scriptorial, systematic 'Gospel' was a relatively late phenomenon, probably at first in the context of a certain weakening of the original eschatological concentration on the future which had characterised early Christianity. Although a start was made on collecting the material together in Israel, it was not by chance that the Gospel as a precise synthetic literary form should have developed outside Israel in the Hellenistic cities where the Christian communities were already composed partly or wholly of non-Jews, who were far removed from the old Jewish prophetic-eschatological mentality but no less eager for redemption and the 'joyous news' brought to them in the name of Jesus. Among them the need for more careful information on the life of Jesus first made itself expressly felt.

The first of the 'evangelists' – as we know, not so much author as editor of the material in the synoptic tradition – Mark, who created or at least first used this literary form about the year 70, was, like Paul, not so concerned with Jesus' *thought*, but concentrated entirely on his *activity*, which was said to be messianic even though not disclosed as such for a considerable time. More important for future developments was the fact that Mark, who evidently felt that the concept of 'Messiah' did not express enough in a non-Jewish milieu, used the title 'Son of God', which was typically Hellenistic. He determined for ever that hermeneutical structure which begins with Jesus' relationship to John the Baptist, continues with his preaching activity in Galilee and his journey to Jerusalem, and reaches its climax on Calvary and in the development of the Easter faith. One need not question the basic validity of this pattern, but at the same time it did give the inaccurate impression that Gospels were a kind of biography, an idea which remained unchallenged until modern scholars began their work. Mark himself – like his successors – was guided above all by theological considerations: he wanted to provide a definite basic structure for the kerygma about Jesus as the Christ. That was Mark's greatest achievement. His combination of the Pauline tradition of Christ with the tradition of the life and work of the earthly Jesus of Nazareth has remained effective ever since. But because Mark personally underestimated the discourses and sayings of Jesus or at least gave them little prominence in his redaction, compared with the others his Gospel seems especially mythical, weak in thoughts but rich in miracle stories.

The second gospel, that of Matthew (edited round about the year 80), which was for centuries regarded as the first owing to

its position in the canon of scripture and the authority of St
Augustine, combined the quasibiographical structure of the
description in Mark (without essential changes) with sayings and
short instructive arguments from Q and elsewhere which preceded Mark's editorial work. Matthew, unlike Luke, shapes Jesus'
sayings into long discourses; he customarily re-works the individual sayings more boldly and courageously than Luke, so
that where there are parallel texts deriving from the same source,
Luke's formulation is in most (not all) cases the most ancient.
Against that, Matthew is less inclined than Luke to give new
stories and legends. His language is more polished than that of
Mark, but even so Matthew is on the whole not a man of letters.
He writes rather stiffly and is plainly more of an exegetical
theologian than a biographer. It is probable that he wrote in Antioch or somewhere else in Syria, but unlike Mark and the others
he always made allowances for orthodox and conservative Jewish
circles. Hence the dominant theme to which his details are subordinated is the demonstration that Christianity is really an authentic form of Judaism and that all the Old Testament prophecies are
fulfilled in Jesus. If the special feature of Mark's Gospel was the
'messianic secret', the leading characteristic of Matthew's Gospel
is the proof from scripture. He is so eager to bring forward his
scriptural proofs that without intending to he undermines his
credibility for the critical reader. For example, he can present the
childhood and youth of Jesus in such a way that it apparently
fulfils Old Testament prophecies, and in his keenness Matthew
does not avoid contradictions such as that Jesus was born in
Bethlehem (Matthew 2:1–12), although he 'came out of Egypt'
(Matthew 2:15) and was known as 'Jesus of Nazareth' (cf.
Matthew 2:23). Matthew puts some order into the various
traditions which give the sayings of Jesus, and in spite of his
defects he performs one inestimable service: he has preserved for
posterity, in the 'Sermon on the Mount' (chapters 5 to 7) one of
the most precious attainments of human culture and the greatest
achievements of the human spirit. Here it is not the theologian
Matthew who speaks, but the Galilean Prophet.

Matthew's method compels us to ponder yet again the influence of Old Testament traditions on the formation of the New
Testament texts. We have already seen how the Old Testament
tradition exerted an influence on Jesus himself, especially through

Daniel's idea of a victorious 'Son of Man' and Isaiah's concept of
the suffering redeemer. These conditioned the success of his
enterprise but were also the cause of his journey to Jerusalem.
Without the Old Testament, one simply could not understand
the meaning of Peter's confession of faith or Jesus' dialogue with
him on what messiahship meant. The surviving synoptic texts are
accurate in that they strive to make clear the deep indebtedness of
Jesus to the Jewish Old Testament tradition. Yet it would be absurd to assume that the real life history of Jesus followed some
detailed prophetic blueprint, and that he fulfilled precise
prophecies in the way Matthew describes. Apart from a general
determination, indeed vocation, to suffer – which was then
brutally fulfilled by his judges and executioners – there was
nothing more precise in Jesus' life and could be nothing more.
And the first disciples of Jesus were so taken up with their eschatological ideas about the dramatic coming of the new age that
they did not attach much importance to the details of Jesus' life,
not even to the details of his trial and execution. Why should
they have bothered? With all their hearts they believed in his exaltation and in his imminent second – and this time decisive –
coming in glory. But thirty or forty years later the situation was
completely different. By now there were few eye-witnesses,
detailed accounts had been forgotten, and faith in Jesus as the
'Redeemer of the world' began to reach different areas and social
classes whose thinking was not so directed towards the future.
They felt the need to know more about the life and suffering of
Jesus. How could this need be satisfied? Apart from those few
women, there had been on Calvary no eye-witnesses from
among the disciples, so how was it possible to find witnesses thirty or forty years later? Yet because there was already a prevalent
conviction that Jesus was the Messiah who had been announced
in a series of Old Testament texts, these texts began to be read
not in any abstract way but as a sort of permanent reminder of
Jesus, indeed as a description of what he went through. And this
resulted in a second and this time more detailed projection of the
Old Testament traditions in early Christianity, not this time into
the thought of Jesus, but into thinking about Jesus.

They wanted to know more about how Jesus had undergone
his suffering. And then they found in the prophet Isaiah a more
vivid and effective description of suffering than they found in the

evangelists. Because of the importance of the text and to help towards a better understanding of this second interpenetration of the Old and New Testaments levels, we shall give this remarkable text almost in its entirety:

For he grew up before him like a young plant,
and like a root out of dry ground;
he had no form or comeliness that we should look at him,
and no beauty that we should desire him.
He was despised and rejected by men;
a man of sorrows, and acquainted with grief;
and as one from whom men hide their faces
he was despised, and we esteemed him not.

Surely he has borne our griefs and carried our sorrows;
yet we esteemed him stricken, smitten by God, and afflicted.
But he was wounded for our transgressions,
he was bruised for out iniquities;
upon him was the chastisement that made us whole,
and with his stripes we hare healed.
All we like sheep have gone astray;
we have turned every one to his own way;
and the Lord has laid on him the iniquity of us all.

He was oppressed, and he was afflicted,
yet he opened not his mouth;
like a lamb that is led to the slaughter,
and like a sheep that before its shearers is dumb,
so he opened not his mouth.
By oppression and judgment he was taken away;
and as for his generation, who considered

that he was cut off out of the land of the living,
stricken for the transgression of my people?
And they made his grave with the wicked
and with a rich man in his death,
although he had done no violence,
and there was no deceit in his mouth.

Yet it was the will of the Lord to bruise him;

he has put him to grief;
when he makes himself an offering for sin,
he shall see his offspring, he shall prolong his days;
the will of the Lord shall prosper in his hand.
(Isaiah 53:2–10)

Similar vivid descriptions of the sufferings of the just man can be found in Job, Jeremiah and some of the Psalms. Some details could be taken directly from the Old Testament: for example Jesus' cry of anguish (Psalm 22:2), and the sharing out of his clothes (Psalm 22:19). This does not of course mean that anything which has an Old Testament basis could not have happened in reality: thus, for example, the division of clothing after an execution was a custom in the Roman army. But it obvious that Matthew takes the method of Old Testament references to the point of absurdity. It is found to a much lesser degree throughout the rest of the New Testament.

The last of the synoptic writers, Luke, who edited his material about the year 90, is the most artistic and the most 'human' of the evangelists. He is the only one who has any feel for artistic description, the only one who can construct a scene and a dramatic dispute, and the only one who attempts to provide a sort of life-description. Formally he adopts the same procedure as Matthew, that is to say, he inserts the preserved sayings of Jesus into the basic structure provided by Mark, but he does it in a way that is essentially different from Matthew. Instead of turning Jesus' sayings into long discourses, he more often provides them with a different setting and a fresh context. It is only in Luke that the characters show ordinary human feelings and act in accordance with the scene, which indicates that the way they behave is not motivated by theological considerations. This is why Luke's Gospel seems to be more vivid, dramatic and natural. His method nevertheless had a certain disadvantage. It opened the door to legendary adornments and fictitious events to which the various apocryphal gospels and later the medieval and baroque stories and legends of popular Catholicism then referred. Although Luke undoubtedly gives us more of the authentic thoughts of Jesus than any of the other sources, he mingles profound thoughts with trivial ones, depth with superficiality, in a way that was to happen frequently in Catholicism.

His personal contribution can be seen in the most beautiful and effective parables: so for example the Pharisee and the Tax Collector (Luke 18:9–14), the Prodigal Son (15:11–32), and the Good Samaritan (10:29–37), one of the most effective human appeals of all time, an appeal to help every suffering human being without consideration for his religion, convictions, origin or nationality, and the subsequent episode of Martha and Mary (obviously a parable like the others originally, later transformed into an actual occurrence: 10:38–42). The Easter legends, too, are much more moving in Luke: one has only to think of the story of the disciples on the way to Emmaus (Luke 24:13–35) who meet the risen Jesus but fail to recognise him, even though their hearts were on fire as the stranger spoke to them. Those natural and moving words – 'Stay with us, for it is toward evening and the day is now far spent' (Luke 24:29) – can still inflame the heart, even when the head does not believe in the resurrection.

Now we must dwell for a moment on a unique, typically Lucan matter, the Christmas story. Luke was in fact its creator, for the older tradition had nothing like it, and Matthew's chapters on the subject are nothing but tedious theologising fabrications. It was Luke who created what has for centuries brought delight to thousands, especially children. Only Luke's Gospel is literally 'tidings of great joy', because of its treatment of the Christmas events. In conservative ecclesiastical circles it is a common opinion that one must at all costs defend the historical character at least of the essentials of the Lucan and Matthean account of Christ's birth and childhood, although historical criticism has long ago shown that these stories cannot be harmonised either between themselves or with the rest of the synoptic tradition or with sound critical judgment. This conservative position, which justifiably believes that the stories have a certain value, has however to propound fantastic hypotheses in order to preserve their historicity, such as for example that Jesus' mother 'kept all these things in her heart' (cf. Luke 2:19; 2:51) and as an old woman recounted them half a century later to Luke or one of his informants. Simpler and more natural explanations are possible.

The ideal and emotional value of Luke's account of Jesus' childhood does not disappear but is rather enhanced when we clearly understand that the Christmas story came into existence only after Easter, that it is the result of the then all-powerful and all-determining idea of the risen Jesus, and that it in fact presents a variant of the Easter message. The Gospel was thereby preached to children too, just as Jesus had wanted. Children could make nothing of the concept of 'Son of Man in all his glory'. Nor could they meditate constantly on the passion of Jesus, and the 'resurrection' was not really a problem for those who had not really begun their life and who did not understand the sting of death. It was therefore obvious and necessary to adapt the message of Jesus and about Jesus to the minds of children so as to make it accessible to them. The Christmas message was the projection of Easter joy into the mentality of children. Consider the climax of the 'Christmas Gospel', the so-called angelic proclamation, which for many people is the most effective passage in the whole Bible: 'Be not afraid; for behold, I bring you good news of a great joy which will come to all the people; for to you is born this day in the city of David a Saviour, who is Christ the Lord' (Luke 2:10–11). Let us compare this with the fundamental eschatological message of Jesus about the Kingdom of the future age: 'The time is fulfilled, and the kingdom of God is at hand; repent and believe in the gospel' (Mark 1:15). Are there not parallels here? Are the two passages not practically the same from the point of view of their psychological effect? In the Christmas Gospel the theme is put in a poetical way and adapted to the popular mentality and to children's ways of thinking. But in both cases there is a similar form of address, a similar emphasis on joy, a similar summons, a similar stress on 'today' – and obviously the same idea of redemption and salvation. There is another element in the Christmas Gospel: 'Glory to God in the highest, and on earth peace among men with whom he is pleased' (Luke 2:14) Originally this meant: 'Glory be to the God of the future age, peace on earth to men of good will'. This text too has a full, human content, and it is not without interest that some of our contemporaries who have rejected nearly all Christian customs should maintain these traditions more stubbornly than anyone else. The three canticles of Mary (Luke 1:46–55), Zechariah (1:68–79) and Simeon (2:29–32), which date essentially from an earlier period than Luke's redaction, contain remarkable peaks of human feeling, for example the expression of maternal or parental happiness: 'And you, child, will be called the prophet of the

Most High; for you will go before the Lord to prepare his ways'
(Luke 1:76).

Of incomparable beauty is Simeon's almost Faustian farewell
to life, in which he glimpses the future realisation of his own
longings:

Lord, now lettest thou thy servant depart in peace,
according to thy word;
for mine eyes have seen thy salvation
which thou hast prepared in the presence of all peoples,
a light for revelation to the Gentiles. (Luke 2:29–32)

If Mark's Gospel is the good news about the Son of Man and if
Matthew stresses the preacher of the future age 'according to the
scriptures', Luke's Gospel is the good news of the humanity of
Jesus.

The fourth evangelist is traditionally known as John. He wrote
sometime around the year 100 in Asia Minor and makes partial
use of an independent tradition which perhaps goes back to John
the disciple, though that is rather uncertain and hazardous. With
John we reach another level and a quite different set of problems.
The notable difference between John and the three synoptics has
always been recognised. Since the canon of the New Testament
books was established, this Gospel has been considered not only a
reliable source but for centuries the most profound of the Gospels
too (which in a sense it is), and therefore as the most credible,
since it was thought to have understood the mind and the
thought of Jesus best. John's Jesus most nearly approximates to
the ecclesiastical image of a Christ who was not of this world, for
he speaks of the pre-existent Christ who enters our world as the
divine Word (*Logos*), is the only one to provide sayings on the
trinitarian nature of God, and his Jesus is in every respect a
powerful figure, full of love, moral strength, human tenderness,
and yet also a solemn and sublime figure. No one paints Jesus so
powerfully, so majestically and yet with such inimitable matter-
-of-factness as John.

It was only as critical methods of historical scholarship
developed in the nineteenth century that the following conclusions were gradually reached. Not only is John's narrative
notably different – that had always been recognised – but it is

historically, psychologically and, more important, in content and conception irreconcilable with the other Gospels, even with the help of fantastic and far-fetched hypotheses. Thus for example one cannot harmonise the fact that in the synoptic tradition Jesus speaks constantly of the 'Kingdom of God' and never about himself with the fact that in John's Gospel Jesus speaks almost exclusively about himself. The synoptics are concerned with the significance of Jesus' preaching, whereas in John the preaching and the preacher, the message and the messenger are fused. This can be seen in the famous 'I'-sayings such as 'I am the resurrection and the life' (John 11:25), 'I am the light of the world' (8:12), and 'I am the living bread which came down from heaven' (6:51). It has been further recognised that the synoptics should have the preference on historical and psychological grounds, on grounds of chronological priority, and because they contain more historical truth. One can explain how Mark and Matthew developed into John, but not the contrary.

As new sources on Gnosticism were discovered and as oriental myths and Hellenistic philosophy were more deeply studied, it became evident that John moved in their conceptual world, and therefore that in his own way he brought Jesus' message into dialogue with Neo-platonic philosophy and Gnosticism, or alternatively that he introduced into the tradition of Jesus the conceptual tools and the problems of Platonism and Gnosticism. Not only Neo-platonic parallels of the *Logos* in John's Gospel but also certain Gnostic parallels for his famous farewell discourse were discovered. Only one conclusion was possible: the author of the fourth Gospel perhaps retained traces of an original element that had escaped the synoptics, and that there may therefore have existed alongside them a specifically Johannine tradition; but that as far as Jesus' history and teaching went, quotations from John were at least highly suspect. Whereas at the beginning of the nineteenth century John was regarded as a reliable source of information about Jesus, in the twentieth century there were certain radical Protestant theologians who were almost ashamed to quote John's Gospel. It is possible that modern exegesis has gone too far in this respect. For example the Qumran documents indicate that certain Gnostic ideas or tendencies existed in Judaism before the time of Jesus (for example the antithesis of darkness and light, which is characteristic both of John and Qumran), and thus that certain Gnostic elements could have found their way into his own thinking or that of his disciples about the world and his own mission, and it is possible that the synoptics were not really able to grasp them. But as far as the general tradition about Jesus goes, it is evident that John is not very reliable.

There is a sense in which John is superior to the synoptics: he is not merely a compiler or an editor, he has an original conception, and he was the first real writer in the history of Christianity. But precisely for that reason the unpretentious synoptics, perhaps more by accident than design, give a much better picture of the historical Jesus of Nazareth. They may make mistakes now and again, but in John it is the whole conception that is unhistorical. The basis for John's extremely effective and original picture of Jesus is that he systematically projects the glorified Christ back on to the historical Jesus. In this respect John's Gospel is an important development in Christian thinking about Jesus. It discloses something of the greatest historical reality – from the period *after* Calvary, of course. The synoptics show that the Easter faith had already begun to appropriate and mould the entire tradition concerning Jesus, but only John took this process to its logical conclusion. The Johannine Jesus speaks like the exalted divine Christ right from the start of his public life. His future glorification, of which, as we have seen, Jesus himself was really convinced, has already invaded his whole life, so that the resurrection fails in its surprise effect, and even Calvary loses its sting. Jesus goes through life as Gnostic divinities traverse the material world, fully conscious of their other-worldly goal, a goal which is already immanent in the journey. That is why in John's Gospel Jesus does not remotely experience the same fears as in the synoptics (cf. Mark 14:33 & par). Not only does he foresee the victory before the suffering starts, but he already *is* the victor, the passion *is* his victory. In the synoptics, Jesus says to his judges: 'But I tell you, hereafter you will see the Son of man seated at the right hand of Power, and coming on the clouds of heaven' (Matthew 26:64). That is courageous, self-possessed and effective; but it is far from the words with which Jesus says farewell to his disciples in John: 'Now is the Son of man glorified, and in him God is glorified' (John 13:31). Calvary here is only a kind of necessary preparatory dissonance before the great final chord of glory and going to the Father' (John 14:12 and elsewhere). In this way the whole history of Jesus from his baptism in the Jordan onwards is divinised. We cannot fail to ask whether this fulness of divinity, this omnipresence of absolute victory, does not detract from the humanity of Jesus' sacrifice and struggles, in that it transforms his heroism and courage in suffering and giving his life for the salvation of his brothers into a divine capacity to endure, an inability to be destroyed by suffering, the shadow-play of a Gnostic divinity who steps down temporarily into the realm of conflict and struggle and appears there as a splendidly gleaming light in the darkness. A Jesus of this kind could certainly not sweat blood (cf. Luke 22:44).

John's transformation of the image of Jesus has had an enormous effect on subsequent history. It is clear that in comparison with the synoptic picture of Jesus, in which social critique plays a dominant part and in whose eschatology there are elements of social radicalism, not to mention revolution, as well as elements of myth, John has underlined the religious and mystical elements – at the expense of Jesus' original eschatological-prophetic dissidence – that therefore in this sense John contributed to Christianity's move away from critique towards ecclesiastical dogma, from prophetic enthusiasm towards opium-like consolation, from the yearnings of the oppressed towards the palaces of ecclesiastical princes. It would be wrong to see only this aspect of John and to underestimate the important positive value of his interpretation. We should not forget that John's Gospel did not replace but complemented Luke and Matthew. It thereby blazed a trail they would never have contemplated. Some of the Hellenistic features which find expression in John's Gnostic-Platonic tendencies are certainly not authentic as far as the historical Jesus of Nazareth is concerned, yet they enabled him and his cause to enter the mainstream first of ancient and then of European thinking in a way that Matthew and Luke and even Paul did not. One could scarcely speak to Galilean fishermen about 'the Word that was with God and that was God', and yet it was this 'Word' (*Logos*) which enabled the message of Jesus to enter into the lucubrations of those phiosophers who based themselves on Plato and Aristotle. It made possible the future synthesis of the Judaeo-Christian intellectual achievement with the intellectual heritage of Greek and Roman antiquity, and finally became the spiritual basis of European history. Likewise the great farewell discourse in John's Gospel (chapters 15–17), which with the Sermon on the Mount is the finest ethical passage in the New Testament, is not credible from the point of view of historical accuracy, and yet it expresses in an unparalleled way the idea of human brotherhood and the future unity of mankind ('that all may be one', John 17:21) as well as the different aspects and potentialities of self-sacrifice and mutual love.

'Now before the feast of the Passover, when Jesus knew that his hour had come to depart from the world to the Father, having loved his own who were in the world, he loved them to the end' (John 13:1). Despite their mystical colouring, such passages have shown again and again in European history (we have only to recall the Hussite movement!) their capacity to arouse the moral strength which is needed for any humanly significant action.

But this book is not concerned with the further influence of John's Gospel in history. Only one question concerns us here: Has all that we consider to be typically 'Johannine' and especially *exclusively* Johannine any connection with the historical Jesus of Nazareth? Or are such elements only the thoughts of John, of the third generation after Jesus, which convey neither his ideas nor a sense of his humanity? As has happened before in this book, we must reject the uncritical approach – willing ignorance – to the documents; but at the same time and for the same critical reasons we have to mistrust a hypercritical approach, which is only another form of lack of critical sense, of lack of readiness to think and to see.

There can be no dispute on the fact that John altered or essentially complemented the image of Jesus characteristic of the synoptic tradition. Likewise beyond doubt is the notable shift of emphasis in John. The question can only be whether the author of the fourth Gospel (or the final editor of the Johannine material, whose name is unimportant) was right to make these changes or not; or whether there was something which justified what he did at least conditionally; and whether again his conception is a late literary fabrication and therefore a misinterpretation, or at least to some extent a compensation for what the synoptic tradition around the year 100 greatly lacked.

In analysing the beginnings of Jesus, we noted that the prophet from Nazareth did not attract his disciples and future apostles –

and it does not matter here whether the initiator of the Johannine tradition was among them – only through his words, discourses and arguments, but that his impact was possible only because of the extraordinary power of his mind, the charismatic quality of his personality; we cannot exclude, either, a certain element of suggestion and even parapsychological influence in his miracles. We have said that the discourses on the Kingdom of God and the need for conversion were influential but only in so far as they were consistent with the whole life and experience of Jesus and grew naturally out of them. The most eloquent of his discourses on the Son of Man could not have been effective if Jesus had not been regarded by those about him as a messianic figure. If Peter had not really thought of him in this way, his confession of faith would have been merely pathetic. Indeed, if his disciples had not already seen in Jesus certain conditions for his future identification with the 'Son of Man in all his glory', that idea would never have taken root. If someone special, a magnetic human personality, had not stood before them, they would have paused to reflect on some interesting parable, perhaps, but they would then have gone home. To *this* man, however, they said: 'Lord, to whom shall we go? You have the words of eternal life' (John 6:68). For Peter's circle of friends, who preserved the synoptic tradition in the first generation after Jesus – for perhaps thirty or forty years – this experience, the experience of being enthralled by the magic of a mature, overwhelming personality, endured despite the continual changes in his words. Otherwise the heroic strength of Stephen who 'saw Jesus' as he was on the point of death from stoning (Acts 7:55–60) would be unintelligible. Otherwise one could not explain the 'effect of the visions of Peter or Mary Magdalen. The others too were mentally prepared, so that after their modest 'visions' they said characteristically: 'The Lord has truly risen indeed, and has appeared to Simon' (Luke 24:34).

Yet the larger group of 'believers', especially in the next generation, had at their disposal only the words, arguments, discourses and parables of the synoptic tradition: they did not have any personal experience of Jesus at whose feet the inflammable Peter had once thrown himself (Luke 5:8). Without such an experience, even the most tempting and splendid words about the Kingdom of the future age were inadequate. Christians could meditate on the truth but not experience the man who was 'full of grace and truth' (John 1:14).

John's Gospel attempts to remedy, not without success, this
lack of direct experience of the person of Jesus, his strength of
mind, his charismatic magic. Its intention, therefore, is not
primarily to make up for something lacking in Jesus, something
Gnostic, Greek, philosophical (it does that too, as we know, but
not only that), but to complement something that was present in
Jesus but that necessarily disappeared with the passing of time:
the experience of a person, of a strong, magnetic person, who
was able to use his strength to make men other, better, than they
were without him. For if Jesus had not been able to 'change'
man, his preaching of change would have been fruitless. And this
gives us a certain historical truth – if that is the word – of John's
Gospel which the synoptics could not grasp. This truth consists
not in the fact that the creator of the joyful message of the future
age which made a total claim on the human soul should really
have said things like 'I am the light of the world' (John 8:12), 'I
am the good shepherd' (10:11), 'I am the way' (14:6), 'I am the
bread of life' (6:48) or 'As the Father has sent me, even so I send
you' (20:21) – these are all words and expressions which belong
rather to Gnosticism than to the world of Jesus – but in the fact
that the man who did not say these things was the type of person
who could affect other people in such a way that he swept them
off their feet not only by the power of his words – the synoptics
had tried to convey that – but also by the power of his person.
For Peter and the others this was a unique experience that could
not be repeated, and so they had to try to find a different way of
expressing the sublimity and majesty of this messianic being. This
was what they were striving to express in the Easter preaching, in
Peter's missionary activity and throughout the early stages of the
synoptic tradition, but it inevitably became weaker as the years
went by, and as the actual presence of Jesus, the wonderful
preacher of the future, faded into the past, memories and images
of him became less and less distinct.

John's Gospel attempts to supply what was lacking in the
words that were preached, but he could do it only through
further words; and here one sees how far it was a mere replacement. Just as one can never adequately describe in words the experience of love or suffering for someone who has never loved or
suffered, so one cannot explain the experience of another human

being to someone who has not himself been fascinated in a similar way by an extraordinary person. And so the celebrated 'I'-sayings of John often became the basis of the empty and sophistic speculations of medieval and also modern pedants; they provided a favourable soil for their lifeless lucubrations. Yet the real basis of John's Gospel was neither Gnostic nor Platonic, nor was it intended to lead away from the essence of the synoptic tradition – the message about the power of Jesus' personality – but rather to renew it. Its aim was to re-establish behind the 'word' of tradition grace-filled contact with the concrete totality of that astonishing person who had been able to inspire fishermen and tax collectors to carry the prophetic tradition of Israel to the Pillars of Hercules. It is therefore quite consistent that the same author who begins his prologue with 'the Word became flesh' (John 1:14) should end with the admission that one should not love simply 'in word and in speech' but rather 'in deed and in truth' (1 John 3:18). He reflects on how happy are those who have believed in Jesus and yet not seen him (John 20:29). He wonders, finally, how this divine work can be continued, and finds the answer in love, just love (1 John 4:16).

Yet in John's Gospel, the beginning of the Platonisation of Jesus' preaching which was then pursued mainly in Greek theology – in Antioch, Alexandria and Caesarea – for the next three centuries, the foundations were laid for the conclusion of that process in which the prophet from Nazareth became first a messianic, then an eschatological and finally an exalted, 'risen' figure. In the subsequent development, the Messiah of the Jewish people and Jewish expectation becomes the universal Saviour, the Light of the nations and the Redeemer of the world, and ultimately an actual divine being, the Son of God who is in the Father and in whom the Father dwells (John 14:10). Thus the dogmatic basis was prepared for the later complete identification of Jesus with the Godhead as the 'second divine person' of the Trinity, while at the same time being truly man. 'Almighty Father, almighty Son, almighty Holy Spirit, and yet not three almighty Gods but only one': this was how Athanasius in the fourth century expressed the conclusion to this process of dogmatisation in spite of Arius' vain attempt to halt and reverse it. It was all perfectly understandable. Even the idea of a 'God-man' was not without value for man's self-knowledge, nor was it simply an error, since it opened up (even though in a way which was remote from the Galilean Master himself) possibilities of transcendence, of overcoming the *status quo* and being open to a more demanding future. Even the so-called christological controversies of patristic and medieval theology were not without a bearing on real human problems, and they often enabled radical thinkers to develop a relevant critique of the social situation. From Augustine to Teilhard de Chardin, 'christological' problems have gone hand in hand with the most important questions of the destiny of the individual and the whole human race, with the interpretation of history and the present. Yet one can and must ask whether that message of the Prophet from Nazareth which he once delivered to his first disciples by the lakeside in Galilee and which then underwent a fantastic process of development in the work of philosophers and artists, in the efforts of pious and godless men alike, has not been so fruitless – in view of all the horror and inhumanity found precisely in the part of the world where it has been proclaimed for 2000 years – as to inspire despair.

Chapter VI

The Significance of Jesus

Where is the promise of his coming? For ever since the fathers fell asleep, all things have continued as they were from the beginning of creation. (2 Peter 3:4)

John's Gospel, which regards Jesus' mission as decisive for real human love as well as for the universe, the mystery of reality and the mystery of life, brings to an end not only the development of so-called New Testament literature later recognised by the Church as 'canonical', 'inspired by God', but also that process of messianic and 'christological' interpretation which began when a few fishermen met a then unknown prophet and were irresistibly attracted to him and sensed that they would experience 'greater things than these' (John 1:50). It ends with the confession of faith: 'My Lord and my God' (John 20:28).

It would certainly be not only beyond the scope and meaning of the present work to plot this history accurately – to arrange Jesus of Nazareth in proper historical order – but also beyond the bounds of human possibility. The Jesus event and dispute over Jesus' philosophy and his significance for mankind have for centuries been one of the fundamental phenomena of the European continent – and later, in part, of other continents too. He has been confessed by great thinkers and simple people, rulers and subjects, martyrs and torturers . . . Thus any attempt to 'plot' his story coincides to a large extent with the assessment of so-called 'Western civilisation' and of the development of European history as a whole. The attempt to 'evaluate' the heritage of Jesus, therefore, is rather like looking for a fixed point in that gigantic and complex movement in which not only we ourselves but also everything around us is caught up, a movement which Jesus once launched on the world but which was then exposed to many other influences.

However, it is a fact that in some sense 'from his fulness have we all received' (John 1:16). That includes those who suppose that his real heritage is to be found in the solid institutional framework of a Church endowed with certain mysterious spiritual gifts, those who are inclined to a more spontaneous, less authoritarian interpretation of the biblical texts, and finally those who in history have rebelled against his authority or protested against the misuse of his prestige. No one doubts that Catholics and Protestants, the Orthodox and the sects have a right to confess his name; but not only does it transpire on closer examination that the 'rebels' of this bimillenary history – 'heretics' and 'atheists', especially Marxists and communists in more recent times – are in their own way an organic part of European history in which the Prophet from Nazareth once, and therefore indelibly, played such a significant part: one may even wonder whether the disciples of Karl Marx, who 1800 years after Jesus set in motion a similarly far-reaching and complex process with as yet quite unforeseeable consequences but similar aspirations to a radical transformation of social relationships and a future conceived in a radically different way, have not in fact the greatest right to regard themselves as the authentic perpetuators of Old Testament messianism and early Christian desires for radical change. Many Marxists, but also many self-critical modern theologians, are aware of the fact that concern for the future – that longing for liberation and radical change once found in Christianity – has been taken over in the modern period almost exclusively by Marxism. Yet such centuries-old tendencies cannot be discussed in a purely academic way. Just as no learned man of the time could have settled the controversy between Jesus and the conservative guardians of Jewish tradition, a controversy that in the end was solved by other methods than looking at the pros and the cons (and was it ever really solved?), so today even the most astute academic argument is not decisive. In the end what counts – and even then only with that relativity which afflicts everything human – is which movement through the centuries makes a greater contribution to progress, and leads to more human values, greater efforts towards the true, the good and the beautiful.

If we study carefully the history of those who opposed Christianity as the worship of a divinised Jesus, we discover the

very interesting and obviously characteristic fact that these
polemicists and critics hardly ever blamed Christians for being
disciples of Jesus, but rather reproached them with *not* being truly
his disciples, with betraying his cause; they claimed that all the
features of Pharisaism detailed by Jesus (Matthew 23:1–36 & par.)
applied to them, and that one saying in particular was true: 'This
people honours me with their lips, but their heart is far from me'
(Mark 7:6 & par.). In such cases it is the Christianity of a particular period that is the object of criticism, not the ideals of Jesus.
We can consider for example the words which Karl Marx addressed to the bourgeois Christianity of his own time: 'Does not
every minute of your practical life give the lie to your theory?
Do you consider it wrong to appeal to the courts when you are
cheated? But the apostle writes that that is wrong. Do you offer
your right cheek when you are struck on the left? . . . Are not
most of your court proceedings and the majority of civil laws
concerned with property? But you have been told that your
treasure is not of this world' (leading article in *Kölnische Zeitung,*
no. 179, given in *On Religion,* Foreign Language Publishing
House, Moscow, p. 35).

From Julian the Apostate to Nietzsche, and since, a really fundamental attack on the thought of Jesus has been a rare and exceptional occurrence. They have been for the most part onesided,
as for example in Nietzsche, who made Jesus responsible for the
development of the supposedly false ideals of passivity and
humility, and for the destruction of the ancient world of beauty
and strength.

Anyone who studies the New Testament texts will at least
have to admit that there is a yawning gap between what Jesus
and his disciples expected and what actually happened. They
awaited the speedy eschatological upheaval – and there followed
the history of Christianity. The expected the Kingdom of God –
and the Church came. Even if we use the most moderate tests and
do not dispute the fact that at least a number of Christians – and
not only famous ones like Augustine, Francis of Assisi, Jan Hus
and John XXIII, but a whole host of anonymous people who
have perhaps lived out their lives no less honestly – have tried to
turn the Church into the Kingdom of God, there remains
nevertheless a discrepancy between the ideal which brought
Christianity into existence and the results. The disproportion is,

to put it mildly, shocking. The question even arises whether one could not blame Jesus himself, whether one could suggest that he was a man of illusions and that subsequent developments proved he was wrong. It is very questionable whether this should be considered a 'fault' in his thinking and his ideal, a deficiency in the strength and influence of his personality. True, all this ought to disturb Christians more than it does, but on the other hand the objective non-Christian has to note that in previous history there has been no case in which there is not a comparable discrepancy between ideal and practice.

It is likewise problematic to criticise Jesus for the fact that mythical elements played an important part in his thinking and indeed that the whole structure of his thought was mythological. That is certainly true as a matter of fact, but precisely for that reason one must ask whether Jesus can be criticised for it. It is true that mythological statements are not suitable for matters for which scientific analysis would be more appropriate. On the other hand, it is well-known that the mythological form can express universal existential and moral problems with particular effectiveness. They can be expressed without mythology, of course, but one should not persuade oneself that our contemporaries who have so much faith in science have really solved the moral and existential problems of their lives. One can certainly say that we know more about the world and ourselves, but whether we *are* more is the real question. Ultimately the important thing is not the mythological form but the depth of human experience which it embodies and expresses.

The question of myth brings us to another objection. It can be urged that the obscurity and ambiguity characteristic of mythological thinking already contains within itself the seeds of those countless interpretations and misinterpretations, uses and abuses, restorations and reformations, so that in the end almost any tendency and value, almost anyone and any historical period can call on Jesus, whether justifiably or not. This adaptive capacity is partly a sign of success, significance and strength. But it has the very grave disadvantage that it enables people to justify the best *and the worst* in history. The history of good and evil in our continent – from the genius of Augustine to the gas-chambers for the children of Jesus' native people – has been profoundly influenced by Jesus and Christianity, but in which direction? To whom must one ascribe the good, to whom the evil? This history was subject to other influences, above all to the rationality of the Greeks which provided the basis for modern science and technology, but also to the political thinking of the Romans which developed such fruitful principles on citizens' rights and legal protection for the individual, although at the same time it also produced imperialism. How, therefore, can one distinguish the good and the evil for which the school of Aristotle or Scipio's victory over Carthage or Caesar's in Gaul or the dialogue between Peter and Jesus has been responsible? All these influences have been inextricably intermingled – even Jesus' 'representatives' have both been inspired by the Sermon on the Mount and read the words of the Roman poet Virgil which they thought had been spoken about Jesus and his Church: 'Observe, he will be the author, and starting from him far-famed Rome shall bound her empire by earth, her pride by heaven' (*Aeneid*, 6:781f.). Are therefore our humanity, our culture, our capacity to raise ourselves to the stars, the result of the legacy of Plato and Aristotle, Caesar and Brutus, or Jesus and Peter? Our humanity, do we say? What is the connection between our meanness, the lack of humanity in our lives, and these traditions? One can scarcely hope for complete clarity on the responsibility of the various traditions for this or that aspect of our time.

For these reasons the attempt to arrive at a definitive 'conclusion' would show not understanding so much as stupidity; yet in practical life, we cannot content ourselves with piling up motives and noting the inextricably complex interrelationships of things; we have to decide and act, and in our action we have to depend on other people, to cooperate with them at least temporarily, even if what they do is not always in accord with our ideals. This is usually where tragedy enters our existence, and everyone has to suffer from it, and the more determined a man is to act honestly, vigorously, fruitfully and with love, the more he will suffer, even if not to the extent that Jesus did on Calvary. But the opaqueness, the impossibility of knowing all the consequences of our actions and desires, is what makes us human: it demands from us the strength to hope again, even though hope has been pushed aside or disappointed or destroyed dozens of times, not to give up, not to fall into cynicism and despair, but to believe, to hope even when one is rejected, misunderstood and unloved. 'Then

Peter came up and said, "Lord, how often shall my brother sin against me, and I forgive him? As many as seven times?" Jesus said to him, "I do not say to you seven times, but seventy times seven" ' (Matthew 18:21–2). The real question today is not whether someone takes the name of Jesus on his lips, especially in a traditional churchy-religious way, but whether he lives out the principles of the Good Samaritan that Jesus put before us (Luke 10:29–37). More and more areas of our personal and social lives today become the object of scientific research and technical control. New nations enter the stage of world history, from sources quite different from those of traditional European culture. In this situation, what does the requirement really and truly to help 'one's neighbour' mean? Although Jesus' message has almost merged with European 'Western' Civilisation and culture, can one leave it in the hands of those to whom the saying perhaps applies, 'Leave the dead to bury their own dead' (Matthew 8:22)?

It would be better to look at the present and the future and to inquire whether historical dynamism today is not leading to certain changes in the balance of power which are preparing the ground for a people of the 'third testament', of which Albert Schweitzer, the greatest investigator into Jesus' life and work of the modern period, had a certain presentiment. It needs the courage which Paul and others once had to stake all in the effort to reach new classes and peoples. But how can that happen today? We can recall that once, after a similar upheaval, the peoples of the 'new' and the 'old' alliance were locked in tragic conflict. Can we people of Western so-called culture (how fantastic and almost pharisaical that seems after Hiroshima!) still offer something of human significance from our traditions?

The controversy we have just mentioned between Jews and Christians, between the first and the second covenant, is one of the most tragic and instructive in the history of the 2000-year-old legacy of Jesus. We can still learn from it. Both took their origin from the same sources; we have seen how the teaching of Jesus was deeply rooted in the Old Testament tradition, especially in the prophetic tradition. There can be no doubt that he wished not to set Judaism aside but rather to bring it to fulfilment. But since Hegel it is easier to understand that 'fulfilment' is really in some sense an abolition, since it raises everything on to another level. Fulfilment destroys the conditions which led to the striving towards what has been fulfilled. In this sense Jesus was a typically Jewish prophet like Moses, Elijah, Daniel and Isaiah. But something happened to him which his predecessors had not known: he was far and away the most successful of Jewish prophets (and that is one kind of 'fulfilment'). His message, which originally brought into existence nothing more than a radical sect within Judaism, now crossed the boundaries of Israel and won whole peoples and continents for the God of Jacob. That was indisputably a success, which – seen theologically – could be considered a success for the God of the people of Israel. But every success easily carries with it the grounds for fresh tragedies. When whole peoples had been won for the message which had originated in Israel – peoples as different as the Greeks and the Germans, the Russians and the Anglo-Saxons – the conception of the God of Israel must have been affected. Was the God worshipped in the Christian churches really the same as the Lord who had spoken to Abraham and Moses or rather a Platonic abstract principle, perhaps even a *Jupiter optimus maximus* in Christian clothing?

The dissolution of the 'old covenant', the counterposition to Judaism into which the cause of the greatest of Jewish prophets has been turned, is the paradox of Jesus' movement. As early as John's Gospel, Jesus is no longer as in Matthew the fulfiller of the Jewish *Law,* but, logically, the adversary of the Jews. From here on it was only a small step to the paradoxical situation in which the worshippers of the one who said that he had come above all for the 'lost sheep of the house of Israel' (Matthew 10:6) and who moreover had preached love and brotherhood should begin to condemn the Jews because they had allegedly 'murdered the Redeemer'. And even some of the greatest guardians of Jesus' heritage – men like Augustine and Luther – showed a tendency to adopt the idea that the survival of the Jews who had once known grace had meaning only in order to permit this now lapsed and guilty people to be permanently punished. So it came about that the Sermon on the Mount could be preached at the entrance to the ghettos: and that illustrates how precarious things are to human consciousness, how dangerous the power of language, since people could live with such a flagrant contradiction between words and reality. There can be no doubt that the origins of Jesus' thought and the meaning of his life and death must be sought in the history of his time and in the context of the oppression of his people. And even if he rejected armed opposition, even if he had a conception of a much more radical liberation than the merely political, it is evident that his ideas implied the defeat of Roman imperialism and the liberation – not condemnation – of the people of Israel.

Partly through Jesus himself, but also thanks to Peter, Paul, John and others of his disciples, there developed a more 'sublime', spiritualised and universal idea of messianism; this undoubtedly had an enormously positive significance for the historical process of man's self-knowledge and for the tasks he had to fulfil. This also explains the heroic enthusiasm of the first Christian generations, as well as that of saints and heretics in later history: this enthusiasm, this readiness to sacrifice oneself for one's brothers and willingness to devote one's life to the cause according to Jesus' example, none of that would have existed without Christian faith in Jesus. In his name they suffered, but also in his name they sinned when they resorted to fanaticism. They were powerfully filled with the idea that they were men of the 'new covenant' (Luke 22:20 and elsewhere): that led them not infrequently to behave intolerantly, cruelly and inhumanly towards those who had other beliefs. An awareness that the idea of Jesus' love and suffering is betrayed if it is used to cause new suffering to members of his people in so-called Christian society – as it was for centuries – has begun to take effect in Christian theology and Church praxis only in the comparatively recent past.

A similar tragic and paradoxical change came with the transformation of Christianity's attitude on social and political questions connected with poverty and wealth, oppression and liberation. We have already seen that early Christianity was not a political and social movement, as many progressive thinkers have imagined – usually because they had not understood eschatological thinking; but on the other hand the vision of the Kingdom of God and the eschatological upheaval implied also a social on political change, and one that would be in favour of the interests of the oppressed, the hungry, the suffering, the exploited. The synoptic tradition contains unambiguous condemnations of those who 'load men with burdens hard to bear' and will not themselves lift a finger to remove them (Luke 11:46 &

par.), and severe judgments on the rich: 'It is easier for a camel to go through the eye of a needle than for a rich man to enter the kingdom of God' (Mark 10:25 & par.). But, most important of all, Jesus ultimately identifies himself for the future with every suffering being: 'For I was hungry and you gave me no food, I was thirsty and you gave me no drink, I was a stranger and you did not welcome me, naked and you did not clothe me, sick and in prison and you did not visit me'. And to the objection that they had never seen him in any of these situations, he replies: 'Truly . . . as you did it not to one of these the least of my brothers, you did it not to me' (Matthew 25:42–5). It is almost unimaginable that feudal, rich, Church authorities should proclaim these words for centuries while relying on political power (as in the time of Constantine and later) or exercising power itself – it would be unimaginable did it not correspond to the historical truth.

We do not want to trivialise or to make the argument too easy for ourselves. The modern period has known many instances where there has been abuse and profanation of ideals other than Christian ideals; that teaches one to be more fair and just towards such happenings in the past. And we do not wish to deny that this process of repressing the socio-revolutionary tendencies of the early Christians who 'were of one heart and soul, and no one said that any of the things which he possessed were his own, but they had everything in common' was protracted and painful. 'There was not a needy person among them, for as many as were possessors of lands or houses sold them, and brought the proceeds of what was sold and laid it at the apostles' feet; and distribution was made to each as any had need' (Acts 4:32–5). Texts like these inspired new movements in almost every century, like the Donatists at the time of Augustine, who wanted a return to the original social radicalism and a break with political power. But even before the canon of the New Testament had been determined, there were rich people who had accepted Jesus and who, even so, continued to oppress the poor and drag them before the courts, and thus blasphemed 'that honourable name' by which they were called (James 2:6–7).

Were all these things simply abuses? Do they not have a basis in the very essence of religion, even though it can contain quasi-revolutionary and non-conformist ideas? Is it not of the essence of religion that it is in its own way a 'promise', that it indicates something which is not present, not here, even though that need not be understood in a dualistic and metaphysical sense? There can be no doubt that Jesus not only intended to make promises but actually expected the real upheaval and that he often called for practical help for those who suffered – and this was not in order to glorify poverty but to banish its tragic causes and consequences. But because the coming of the Son of Man in his glory was not in the end realised, and though Jesus was not concerned simply to bring consolation, the fact that 'the poor have good news preached to them' (Matthew 11:5 & par.) had to have the effect ultimately of administering 'opium to the people'.

The essential function of every religion to console and promise (people often need real consolation) is particularly appropriate to the radically eschatological movement. The eschatological-prophetic phenomenon – which can be studied not only in Judaism and early Christianity but in other schools and at other times – is always a particular way of rebelling against current religion, possesses vivid social relevance, smashes formalism and stagnation, develops the remarkable utopias of fanatics and sectarians, is always associated with great social dynamism and social upheavals. It can reach a point of astonishing revolutionary intensity, and that can be studied better in movements other than early Christianity. It kindles noble feelings and passions. But along with these positive features there is a drawback: when the anticipated collapse of existing society fails to come, when, with the passage of time, the chiliastic revolution seems less and less likely, the intellectual wealth, the depth of feeling and the lofty morality of the movement necessarily take on a different meaning.

We have seen clearly for example that for Jesus the idea of loving one's neighbour, including enemies, of forgiving and not resisting others, were certainly not understood in a defeatist sense, as a sort of capitulation. They were not religious appeals for humble patience with the promise of rewards after death. They were rather examples of a total claim on oneself in all activities. They were the projection of the vision of the Kingdom of God on the present. They were certainly not a recommendation to come to terms with the given situation of privilege for the rich, the Pharisees, the Romans. All that would be in utter con-

tradiction to the preaching of Jesus. Yet when the expected eschatological transformation failed to materialise and as
Christianity spread among people who were less revolutionary-
minded and who had less sympathy for the eschatological view
of the world and life, the original radical principles of love, conversion and reconciliation took on a different and often even opposite meaning. When eventually members of the property-ow-
ning classes, overcome by the desire for redemption and love,
became 'believers', the hopes of the oppressed and the poor were
turned into something which suited the interests of the ruling
classes; and worse than that, the idea of authority was justified by
an appeal to God himself. It was enough to love, one should not
try to disturb class privileges. The words of Paul sound almost
like a parody of Jesus' message: 'Let all who are under the yoke
of slavery regard their masters as worthy of all honour, so that
the name of God and the teaching may not be defamed. Those
who have believing masters must not be disrespectful on the
ground that they are brethren; rather they must serve all the
better since those who benefit by their service are believers and
beloved' (1 Timothy 6:1–2). 'Let every person be subject to the
governing authorities. For there is no authority except from God
. . . Therefore he who resists the authorities resists what God has
appointed' (Romans 13:1–2). 'Bid slaves to be submissive to their
masters and to give satisfaction in every respect; they are not to
be refractory . . .' (Titus 2:9).

When one begins to think in this way, the idea of the
Kingdom of God may survive in some remote corner of the
mind, but it has become a simple instrument in the hands of the
rulers. Redemption is postponed until eternity and is seen in
dualistic terms as the liberation of the soul. Jesus' countless examples of the stringent demands made on the self are understood
merely as the cultivation of inwardness, as an end in themselves,
and they are not related to the overwhelming vision of the
radical upheaval. Obviously one can attain particular values of
the intellectual and moral life even in this way, but it is not what
Jesus intended. It is said now that Jesus came into the world as
into his own house, but 'the world knew him not' (John 1:10),
and in the end his Kingdom is 'not of this world' (John 18:36).
Christianity is understood as a programme for the reform of the
heart, one can do nothing about the state of the 'world'. This, we

repeat, can produce certain excellent results, but it is no longer in harmony with the principle, 'Behold, I make all things new' (Revelation 21:5).

Yet it is a principle of history that the work and the spirit of great personalities can never be entirely destroyed, no matter how hard their enemies but even more their friends and supporters try. The dream of those who resisted the absolute power of tyranny and despotism and who did not fall into passivity and despairing resignation – the dream of a more just and more human society – cannot go under. You can corrupt the heritage, overlay what is best in it or push it into the background, but those who seek it out tomorrow will find life and new hope beneath the layers of dirt and the petrified outlines – simply because they are attuned to it. Thus in Christianity the dogmatised image of Jesus Christ has never been able thoroughly to banish the image of the man Jesus of Nazareth. This has often been driven underground, preserved by saints or heretics who often were brought to the very limit of their human strength and possibilities because they asserted the meaning of Jesus' work against the authoritarian guardians of dead conventions. 'You are the salt of the earth; but if salt has lost its taste, how shall its saltness be restored?' (Matthew 5:13). And it is these men, constantly persecuted and only rarely rehabilitated, who have certainly the greater moral right to confess the crucified one – from which one cannot conclude that every heretic is necessarily always and in all things right. 'Established heresy', fashionable opposition for its own sake: these are only the obverse of self-satisfied habit and defence of the *status quo* at any cost; they are inauthentic, perverted forms of the 'salt of the earth' and they are not without a certain resemblance to Pharisaism.

'Come to me, all who labour and are heavy laden, and I will give you rest. Take my yoke upon you, and learn from me; for I am gentle and lowly in heart, and you will find rest for your souls. For my yoke is easy, and my burden is light' (Matthew 11:28–30). The usual and traditional ecclesiastical conception stresses the suffering Christ, the one who consoles in every difficulty, and on the other hand Christ in his glory, in his victory over evil, death, the 'world'. 'I glorified thee on earth, having accomplished the work thou gavest me to do; and now, Father, glorify thou me in thy own presence with the glory

which I had with thee before the world was made' (John 17:4–5).
Beyond doubt human existence needs both poles: it needs to
overcome difficulties, pain, failure; but it also has a need to rise
above humiliations and the greyness of the everyday. That is why
the two aspects in the presentation of Christ by the Church have
always attracted millions of people; yet the opposition
movements which expressed social interests and the
revolutionary mood of the masses could also discover, besides the
two aspects of the divinised Christ, Jesus of Nazareth's desire to
bring fire and sword into the world to effect the radical upheaval: 'I came to cast fire upon the earth; and would that it were
already kindled!' (Luke 12:49). This understanding is very much
alive in Christianity today; in fact it has become more intense
than in the past two centuries. No doubt this has something to do
with the development of Marxism and communism as a world
movement which on the one hand has forced Christians to ask
new questions, and on the other has taught them to see traditional
problems through other eyes – and this in its turn has led them to
take a fresh look at their most ancient and genuine traditions.

We believe that we have given a picture of Jesus which is
faithful to a critical study of the sources and times of Jesus and his
environment, a picture that conceals and glosses over nothing. At
the same time we believe that the picture at which we have arriv-
ed without needing to appeal to the 'supernatural' and the
'miraculous' in no way diminishes what Jesus stood for either in
general or in particular, but that on the contrary it shows the far-
reaching significance of his message and explains why it had
such a great impact on world history and why it should be at the
origin of so much controversy and conflict. We think that today
the understanding or lack of understanding of Jesus' message does
not depend on the religious denomination. The frontier cuts
across all denominations, world-views and ideologies. Jesus did
not, however, as we have emphasised throughout this book,
propound an ideology. But he *was* concerned with man, with his
future and his present, his victories and failures, his love and pain,
his despair and unconquerable hope.

APPENDIX

The Life and Thought of Jesus as an Object of Research

We have studied the process by which accounts of the life, thought and death of Jesus of Nazareth began to be rapidly and almost imperceptibly transformed into the message about Christ, the Redeemer of the world, until finally a more or less stable theological interpretation of Jesus as 'the Son of God', 'consubstantial with the Father', the 'Second Person of the Trinity' was reached. In this process the human features of Jesus which the synoptics and especially Luke had presented were not so much suppressed as overlaid. The idea of the God-man then lived on in the whole of Christianity without any essential change until the eighteenth century. The ferment and countless controversies which patristic theology, then Scholasticism, medieval mysticism and sectarian opposition, and finally even the Reformation waged did not essentially change this conception, although different Christian bodies stressed different aspects of it and highlighted different real or imaginary characteristics of Jesus. Jesus was an object of faith and hope, devotion and love. Rational considerations were brought into the study of Jesus not primarily in order to establish the historical truth, but to provide theological certainty and a foundation for piety. Unintentionally, however, this created, or at least sowed the seeds for, many problems, some of them in the very structure of theological thinking, to which strictly scientific research, for other motives, later succeeded.

Thus for example during the period of patristic theology, from the second to the sixth century, although the basic outline of faith in the God-man remained the same, there developed an important distinction between theology in the East and in the West. Eastern or Greek theology, especially under the influence of Origen, stressed metaphysical, Gnostic problems of 'christology' in the sense of a philosophical knowledge of the world and being, while the Western Latin tradition, under the influence of the impulsive personality of Augustine, brought out rather the psychological and moral aspects of the Jesus tradition, stressed experiences, feelings, real communication of heart to heart, and not so much learning and knowledge of the world. The Western approach enabled the human side of Jesus to be better and more vividly preserved, and the old traditions to be updated by contact with recurring time-bound social problems. No doubt this is a partial explanation of the relatively greater dynamism of Western Christianity and Western history taken as a whole. For Augustine, the believer came as directly to Jesus' feet as Peter and Mary Magdalen had done, with his heart and sentiment rather than with his reason, and in itself this is quite foreign to the concerns of later research into Jesus' personal history. Nevertheless, the emphasis on Jesus' concrete human individuality and the Christian's direct personal contact with him has impeded Jesus' total incorporation into the structures of the Church and of dogma and the conservative interests of the authorities. Similarly in the high Middle Ages in the West the understanding of Jesus' person was polarised in the dispute between the rational theology of the Scholastics, which culminated in Thomas Aquinas, on the one hand, and mystical tendencies both orthodox and heterodox on the other. But here the destruction of the dogma of Jesus' dual nature came not so much from the attack on his divinity as from the emphasis on the universality of theandrism, the tendency to identify every human being with the godhead.

The Reformation too fulfilled an important progressive or evolutionary function. Once again there was no question of challenging the divinity and uniqueness of Christ. On the contrary, right from the beginning of the Czech Reformation in the fourteenth century to the German and Swiss Reformations of the next two centuries, it was the emphasis on the divinity, uniqueness and irreplaceability of Jesus which enabled the reformers to combat the worldly power of Church authority, the medieval cult of the saints, the proliferation of non-biblically founded feasts, rites and services, and the usurpation in practice (even though it would be denied in theory) of Jesus' prerogatives by sinful men. Jan Hus, Martin Luther and John Calvin, not to mention Dutch and French Jansenism and Gallicanism (Blaise Pascal), used the absolute uniqueness of Jesus to fight everything which had clustered around him in centuries of tradition — from the cult of his 'virgin mother' to the splitting up of Christian life into a host of little actions and prescriptions in which the real significance of Jesus was lost. They fought against the Constantinian temptation to be dazzled by worldy power, wealth and external splendour, and they attacked the Scholastic rational efforts to harmonise faith and reason. Hence the paradox that even while the Reformation emphasised the absolute supremacy of faith and the Bible and the absolute uniqueness of the God-man, by its critical and courageous attacks on ecclesiastical authority, tradition, liturgy and doctrine it in many respects prepared the ground for the following age of enlightened understanding and incipient critical research which did not hesitate to investigate the life and thought of Jesus himself. Despite this, faith in Jesus as the mysterious God-man lives on in theology to this day, especially in Catholic theology, even though the leading thinkers of modern Protestantism (such as Karl Barth, Paul Tillich and Josef Hromádka) and of Catholicism (such as Teilhard de Chardin and Karl Rahner) try to build bridges to the present by liberating dogmas from their medieval formalism and, through historico-critical interpretation, by working out their significance for the struggles of modern man.

If faith in Jesus as God-man and Redeemer of the world was critically attacked at all in antiquity and in the Middle Ages, it happened predominantly in non-Christian circles which came into contact with Christianity, and the contacts were often marked by pain and tragedy. It was consequently a matter not of criticism in the sense of scientific scepticism and analysis but of attack on a different orthodoxy. Thus, for example, the devotees of Islam, who regarded Jesus as an important prophetic figure, rejected the Christian dogmas about his divinity and the Trinity as a betrayal of the pure monotheism which had been proclaimed from Abraham to Muhammad. In Judaism the question which naturally occupied the foreground was whether the messianic process had in fact been accomplished by Jesus: was he 'redeemer of the world'? But what had changed? There was just as much poverty and evil in the world as before Jesus. This was the objection of Orthodox Jews, a view shared on the whole only by isolated non-Jews.

Within Christianity itself, however, it was not so much the effects of Arab expansion or the Jewish diaspora as the echo of primitive radical dualism from Persia which made itself most felt. A considerable influence was exercised by the various Gnostic currents, which had already made inroads, in pre-Christian times, in the same centres of the Hellenic world in which Christianity was also successful, and which evinced a powerful inclination to a redeemer mysticism. Later, from the third century, under the influence of Manichaeism which as late as the Middle Ages spread over the Iberian and Balkan peninsulas into central Europe (with the Albigensians, Cathars, Bogomils, etc.), radical dualism temporarily affected, directly or indirectly, even some prominent Christians. So from Marcion, who was one of the important theologians of the second century, to the Reformation (and in certain secondary forms right up to the present), there was always in Christianity a kind of cryptomanichaean radical contempt for matter, for the 'world', an increased aversion to Judaism and Jewish traditions, a onesided stress on the differences between the Old and New Testaments, a onesided stress on the divinity and holiness of Christ, an undervaluing of his humanity, a tendency to exclusivism, asceticism and esoteric groups of élite individuals. Nevertheless – precisely because of their radical idealism and dualism – these and similar tendencies enabled theology (Marcion did, for example) to distinguish various strands in the New Testament tradition and attempt their classification and selection.

The tension which existed from the Reformation onwards between Protestant and Catholic scholars also helped to lay the foundations of biblical criticism. The Protestants wished to demonstrate that the 'Word of God' in the Bible was sufficient for faith. The Catholics wished to illustrate the insufficiency of the Bible from the Bible itself, the need to complement it with Church tradition and papal authority. In this way biblical studies owe their origin to the mutual dislike of Catholics and Protestants, knowledge of the original languages began to develop, various nuances and alternative readings in the ancient manuscripts were studied. In the period from the seventeenth to the eighteenth centuries, all this scholarly activity, which had originated in purely ecclesiastical concerns, went beyond immediately confessional aims in the contributions of Christian theologians and scholars like Muratori and prepared the way for critical research – contrary to the intentions of its sixteenth-century initiators.

The eighteenth century, however, which saw the beginning of the Enlightenment, of philosophical rationalism and scepticism, the connected boom in empirical science and the methods of historical and philological criticism, witnessed the revolution in the study of the life and thought of Jesus. Leading thinkers, especially English and French, from David Hume to Voltaire, destroyed belief in miracles and divine revelation. Resistance to fundamental Christian dogmas (particular casualties were miracles, the resurrection and Jesus' dual nature) began to spread first among the educated and later, as a result of the revolution – especially in France – among the less-educated classes of society, even when they made no specific study of religious matters. Here again it was not strictly scientific concerns so much as the growing opposition to the Church as one of the mainstays of the old feudal, absolutist social system that created a wider basis for the non-confessional, non-theological study of Jesus. True, anti-confessional bias and outright opposition to the Church played its part in this study, and much time was devoted to the refutation of ecclesiastical positions; certain experiences with the clergy of their time led them to propose the naive theory of deceit (with the theft of the body of Jesus, the resurrection as a piece of Essene *mise-en-scène* etc.), which even occurred in the better books of the period (Bahrdt, Venturini and others). Even so, these conflicts between an old and a new naiveté began to create more favourable conditions for the beginnings of genuine scientific research. The development of sea trade and colonialism gave Europe a better and more reliable knowledge of Chinese and Indian spiritual traditions, to whose significance and analogies to Christianity scholars as early as Leibniz drew attention. Thus there came to exist among educated men in Europe a mistrust of the legends and myths in the Christian tradition.

At the time of the French Revolution, the attacks on the fundamentals of Christianity were so strong that, radical in their methods and nihilistic in their consequences as they were, they destroyed with dazzling effort but constructed nothing, they freed the people from medieval superstition and obscurantism but provided no new moral, emotional and ideological convictions. The typical representatives of the Enlightenment period had not the slightest feeling for the very real desire for a Saviour which the early Christians and later generations experienced, nor could they understand the emotional power which generations of men had found in Christian worship. The result was that as soon as the revolutionary enthusiasm weakened, through either the fulfilment or the non-fulfilment of its demands, people returned to the churches in their thousands. The aggressive broadsheets of the Enlightenment soon turned yellow and faded, and the light they had provided was dimmed.

In Germany, traditionally considered immature politically but the most progressive country in Europe as far as speculative thought is concerned, the philosophy of Lessing, Kant and others laid the foundations, as early as the eighteenth century, for the realisation that the destruction of religion, medieval thought and especially Christian tradition could not be so facilely, ingenuously and negatively conceived, but that careful distinctions and the positive construction of new convictions were necessary. This realisation, which gradually prevailed and eventually reached its climax in the nineteenth century with the work of Hegel, Feuerbach and Marx, the ability to separate what was humanly real from what was merely mythical, had produced as early as Lessing the first notable event in the developing specialist study of Jesus' life and thought. Lessing's colleague Hermann S. Reimarus (*Von dem Zwecke Jesu und seiner Jünger*, Brunswick, 1778) was the shrewd pioneer of a new age. Even he still worked on the hypothesis of the theft of the body, but he was the first to understand that the basis of Jesus' activity was his eschatological-prophetic preaching of the Kingdom of God and the need for inner conversion, and that later faith in the resurrection was in effect the substitution of one conception of the messiahship for another, even though they both belonged to the same tradition. He was already aware of the identity of Easter and Pentecost and knew that the understanding of the various messianic titles was much simpler and more natural among Jesus' contemporaries than it was later to become. Reimarus, who was Professor of Oriental languages at Hamburg, was also aware of Jesus' Jewishness and knew that Jesus was very far from wanting to found any kind of new religion, that he was concerned rather with the eschatological transformation of human history. Reimarus was a kind of John the Baptist for the new-style research on Jesus, but there was still a long way to go before the different levels of the synoptic tradition were recognised and the complexities involved in the transmission of the texts admitted. Atheists, most of whom were interested in the natural sciences or contemporary politics, had on the whole little interest in questions of this kind and did not realise (and do not to this day) that these problems affect them too. Until recently, up to Pius XII, the Catholic Church hindered and checked serious research. It seemed that to apply systematically and logically all the methods of historical and philological criticism to Jesus was a contradiction of faith. The result was that research into Jesus throughout the nineteenth century was almost exclusively the preserve of Protestant theologians and pastors, who nevertheless managed to formulate almost every possible hypothesis on the subject.

A series of important historical questions were finally solved. A condition for any serious scientific approach to the sources was the separation of John's Gospel from the others. Herder (*Vom Erlöser der Menschen,* Riga, 1797) recognised the basic impossibility of harmonising the narrative of the synoptics with that of John; and yet Schleiermacher (1768–1834) could still be taken seriously when he unequivocally gave John's Gospel precedence. In the second half of the nineteenth century, the problem of John's Gospel became secondary, and in the foreground was the question of the classification of the synoptic Gospels. Christian Hermann Weisse (*Die evangelische Geschichte kritisch und philosophisch betrachtet,* 1838) recognised the priority of Mark's Gospel. Thanks to the influence of Bruno Bauer (*Kritik der evangelischen Geschichte des Johannes,* 1840), it was gradually recognised that the synoptics had not been trying to write biographies (the problem of the 'messianic secret' was one of the key pieces of evidence) and that they too ordered their material in the light of an overall theological conception, even though not quite so explicitly as John. At about the turn of the century it was discovered with irrefutable certainty that one could solve the various contradictions of the synoptic tradition only if one supposed that it was made up of two levels of tradition coming from two different periods, one composed without taking the messiahship into consideration and the other being its messianic reworking. In particular William Wrede (*Das Messiasgeheimnis in den Evangelien,* 1901) and Albert Schweitzer (*Das Messianitäts- und*

Leidensgeheimnis, 1901; trans. *The Mystery of the Kingdom of God*, with an introduction by Walter Lowrie, A. & C. Black, London, 1925) listed a whole series of problems which could make sense only on the supposition that the synoptic Gospels were the reworking of older accounts. But then almost everything began to appear uncertain – even whether faith in Jesus' messianic vocation existed at all before Calvary.

To the liberal intelligentsia or bourgeois society in the second half of the nineteenth century, the problem of what the thought and life of Jesus had really been like seemed insoluble: no view was put forward which was not immediately contradicted by someone else. Thus the more important question of what Jesus meant for contemporary man seemed to be a desperate enterprise. The most notable of such works, and in fact the only non-ecclesiastical presentation of Jesus' life, was Ernest Renan's *La Vie de Jésus* (1863; trans. *The Life of Jesus*, Dent, London, 1927), but the results were achieved at the expense of such doubtful modernisations and adaptations (his Jesus is essentially the preacher of sentimental love for its own sake) that his method led to absurdity because of its totally arbitrary nature. Even, however, when the Protestant historian Adolf von Harnack, the greatest and soundest scholar of this whole period and the author of a series of historical works of abiding value, left the realm of history and attempted to discuss the question of what significance Jesus' teaching might hold for contemporary bourgeois society (in *Das Wesen des Christentums*, 1900; trans. *What is Christianity?*, Theological Translation Library, London, 1901), he could direct his readers only to a kind of sublime morality, a greater joy than the world can offer; and this, in comparison with the Epicurean joys and social misery of bourgeois society, must have seemed rather absurd to thinking people even in peacetime and, in comparison with the great sayings on the 'salvation of men', laughably lightweight. Soon afterwards, as these 'Christian peoples' plunged into the bloody carnage of the First World War, the most terrible catastrophe in their entire history, Renan's thesis appeared universally indefensible. Christianity, quite happy to go along with almost anything, no longer worked in society, practically speaking; it became an appendage to social status and therefore a matter of purely personal significance. At the end of the great period of liberal Protestant studies on Jesus, Albert

Schweitzer, in his epoch-making work *Geschichte der Leben-Jesu-Forschung* (1st edn. 1906, 2nd revised edn. 1913; trans. *The Quest of the Historical Jesus,* A. & C. Black, London, 1954), offered a basically negative appreciation: apart from the general eschatological preaching of the Kingdom of God, the only thing one could be certain of was that the basic ideas of Jesus were wholly foreign to the modern world. The departure of one of the greatest Christian thinkers of modern times from 'Christian' Europe for Africa was no less symbolic than his abandonment of theology in favour of medicine. His action, like his book, in some sense brought the period of liberal bourgeois Christianity to a close as effectively as the First World War was soon to do.

If nevertheless today, more than half a century later, the study of Jesus seems not nearly so hopeless, it is due to three new circumstances which enable us ideologically and methodologically to go beyond the horizon to which the liberal Enlightenment tradition, from Reimarus to Schweitzer, led. First there was the development and the critical rejection of the so-called 'mythological school', secondly the advance of socialist ideals and Marxist methodology, and finally the application of the new methods of so-called form-historical research. These three factors affected the study of Jesus separately and had only very slight influence on each other: but in our opinion a synthesis between them is the only way to avoid onesidedness, vicious circles and extreme points of view.

The founder and classic author of the 'mythological school' was David Friedrich Strauss (*Leben Jesu,* 1835; trans. by George Eliot, *The Life of Jesus,* Sonnenschein, London, 1898); he was the first to make modern scholars aware of the conceptual peculiarities in mythology in general and in Jesus' time and primitive Christianity in particular. Once he had consigned John's Gospel to the realm of the purely theological, he was in a position to discriminate between the mythological and the historical in the synoptics, especially as regarded the term 'Son of Man' and Jesus' relationship to it. He was the first to shift the emphasis away from the metaphysical-Gnostic conception of messianism, which had prevailed for centuries under the influence of John's Gospel and Origen, towards a more phenomenological and existential approach: the question was no longer whether Jesus 'was' God and man or the Messiah, whether revelation had actually taken place, but rather what the idea of the God-man meant for human history. Jesus himself had not originally thought that he was the Messiah, but he came to think so by a natural development – and he was then mythologised and divinised. It follows, therefore, that the question about the meaning of Christianity for the modern world can be solved only by 'demythologising' the Bible. That does not mean, however, that Strauss wanted to present Christianity as pure myth, as his opponents alleged, nor did he at all intend to reduce the content of the New Testament to myth. He recognised the historicity of the person of Jesus and also a certain historical kernel in the New Testament tradition. Yet at about the turn of the century, the highly important discoveries of Strauss on the significance and extent of mythical thinking were taken to the point of absurdity, and the attempt was made to reduce everything in the New Testament to myth, including the historical existence of Jesus himself. An example of this school was Arthur Drews (*Die Christusmythe,* vols I and II, 1910 and 1911; trans. *The Christ Myth,* T. Fisher Unwin, London, 1910), who sought to explain Christianity entirely through the influence of Oriental myths, and this led him totally to neglect properly Jewish eschatological thinking. The extreme versions of the 'mythological school', which found a certain amount of support among some Marxist students of early Christianity (Vipper, Ranovic), would today be rejected by the majority of both Christian and atheist scholars; and yet Strauss' emphasis on the place of myth in the thought of Jesus himself and in early Christianity remains of decisive importance, and his contribution is today recognised by Protestant and atheist scholars, and partly also by Catholics.

The significance of the rise of the socialist and especially the communist movements, and consequently of Marxist theory, for the fate of Christianity and for research into Christ in particular has been enormous and multiform. We refer not simply to the historical-materialist method in the study of the past, which has enabled us to approach the sources from essentially different standpoints, but also to the fact that the Marxist stress on the future has provided new assumptions for the understanding and evaluation of the eschatological-prophetic phenomenon in ancient Jewish and especially early Christian tradition. Also relevant is the fact that aggressive atheism, which as Marxism appears for the first time in history as a mass phenomenon, ultimately forces those responsible for Christian traditions radically to re-evaluate the history of Christianity, including its origins, sheerly by way of reaction. And very probably (although this belongs to the future) in Marxism a dynamic movement of typically Western origin will for the first time penetrate the Eastern empires which have not essentially been influenced by Judaeo-Christian traditions. Sooner or later this will force such an intense and total dialogue of millennial intellectual structures that completely new scales of value will gradually be created. These last two effects of the advance of Marxism are still only at the germ stage; but the first two effects have already borne considerable literary fruit to assist in their further development.

It was Friedrich Engels, Marx's collaborator, who first tried to apply his method to early Christianity in a series of essays and book-reviews. Marxist methodology consists essentially in investigating social ideas, including religious ones, not in isolation but as component parts of the concrete totality of human society, in whose crises socio-economic contrasts play a basic part, especially the contrast between the gradual increase of productive capacity and the state of relationships in the organisation and property of the social classes. From the point of view of the classical problems of religion, this means that emphasis is transferred from the question of whether there actually is a God or an afterlife to the question of what influence was exerted by this or that concept of God on each period of the class struggle and conversely of which social situation favoured or produced which idea of God. Of special interest is the fact that the basic condition for the development of Christianity was the critical situation of the Roman Empire's slave system which demanded a new way of expressing the situation of the enslaved masses, and the development of an ideal of liberation and redemption. Although Christianity located its highest ideal in 'the beyond' (at least as it was commonly understood in the New Testament scholarship of the nineteenth century) and the incipient socialist movement in the transformation of this visible world, Marx and Engels were aware of a whole series of important parallels between the situation, ideals and development of early Christianity and those of the socialist movement in their own time. Marx was much more cautious and restrained than Engels as far as interpreting material of which he had not made a specialist study was concerned; he concentrated far more on combining the vision of the communist future with scientific analysis.

When, however, in the twentieth century many analogies between the two movements became apparent to socialist and also to non-socialist intellectuals, and as the archetypes of social events and great personalities were studied, the idea began to grow that perhaps Marx himself represented a 'prophetic type' who in some sense would fulfil in future ages a complex, great and multifarious mission and role comparable with that of the Master from Galilee (Löwith, Popper, Künzli). This was based not only on his success in creating a new international revolutionary movement, not only on his analyses and his whole rousing programme of renewal, but also on a certain onesided attitude.

The first systematic study of early Christianity based on Marxist methodology came from Karl Kautsky (*Der Ursprung des Christentums,* Stuttgart, 1908; trans. *Foundations of Christianity,* Allen & Unwin, London, 1925). Lenin acknowledged that Kautsky had made a permanent contribution to socialist culture, although he had violent political clashes with him. Kautsky demonstrated the justice of Engels' views on the basic characteristics of the crisis of the Roman system of society which was built on slavery by pursuing a solid and extensive study of the material, especially of Jewish documents from the Essenes to the particular situation of diaspora Judaism; he did not allow himself to be too impressed by the then fashionable pan-babylonianism and the extravagances of the 'mythological school'. Kautsky also painted a convincing picture of the intellectual decay of antiquity, the mood of uncertainty and scepticism which dominated Greek and Roman society at that time. He described very credibly how the real conditions of the age, and especially the impossibility for the working masses to find any economic solution to their difficulties, so conditioned things that all attempts at renewal, however practical to start with, eventually took on a religious form and appeared as faith in the redeeming work of Jesus. Kautsky's work is particularly valuable, however, in that it was the first book in the field of the study of Jesus to be based on the spirit of strict determinism: Christianity is seen here not as the work of a God who steps down from heaven or as the result of sheer human design, the intentions of the apostles or the visions of fanatical women, but as a real answer of millions of men to the crisis of their time. The origin of Christianity, therefore, does not lie in any kind of miraculous revelation, or even in a moral miracle; on the contrary, in the given social situation, it would rather have been a miracle if Christianity had *not* come into being. And even if Kautsky underestimated the importance of personal activity, his approach proved to be important and fruitful, simply as an antithesis to all previous work on the subject quite apart from anything else. But on the other hand, after more than half a century in which Marxist thought itself has undergone considerable development, there is scarcely a Marxist today who would defend the thesis of the social origins of Christianity in so simple a way as Kautsky. In the end he reduced the entire content of Christianity to social interests, and religiousness became merely a form of self-expression, so that in Kautsky's conception Christianity became simply a social revolutionary movement, indeed a sort of communist movement of antiquity. Kautsky's Jesus is a politically active dissident and a social revolutionary. It is not nonsense to suggest this, and we have already seen that Jesus' prophetic-eschatological thinking undoubtedly has social and political consequences. This view, however, does not go to the heart of Jesus' position, and it betrays a total lack of understanding of what his eschatological thinking really was: it contained socio-political elements but is not reducible to them.

The subsequent development of the Marxist interpretation of Christianity has led to a more accurate and far-reaching distinction between Marxism and Christianity than was found in Kautsky; among the monographs we may mention the study by the British Marxist Archibald Robertson, *The Origins of Christianity* (Lawrence & Wishart, London, 1953). But this sharper differentiation has enabled a fruitful dialogue between Christianity and Marxism to take place in the name of humanist goals. Leading European Marxists have taken part in this dialogue: Roger Garaudy, Ernst Bloch, Lucio Lombardo-Radice, Branko Bosnjak, Konrad Farner and others. They are answered without any hatred, and indeed with a recognition of the contribution of Marxism to the renewal of society and the new dynamism found in traditionally Christian countries, by men like

Helmut Gollwitzer, Jürgen Moltmann, Giulio Girardi, Wolf-Dieter Marsch, John C. Bennett, Johann B. Metz, Albert J. Rasker and others who carry still further the tradition begun in an earlier generation by classical theologians like Barth, Teilhard, Rahner, Hromádka and Tillich. Because of its central position to Europe, between East and West, Catholicism and Protestantism, Orthodoxy and modern atheism, not to mention the tradition of the Czech Reformation which always had a stronger social sense and a deeper understanding of eschatological thinking, Czechoslovakia soon took a special place in the dialogue between Christianity and Marxism. Of the many Czech studies concerned directly with Jesus we can mention Vitézslav Gardavsky's *God is not yet Dead* (Pelican, 1973), Jan Kamelsky ('On the Trial of Jesus', in *Encounter Today*, Issy-les-Moulineaux, 1969, no. 3) and Petr Pokorny (*Der Kern der Bergpredigt*, Hamburg, 1969).

Finally, the most important contribution to the renewal of the study of Jesus since Albert Schweitzer has come from the form-historical school. It has to its credit important achievements, especially in the discovery of the chronological development of the synoptic tradition through a study not simply of the content but also of the form of the New Testament sayings, episodes, legends, stories, parables and so on. The basic works of this school, which today would be accepted by the majority of scholars, are those of Martin Dibelius (*Die Formgeschichte des Evangeliums*, 1919, 2nd edn. 1933) and Rudolf Bultmann (*Die Geschicthe der synoptischen Tradition*, 1921; trans. *The History of the Synoptic Tradition*, Oxford, 1963). Making use of this method, Bultmann in particular worked out a new picture of Jesus which is very convincing (*Jesus*, 1926; trans. *Jesus and the Word*, Scribner's, New York, 1934. *Das Urchristentum im Rahmen der antiken Religionen*, 1949. *Theologie des Neuen Testaments*, 1948–53; trans. *Theology of the New Testament*, S.C.M., London, vol. I 1952, vol. II 1955). The comparative study of the different literary forms of New Testament tradition and times, ranging from 'familiar quotations' and short didactic phrases (paradigms) to complicated narratives and parables, made it possible to come very close to Jesus with a high degree of probability. New methods of form-history research also enabled scholars, indirectly, to undertake a fresh study of the content of new Testament tradition. In this they subsequently agreed, in the many thousands

of monographs and countless studies of the last century, with the
line of older research from Reimarus–Strauss to Schweitzer – a
line which had unequivocally disclosed the
prophetic-eschatological features of Jesus of Nazareth's authentic,
original thought. The successors of Bultmann today form a
school which has already developed several branches: Joachim
Jeremias (*Die Gleichnisse*, 1926; trans. *The Parables of Jesus*, S.
C.M., London, 1954. *Das Problem des historischen Jesus*, 1960, and
other works); Oscar Cullmann (*Petrus*, 1952; trans. *Peter: disciple
– apostle – martyr*, S.C.M., London, 1953. *Die Christologie des
Neuen Testaments*, 1956; trans. *The Christology of the New Testament*, New Testament Library, London, 1963, and other works);
Günther Bornkamm (*Jesus von Nazareth*, 1956; trans. *Jesus of
Nazareth*, London, 1960); Willi Marxsen (*Die Auferstehung Jesu*,
1964); Herbert Braun (*Jesus*, 1969); and others.

Bultmann's school enjoys such a degree of competence in the
critique of religious matters that although there may be specialist
disputes over some details of their work, neither the non-Christian nor the atheist is forced to advance objections of an
ideological or philosophical nature against their conclusions. The
'supernatural' and the 'miraculous' are taken into account only as
current elements in the mythical view of the world which
belonged to that age: therefore something *in need of* explanation,
and not the explanation itself. Precisely because faith in Jesus'
miracles was found among both his supporters and his opponents,
miracles cannot be the essence of his preaching. Even the
resurrection is not understood literally as the reanimation of a
corpse: it is rather 'resurrection in the word', in the kerygma, in
faith, in the thought of Jesus' followers – something that can ultimately be asserted of any great man. It is not surprising, then,
that Bultmann should be attacked by a host of conservative
theologians as a cryptoatheist. Yet Bultmann himself – although
the same cannot be said of all his disciples – retains a link with the
tradition of the Church in his life-style and his theoretical conclusions, and the key to his position is that he attributes an eschatological meaning to everything that happened from the first
appearance of Jesus to the constitution of the Easter faith – and
here 'eschatology' manifestly takes on a new meaning. There is
an almost imperceptible shift of emphasis here: whereas eschatological thinking presupposed the relatively rapid transfor-

mation of the situation through the mysterious irruption of higher powers, an idea which Bultmann regards as mythical and in need of demythologisation, he himself considers the 'eschatological event' to be not what Jesus and the apostles thought was going to happen, but what they themselves did (and that includes their expectations). The expectation of the objective eschatological upheaval was therefore a myth, but Jesus' own faith is eschatology. Eschatology, which originally was a part of what needed explaining, now becomes the key to the explanation. Here one can ask whether there is not a vicious circle. Bultmann was strongly influenced by the philosophy of Heidegger, and although his historical work is universally recognised, as a theological interpreter of the preaching of Jesus he is attacked on almost all sides: atheists find that his ideas are still too Christian, most Christians find them too atheistic. But whatever view we have of his theological conclusions, there can be no doubt that his programme of 'demythologisation', alongside Barth's dialectical theology and Teilhard's cosmic christology, has shown itself to be one of the most dynamic factors in Christian tradition in the middle of the twentieth century.

Index of Subjects

Aaron 130, 144
Abel 57
Abraham 54, 57, 61, 207
Afterlife, the 56, 96, 170, 215
Akhenaton 58
Albigensians 208
Anonymous Christianity 15
Anthropomorphism 59, 62, 134
Apocrypha 41
Aquinas, see Thomas Aquinas
Aristotle 22, 38, 196
Arius 190
Athanasius 190
Atheism 13, 21, 49, 211, 214–15, 220
Augustine 48, 88, 112, 177, 191, 194, 195, 198, 200, 206
Auschwitz 49, 103, 153

Bahrdt 70, 209
Baptism 71, 78
Bar Kochba 129
Barth K. 62, 207, 218, 220
Bauer B. 211
Beatitudes, the 96, 110
Benedict 101
Bennett J. C. 218
Bible, the 63, 207, 214
   see also Old Testament, New
   Testament
Biblical studies 208–20
Bloch E. 19, 62, 217
Bogomils 208
Bornkamm G. 219
Bosnjak B. 217
Braun H. 219
Brecht B. 12
Brutus 196

Buber M. 21
Buddha 40, 80
Bultmann R. 14, 15, 49, 83, 218–20

Caesar 196
Cain 57
Calvin J. 206
Carmichael J. 70, 132, 149
Casalis G. 19
Cathars 208
Catholicism 49, 174, 180, 211
Chance 48
Childhood, example of 99–103, 117
Children of the Pure Life 100
Christianity 10, 18, 48, 75, 90, 102, 111–12, 128, 169, 170, 193–4, 195, 199–204, 206, 214
   and the Law 174
   origin of 23–4, 161, 217
   universalism 173–5
   see also Anonymous Christianity, Catholicism, Church
Christmas narratives 101, 181–3
Church 125, 162, 193, 194, 205, 209
Communism 204
   see also Atheism, Marxism
Confucianism 98
Confucius 40, 47
Conversion, see Metanoia
Covenant 58, 60–2, 170
Criticism 37–8
Crucifixion, method of 154–5
   on whom used 40, 154
   see also Jesus Christ, death of
Cullmann O. 219
Cyrus 129

Daniel 63, 147, 178, 198
David 53, 54, 59, 65, 107, 118, 129, 130, 131, 143, 147
Death 48, 62, 95, 155, 169
Demythologisation 49, 214, 220
'Dialectic of the cross' 84
Dialogue 9, 38, 128
  Christian-Marxist 16–17, 19, 26–8, 38, 50
Dibelius M. 83, 125, 218
Docetism 14
Donatists 112, 200
Dostoievski F. M. 81, 155
Drews A. 214
Dubček A. 10, 16
Dvořak A. 155

Easter experience, the 42, 137
Easter faith 125, 165–72, 176, 185
Ebionites 174
Ecclesiastes 62
Einstein A. 52
Elias 63
Elijah 125, 156–9, 198
Engels F. 35, 215, 216
Enoch 157
Eschatology 64
Essenes 70–3, 82, 216
  see also Qumran
Eucharist 71
European tradition 49
Exodus 54, 57, 148

Failure 48, 62
Faith 20, 90, 91–2, 99, 111, 128, 167, 173, 207, 208
Farner K. 19, 217
Fate 48
Feuerbach L. 10, 13, 35, 210
Force, use of 33, 105–7, 109
Forgiveness of sins, see under Jesus Christ
Form criticism 83
Form-historical research 213, 218–20
Francis of Assisi 100, 101, 194
Freedom 48
Freud S. 52, 99
Fromm E. 19, 62
Future, the 37, 42, 65, 88

claim of on the present 86–8, 102, 117, 119, 166–7, 201

Gandhi M. 101, 102, 109
Garaudy R. 19, 217
Gardavsky V. 13–14, 19, 218
Girardi G. 16, 19, 218
God 48, 54, 57–62, 92, 99, 106, 129, 132, 135, 137, 153, 186, 198, 215, 216
  fatherhood of 99, 102–3
  in Braun 21
  in Buber 21
  in Hromádka 21
  in Rahner 21
  Jewish concept of 56
  Platonic concept of 59
  variety of concepts of 21, 215
  see also Bible, Covenant, Monotheism, Trinity
Goethe J. W. 47, 151
Gollwitzer H. 19, 218
Gospel 16, 40, 84, 90
Gospels, the 41, 52, 83, 144
  contradictions in 44–5
  formation of 175–91
  see also John, Luke, Mark, Matthew, Myth, Thomas
Greeks 49, 56, 59, 60, 63, 67
Guilt 41, 60

Harnack A. 212
Heaven 90
Hebrews, Epistle to the 71, 144
Hegel G. W. F. 13, 38, 112, 197, 210
Heidegger M. 11, 220
Herder J. G. 211
Herod the Great 67–8
Hiroshima 49, 197
History 33
Hromádka J. L. 19, 31, 207, 218
Humanism 103, 109
Hume D. 209
Hus J. 112, 116, 139, 174, 194, 206
Husserl E. 11

Immortality 170
  see also Afterlife, Soul
Injustice 34, 110

Inquisition, the 16
Institutionalisation 19–20
Isaac 57
Isaiah 38, 57, 63, 137, 147, 178–9, 198
Islam 170, 207

Jacob 54
Janov M. 116
Jansenism 206
Jeremiah 180
Jeremias J. 83, 219
Jerusalem, fall of 67, 70, 154
Jesus Christ: (1) *general*
  and Jewish tradition 112–16, 193, 197, 199, 210
  and John the Baptist 77–8, 91
  and revolution 14, 97, 217
  and the Essenes 70–3
  and the Pharisees 68, 98, 104, 113, 148
  at one with his preaching 86–90, 100–1
  different interpretations of 40
  difficulty of biography of 41, 46, 192
  distinction between Jesus and the Christ 14–15, 203
  divinity 206, 208
  healing power 82
  historical background 51–73
  'historical Jesus' 41, 185, 187
  historicity 41–7, 181, 214
  influence 40–1, 191, 204
  in Marxist theory 13, 23–4, 31
  'kerygmatic Jesus' 41
  magnetism 81, 188–9
  'messianic awareness' 128
  'messianic secret' 211
  personality 81–3, 188–9
  significance 192–204
  uniqueness 206
Jesus Christ: (2) *ministry*
  eschatological nature of 86, 93, 97, 115
  basic scheme of 39, 42, 176
  infancy 177, 181
  youth 75, 77, 177
  baptism by John 78–9, 127
  stay in the desert 77, 79
  temptations 79–80, 127, 167
  start of public life 75, 77, 80, 87
  call of first disciples 81

miracles 125, 146, 204, 209, 219
transfiguration 157–8, 160, 164, 168
journey to Jerusalem 148–9, 158, 159, 174, 178
transfiguration 157–8, 160, 164, 168
journey to Jerusalem 148–9, 158, 159, 174, 178
entry into Jerusalem 132
cleansing of the Temple 149
last supper 149
betrayal 150–1, 153
arrest 106, 149–50
trial 149, 150, 151–3
suffering 137–142, 159, 178, 182, 196
'Way of the cross' 155
'Seven Last Words' 155
call to Elijah 155–9
death 139–41, 150, 155, 160, 163, 176
burial 155, 168
resurrection 145, 160–71, 172, 181, 182, 209, 219
post-resurrection appearances 160–1, 165–9, 188
Emmaus 161, 181
exaltation 163–4, 168
victory 34, 163–4, 185–6
parousia 125, 139–40
see also Christmas narratives, Crucifixion, Prophecies of the passion
Jesus Christ: (3) *teaching*
  attitude to non-Jews 114, 175
  attitude to social outcasts 110–11
  childhood 22, 99–103
  ethic 107
  extra-biblical parallels 82, 86
  forgiveness 105, 108–9, 201
  forgiveness of sins 144
  full living of the present 94–5, 102, 119
  love of enemies 107–8
  love of neighbour 49, 105
  pacifism 33, 70, 105, 108
  parables 93–4, 126, 146, 171, 181
  poverty 96–7
  prayer 90
  rejection of vengeance 105
  self-denial 101–2
  the Law 104, 112
  the Our Father 90–1, 99

the sabbath 115
violence 106
wealth 97–8
see also Kingdom, Metanoia, Sermon
on the Mount
Jesus Christ: (4) *titles*
Christ 127, 152, 166, 170, 173, 176, 205
King of the Jews 132, 152
Logos 183, 184, 186
Lord 175
Man of Sorrows 136, 159
Messiah 126–59, 170, 174, 176, 178, 213–14
Pantocrator 175
Prophet 126, 129–30, 198
Redeemer 48, 166, 170, 173, 174, 178, 190, 205, 207
Saviour 40, 51, 175, 190
'Saviour of the Gentiles' 175
Servant of the Lord 143
Son of David 132
Son of God 40, 45, 48, 129–30, 176, 190, 205
Son of Man 118, 120–5, 127, 128, 129, 130, 139, 143, 144–5, 156, 159, 162, 164, 165, 166–8, 169, 172, 178, 182, 188, 201, 213
Job, Book of 58, 62, 80, 135, 180
John 41, 42, 81, 87, 101, 127, 129, 145, 183–90, 191, 198, 199, 211, 213
John the Baptist 63, 70, 72, 75, 77–8, 82, 91, 98, 101, 113, 125, 128, 137, 158, 166, 176
John XXIII 9, 20, 51, 49, 153, 194
Johnson S. 8
Joseph 144
Joseph of Arimathea 168
Joseph of Egypt 54, 130
Josephus 42, 70, 106, 136–7
Judaism 51–73, 106–7, 120, 147, 175, 198, 207
and Christianity 154, 174, 177, 197
and Jesus' death 153, 198
capacity to endure 55
concept of God 56
concept of man 52, 56
diaspora 67, 207, 216
fusion of sacred and profane 53–5

monotheism 57–62
see also Covenant, Ebionites, Essenes, Law, Messiah, Old Testament, Pharisees, Prophets, Sabbath observance, Saducees, Scribes
Judas Iscariot 150–1, 153
Julian the Apostate 194

Kadlecova E. 16–17
Kamelsky J. 218
Kant I. 38, 210
Kautsky K. 14, 17, 22, 23–4, 35, 43, 98, 149, 216–17
Kingdom, the 36–7, 47, 64–6, 78, 84–105, 108, 110, 119–20, 123, 126, 133, 139, 140, 145, 158, 160, 166, 169, 171, 172, 182, 188, 194, 199, 201, 202, 210
Klíma O. 91
Kolakowski L. 11, 12
Künzli 216
Kutter 32

Lao-tse 98
Last Judgment 122, 124
Last Supper 149
Law, the 63, 68, 104, 153, 174, 198
Leibniz G. W. 38, 112, 174, 209
Lenin 18, 32, 49, 216
Lessing G. E. 38, 210
Lombardo-Radice L. 19, 217
Lot's wife 57
Love of enemies 107–8, 201
Love of neighbour 49, 105, 110, 197, 201
Löwith 216
Lukacs G. 34
Luke 46, 83, 91, 121, 156, 162–3, 177, 180–3, 186, 205
Luporini 19
Luther M. 198, 206

Maccabees 107
Macek J. 11
Machovec̆ M. 8–17
Malachi 158
Man, supreme in the cosmos 21
'Man of Sorrows' (Isaiah) 136, 159
Manichaeism 111, 208
Mann T. 81

Marcion 208

Mark 46, 75, 83, 87, 90, 121, 123, 125–6, 149, 160, 172, 173, 176, 177, 180, 183, 184, 211

Marsch W.–D. 218

Marx K. 10, 13, 18, 21, 22, 25, 28–9, 32, 33, 35, 37, 49, 52, 69, 100, 104, 111, 174, 193, 194, 210, 215–16

Marxism 9–17, 24–38, 89, 112, 193, 204, 213, 214–18

Marxsen W. 219

Mary Magdalen 111, 160, 161, 168, 188

Mary mother of Jesus 75–6, 155, 168, 181, 207

Materialism 21

Matthew 46, 83, 87, 91, 112, 121, 123, 132, 172, 175, 176–80, 181, 183, 184, 186, 198

Merleau-Ponty M. 11

Messiah 65–6, 71, 130–41, 143–5, 190, 210

Metanoia 36–7, 64, 87, 107, 111, 123, 167, 171, 172, 210

Metz J. B. 9, 19, 218

Michelangelo 155

Modern man and Jesus 47–8 and the Gospels 52

Moltmann J. 9, 19, 218

Monotheism 57–62, 88, 207

Moses 48, 52, 54, 57, 58, 59, 61, 65, 80, 107, 130, 134, 144, 157, 198

Muhammad 98, 207

Muratori L. A. 208

Mythological school 44, 213–14

Mythology 72, 85, 195

Myths 44, 54, 120, 184
   creation myths 56
   German 140
   Greek 54, 140
   Indian 54, 140
   in the Bible/Christianity 26, 30, 34, 35, 43, 88, 186, 195, 210, 219–20
   resurrection myths 170
   Slav 140
   Aeneas 57
   Adonis 35
   Andromeda 140
   Apollo 59
   Heracles 35

Hermes 59
Iphigenia 57
Niobe 57
Oedipus 57
Osiris 35, 170
Perseus 35, 141
Remus 56
Romulus 56
Shiva 58, 170
Tammuz 170
Zeus 57, 58

Napoleon 47

Neo-platonism 68, 184

New Testament 70–1, 87, 126, 145, 177, 180, 192, 194, 200, 214, 218
   see also Gospel(s), John, Paul, Pauline Letters, Peter, Synoptics

Novotny 8

Old Testament 82, 85, 88, 120, 134, 170, 177, 178, 197

Origen 213

Our Father, the 90–1, 99

Pacifism 33, 70, 105, 108–9

Parousia 125

Party, the 12, 13
   see also Communism

Pascal B. 206

Passover 54, 148

Paul 52, 57, 68, 73, 75, 112, 117, 161, 168, 169, 170, 171, 172, 173–5, 176, 186, 197, 199

Pauline Letters 41, 75, 87, 144

Paulusgesellschaft 10

Peter 15, 23, 34, 70, 73, 81, 117, 127, 128, 129, 138, 142, 143, 146, 151, 157, 159, 160, 161, 163–71, 172–3, 174, 188, 189, 196, 199
   confession of 127, 128, 144–5, 178
   denial of Jesus 163
   mystery of 128–9, 163
   primacy of 161–3

Pharisaism 32, 68, 111, 114–15, 203

Pharisees 68, 98, 113–14, 201

Philo 70

Pilate 132, 149, 152, 154

Pius XII 211

Plato 22, 59, 196
  see also Neo-platonism, Platonisation
  of Jesus' message
Platonisation of Jesus' message 190
Pokorny P. 218
Polemic 113
Polytheism 59
Popes, primacy of 161
Popper K. 216
'Prague School' 11, 36
'Prague Spring' (1968) 12
Prophecies of the passion 137–8, 141, 142, 172
Prophets of Israel 10, 64–7, 84–5, 88, 89, 97, 98, 118, 152, 166–7, 169
Pruha M. 11
Psalms, the 55, 58, 62–3, 131, 136, 180

Q 101, 121, 123, 172, 173, 177
Qumran documents 43, 70–1, 144, 184
Qumran-Essene sect 71–3, 74, 77, 78, 91, 111, 149, 174

Ragaz L. 32
Rahner K. 15, 19, 207, 218
Ranovic 214
Rasker A. J. 218
  Redemption, see Salvation
Reformation, the 208, 218
Reimarus H. S. 210, 213, 219
Religion 201, 215
Renan E. 212
Repentance, see Metanoia
Resurrection 68, 169–70
  see also under Jesus Christ (2)
Revelation 62
Revelation, Book of 86
Robertson A. 23, 217
Romans and Jesus' death 153–4

Sabbath observance 72, 115
Sacrifice 61, 133–6
Saducees 68–9, 98, 114, 115
Saints, cult of 206
Salvation 96, 135, 173, 176, 182, 202, 212
  concept of 34
  man's need of 48
  quest for 51, 65, 85, 202, 215

Samaritans 67
Schaff A. 11
Schleiermacher F. 211
Schopenhauer A. 110
Schweitzer A. 49, 107, 165, 197, 211, 213, 218, 219
Science 37–8, 196, 207
Scipio 196
Scribes 68–9, 98
'Secret epiphanies' (in Mark) 125, 128
Self-sacrifice 134, 138, 140, 187, 199
Seneca 109
Sermon on the Mount 33, 87, 101, 104, 106–7, 112, 146, 153, 177, 187, 198
Servant of the Lord 66, 133
Shaw G. B. 29
Sheol 170
  see also Afterlife, Immortality, Soul
Simeon 183
Simon of Cyrene 157, 165
Simplicity of life, see under Childhood
Socialism 12, 18, 26, 112, 213, 214–18
Socrates 40, 47
Soul 96, 170
  see also Immortality
Stalin 9, 16
Stalinism 8, 11–12
Stephen 124, 188
Strauss D. F. 213, 219
Suffering 134–5, 155
Svoboda K. 99
Synoptics, Synoptic tradition 41, 42, 46, 68, 70, 77, 81, 83, 86, 96, 100, 104, 106, 108, 115, 117, 121, 124, 125, 127, 132, 142, 144, 146, 150, 156, 157, 160, 163, 167, 173, 175, 184, 185, 188, 189, 190, 199, 205, 211
  see also Luke, Mark, Matthew

Tacitus 42, 133
Talmud 42, 62, 116, 136
Taoism 98, 99
Teilhard de Chardin P. 11, 74, 191, 207, 218
Theology 8
  Eastern theology 205–6
  Western theology 205–6
Thomas Aquinas 206

Thomas, Gospel of 41
Threatenedness 48, 52
Tillich P. 207, 218, 220
Tolstoy L. 81, 101
Trinity, the 190, 205, 207
  see also God
Truth (fulness) 35, 38, 49, 89, 109, 140

Venturini 70, 209
Vespasian 129
Violence 105, 109, 110, 117, 134
Vipper 214
Virgil 196

Vishnu 136
Voltaire 209

Waldensians 112
Weakness, human 41
Weisse C. H. 211
Wittgenstein L. 11
Wrede W. 211

Yahweh, see God

Zarathustra 80, 111
Zealots 39, 70, 74, 108, 149

Index of Biblical References

Old Testament

Genesis
6:18	60
19:17	24
32:38	60
49:25	48

Exodus
3:14	60–1
32:4	61
34:28	80

Leviticus
19:18	107

Deuteronomy
5:6–10	51
6:4–5	51
6:5	107
18:20	153
32:15	61
34:6	157

2 Samuel
5:3	129

1 Kings
19:16	129

2 Kings
2:11	157
8:1	170
13:21	170

Job
9:3	135

Psalms
2	131
2:8	131
8:4	121
22	135, 156
22:2	180
22:19	180
24	131
31	135
38	135
45	131
69	135
72	131
72:4–10	131
80:17	121
89	131
110	131
121:1	62
132	131
137:1–5	55
142	135

Ecclesiastes
4:1–3	135

Isaiah
2:4	65
45:1	129
53	135
53:2–10	180
53:3	136
53:4	136
53:5	136
53:7	136
61:1	129

Ezekiel
37	170

Daniel
7:13	121
7:13–14	66

Malachi
4:5	158

New Testament

Matthew
2:1–12	177
2:15	177
2:23	177
3:2	78
4:1–11	79
4:8–10	167
4:9	132
4:17	87, 119
5–7	33, 104, 177
5:3–12	96
5:5–9	110
5:11	139
5:13	203
5:13–14	92
5:16	92
5:17	174
5:17–20	112
5:20	109
5:21–37	104
5:22	112
5:28	112
5:32	112
5:34	112
5:38–6:3	105
5:39	112
5:43–8	109
5:44	112

6:8	103	18:12–13	93	1:17	81
6:9–15	90	18:20	138	1:22	81
6:19–24	98	18:21–2	197	1:34	125
6:26	101–2	20:1–16	93, 94	1:36	128
6:28	102	20:25–8	142	1:44	125
6:33	87, 104	20:30–1	132	2:15	110
6:34	102	21:9	132	2:17	105
7:3	111	21:15	132	2:27–8	115
7:7	92	22:42	132	2:28	122
7:13	92	23:1	148	3:12	125
7:15	39	23:1–4	114	3:17	70
7:16	92	23:1–36	194	3:28–30	122
7:21	92	23:2	32	3:31–5	75
8:10	110	23:2–4	148	3:32	44
8:11	175	23:5–28	114	4:11	127, 141
8:20	122	23:17–33	104	4:12	126
8:22	105, 197	23:27	148	4:19	98
9:27	132	23:29–39	115	4:28	93
9:28–9	99	23:32–6	148	4:30–2	92, 93
10:6	198	23:37	137	5:34	99
10:8	111	25:14–30	94	5:38–43	125–6
10:16	101, 103, 139	25:31	122	6:2	98
10:22	139, 165	25:31–46	124	6:3–4	81
10:27	165	25:34–40	122	6:4	126
10:30	102	25:40	38, 97	6:34	96
10:32	139	25:42–5	200	7:6	194
10:34	45	26:14–16	151	7:36	125
10:38	84	26:52	45, 106	8:2	96
10:38–9	139	26:64	124, 127, 185	8:27	122
11:15	201	26:73	77	8:27–8	125
11:28–30	203	27:25	153	8:27–33	166
12:23	132	27:46	156	8:28	158
12:31–2	122	27:47	156	8:29	127, 147
13:33	93	27:49	156	8:31	137, 141, 146
13:33–46	95	27:55	150	8:32	138, 173
13:44–6	93	27:64	165	8:34	84
14:28–31	165	28:10	142	8:38	123
15:22	132	28:15	165	9:2	168
15:24	175	28:16	142	9:2–8	157, 165
16:13	122	28:19	72, 175	9:11	158
16:13–23	142			9:31	137, 141, 146
16:18–19	162	**Mark**		9:32	141, 167
16:21–3	138	1:6	78	9:37	100
16:22	142	1:7	73	10:14	101
17:13	158	1:9–11	78	10:23	97
17:21	99	1:12	79	10:25	200
17:23	173	1:15	73, 74, 87, 182	10:29	84
18:3	100	1:16–20	166	10:33	137, 141, 146

11:1–10	149
11:10	132
11:11–12	150
11:11–12:37	148
11:15–17	149
12:18–27	98
12:29–31	107
12:31	49
13:1–32	123
13:26f	93, 123
13:28–9	93
14:9	175
14:10	150
14:21	141, 146
14:22–5	149
14:27	151, 160, 163
14:28	142, 160
14:33	185
14:36	99
14:38	91
14:41	141, 146
14:43–5	151
14:45	151
14:58	150
14:62	127
14:66–72	163
15:2	146, 152
15:13	149
15:14	154
15:16–19	132
15:21	157, 165
15:26	132
15:34	156
15:35	156
15:36	156
15:40	150, 157
15:42–7	168
15:47	168
16:1–8	168
16:7	161
16:11–18	160
16:15	72
16:17	142

Luke

1:46–8	76
1:46–55	182
1:68–79	182

1:76	183
2:10–11	182
2:14	182
2:19	181
2:29–32	182, 183
2:50	76
2:51	181
3:3	87
3:23	80
4:20	76
5:8	81, 188
5:28–6:36	105
6:6–11	115
6:15	70
6:20–1	96
6:20–3	110
6:20–49	104
6:37	111
6:38	111
6:43–5	92
6:46	92
7:1–10	175
7:36–50	94
7:40ff	68
7:47	111
8:2	111
9:18	122
9:32	128
9:45	172
9:60	26
10:23	93
10:29–37	181, 197
10:37	92, 109
10:38–42	181
10:41–2	100
11:2–4	90,99
11:46	199
12:10	122
12:48–9	117
12:49	204
15:11–32	93, 94, 181
16:15	114
17:6	99
17:20–1	88
17:24	120
18:9–14	181
18:10–14	93, 94
18:11	32, 114

18:31	148, 158
18:34	141, 148, 167
21:27–8	123–4
22:18	149
22:20	199
22:24,	142
22:29–30	96
22:32	142, 163
22:33	142
22:44	186
22:67	152
22:70	127
23:2	152
23:46	156
23:49	150
23:50–1	153
24:13–35	181
24:17	160
24:29	181
24:32	50
24:34	188
24:35	161

John

1:10	202
1:14	82, 101, 188–9, 190
1:16	14, 193
1:17	82
1:29	101
1:50	192
3:1ff	68
3:3	87
3:30	128
6:48	189
6:51	184
6:68	188
7:15	98
8:12	184, 189
10:11	139, 189
10:30	99
11:25	184
13:1	187
13:23	129
13:31	185
14:6	189
14:6–13	99
14:10	190

14:12	185	5:34–9	68	**1 Timothy**	
14:16	145	7:56	124	6:1–2	202
14:26	145	7:55–60	188		
15–17	187	10–12	165	**Titus**	
15:12–13	138	23:6 68		2:9	202
15:26	145				
16:7	145	**Romans**		**1 Peter**	
17:1	99	7:6	174	1:19	101
17:4–5	204	13:1–2	202		
17:21	187			**2 Peter**	
18:36	202	**1 Corinthians**		2:9	91
19:20	150	1:10–16	171	3:4	192
19:25–7	155	5:7	101		
20:2–3	101	15:1–58	168	**1 John**	
20:21	189	15:5	161	3:18	190
20:28	192	15:14	168	4:16	10,190
20:29	190	15:51	164		
21:15	129	15:51–5	95	**James**	
21:16–17	162	15:51–8	169	2:6–7	200
21:17	129				
21:23	101	**2 Corinthians**		**Revelation**	
		3:6	113	3:10	91
Acts		5:17	171	5:6	119
1–5	161			5:8–15	101
2:4	171	**Galatians**		5:11–12	119
3:16	40	1:18–2:14	168	21:2ff	86
4:32–5	200	2:14174		21:5	87, 171, 203
				21:8	86